NATALIA GINZBURG

EDITED BY

ANGELA M. JEANNET AND GIULIANA SANGUINETTI KATZ

A prominent and prolific Italian writer, Natalia Ginzburg (1916–1991) is known for her novels, plays, short stories, and essays. This collection brings together for an English-speaking audience a variety of critical perspectives on Ginzburg's work.

The essays, all by North American scholars, examine the author's entire production. The topics examined include Ginzburg's struggle to define herself as a woman, a writer, and an intellectual; her interpretation of the relationship between historical events and private lives; her reflections on the women's movement and the changing nature of the family; and her mastery of a distinctly personal writing style. What emerges here is a nuanced and complex portrait of Ginzburg and her work. The reader is given a sense of the importance of her contribution, not only as a writer but as a witness to the events of the twentieth century. The volume also includes a chronology, a bibliography, and translations of some of Ginzburg's lesser-known writings, including three articles, a poem, and a one-act play.

(Toronto Italian Studies)

ANGELA M. JEANNET is Charles A. Dana Professor of Romance Languages, Emerita, Franklin and Marshall College.

GIULIANA SANGUINETTI KATZ is Professor, Department of Italian Studies, University of Toronto.

NATALIA GINZBURG

A Voice of the Twentieth Century

Edited by
Angela M. Jeannet and
Giuliana Sanguinetti Katz

UNIVERSITY OF TORONTO PRESS
Toronto Buffalo London

Toronto Buffalo London
Reprinted 2017

ISBN 978-0-8020-4722-9 (cloth)
ISBN 978-1-4875-8727-7 (paper)

Printed on acid-free paper

Toronto Italian Studies

Canadian Cataloguing in Publication Data

Main entry under title:

Natalia Ginzburg: a voice of the twentieth century

(Toronto Italian Studies)
Includes bibliographical references.
ISBN 978-0-8020-4722-9 (bound) ISBN 978-0-8020-8342-5 (pbk.)

1. Ginzburg, Natalia – Criticism and interpretation.
I. Jeannet, Angela M. II. Katz, Giuliana, 1938– .
III. Series.

PQ4817.I5Z82 2000 853′.912 C99-932171-4

This volume was published with the financial assistance of the Emilio Goggio Chair of Italian Studies, University of Toronto.

University of Toronto Press acknowledges the financial assistance to its publishing program of the Canada Council for the Arts and the Ontario Arts Council.

University of Toronto Press acknowledges the financial support for its publishing activities of the Government of Canada through the Book Publishing Industry Development Program (BPIDP).

Cover photo courtesy Stefano Baroni, Lucca, Italy

Contents

Editors' Foreword

Natalia Ginzburg: A Voice of the Twentieth Century originates from our desire to highlight the importance of this modern Italian author, who is not sufficiently read in North America. Although her name is well known in Italian critical circles and among the Italian reading public, the deceptive simplicity of her writing has prevented even her most devoted readers from appreciating fully the depth of her analyses and the complexities of her style. Because Italian readers were accustomed to the flamboyance of a rich rhetorical tradition, they considered Ginzburg a plain, minor writer. Her novels and plays were treated casually, as one more pleasing example of the traditional marginality of a woman's perspective on the world. On the other hand, her lucid and disillusioned explorations of the daily lives of an alienated Italian middle class are disturbing, with their lack of sentimentality and peculiarly understated style. As a new critical atmosphere prevails, it is imperative that Ginzburg be reread in a way that will reveal her unique contribution to the wider Western literary tradition, as well as address the seriousness and timeliness of her themes, her consummate stylistic skill, and a sharp sense of the comic that one seldom finds in twentieth-century Italian writers.

Natalia Ginzburg was born in Palermo in 1916 as Natalia Levi, last of the five children of Giuseppe Levi, a prominent biologist from Trieste, and Lidia Tanzi, whose family included lawyers, musicologists, literary critics, and friends such as Filippo Turati, a prominent socialist lawyer. In 1919, the Levis moved to Turin. After some private schooling and enrolment at the University of Turin as a student of letters, the young woman began publishing her first short stories in literary journals. Turin's cultural atmosphere favoured political reflection. Among the many young intellectuals of the budding left, Leone Ginzburg, an accomplished scholar of Russian literature, was one of the brightest. He and Natalia married in 1938, and soon they were sent by the Fascist regime into confinement in the Abruzzo region because of Leone's anti-Fascist activities. His imprisonment, torture, and murder represent one of the many well-known episodes in the history of the attempted repression of the Italian Resistance. Natalia Ginzburg was left alone with their three children, but managed to survive the persecution of Jewish people that was then at its most pitiless. In 1950, she married Gabriele Baldini, an Anglicist scholar, and in 1952 they moved to Rome, which became their permanent home and where Ginzburg died in 1991.[1]

In 1942, Ginzburg had published her first book with Turin's Einaudi publishing house, *La strada che va in città* (*The Road to the City*), under the assumed name of Alessandra Tornimparte. After the war, she became an editor at Einaudi, marking the beginning of her lifelong publishing association with that house. Her novels include *È stato così* (1947; *This Is How It Happened*), *Tutti i nostri ieri* (1952; *All Our Yesterdays*), *Le voci della sera* (1961; *Voices in the Evening*), *Lessico famigliare* (1963; *Family Sayings*), *Caro Michele* (1973; *Dear Michael*), and *La città e la casa* (1984; *The City, the House*). She also wrote short stories, such as 'Sagittario' (1957; 'Sagittarius') and 'Famiglia' (1977; 'Families'). Her essays are collected under the titles *Le piccole virtù* (1961; *The Small Virtues*), *Mai devi domandarmi* (1970; *You Must Never Ask Me*), and *Vita immaginaria* (1974; *Life of the Imagination*). In the mid-1960s, she began writing a successful series of comedies, collected in *Ti ho sposato per allegria e altre commedie* (Turin: Einaudi, 1968; *I Married You to Have Fun, and Other Comedies*) and *Paese di mare e altre commedie* (Milan: Garzanti, 1973; *By the Sea, and Other Comedies*).[2]

In 1983, Ginzburg entered the political arena when she ran among the Independents of the Left and was elected representative in the Chamber of Deputies.

This book is the first attempt to engage in a multifaceted reading of Ginzburg's works. It contains a series of articles written by a number of North American critics, who look at Ginzburg's universe from different perspectives. The topics examined include: Ginzburg's struggle to define herself as a woman, a writer, and an intellectual; her critique of herself and her fictional characters; her insights into the psyches of female characters who are involved in complex relationships with family and friends; her interpretation of the relationship between historical events and private lives; her exploration of the changing definition of family; her mastery of a *staccato* writing style; and her use of dialogue and physical description to capture and fix her characters.

The articles span Ginzburg's entire production: her early novels (Giuliana Sanguinetti Katz and Angela M. Jeannet), her newspaper articles (David Ward), her most popular novels *Le voci della sera* and *Lessico famigliare* (Angela M. Jeannet, Luigi Fontanella, and Jen Wienstein), her later novels (Peg Boyers and Judith Pastore), her essays (Eugenia Paulicelli), and two of her plays (Serena Anderlini-D'Onofrio).

The volume opens with an Introduction by Rebecca West, which provides a context for the writer and the readings, and an interview with Natalia Ginzburg by Peg Boyers. At the end of the volume are samples of Ginzburg's writing in various genres: three articles translated by David Ward and the first English translation of one of Ginzburg's plays, *The Wig*, done by Jen Wienstein.

The contributors to this collection of articles were purposely invited to study Ginzburg's writings from the different perspectives each one of them privileges – historical, psychoanalytic, stylistic, and feminist – so that the author's work can be seen in its originality and power, not one-dimensional but varied, and open to ever new readings. Natalia Ginzburg emerges from these pages as a gifted, innovative, and complex writer who deserves greater visibility in the literary landscape of the twentieth century.

NOTES

1 For more biographical information, see Maya Pflug, *Natalia Ginzburg: Arditamente timida* (Milan: La Tartaruga, 1996), which is translated from the German *Natalia Ginzburg: Eine Biographie* (Berlin: Verlag Klaus Wagenbach, 1995).

2 For bibliographical references, see Alan Bullock, *Natalia Ginzburg: Human Relationships in a Changing World* (Oxford: Berg, 1991). Maria Luisa Quarsiti's *Natalia Ginzburg: Bibliografia 1934–1996* (Florence: Giunti, 1996), although quite complete, does not include Ginzburg's fiction published from 1965 to 1974.

Credits

David Ward's article 'Natalia Ginzburg's Early Writings in *L'Italia libera'* is a slightly amended version of a chapter published in his book *Antifascisms: Cultural Politics in Italy, 1943–46. Benedetto Croce and the Liberals, Carlo Levi and the 'Actionists'* (Madison, NJ, and London: Fairleigh Dickinson University Press, 1996). His translations of the Ginzburg articles included in this book were also previously published in *Antifascisms.*

Serena Anderlini-D'Onofrio's article 'Feminism and the "Absurd" in Two Plays by Natalia Ginzburg' was previously published in her book *The 'Weak' Subject: On Modernity, Eros and Women's Playwriting* (New York: Associated University Presses, 1998).

Peg Boyers' interview with Natalia Ginzburg was previously published in *Salmagundi* 9 (1992): 130–56.

Chronology

1916 Natalia Levi is born in Palermo, on 14 July, the last of five children of Giuseppe Levi and Lidia Tanzi. Her father, originally from Trieste, teaches anatomy at the University of Palermo. Her mother's family lives in Lombardy and includes among its members a lawyer (her father), scholars, a psychiatrist, and a musicologist.

1919 The Levis move to Turin. Natalia is tutored at home.

1921 The Fascist Party and the Communist Party are born, in Milan and Livorno respectively, from splits within the Italian Socialist Party.

1927 Natalia Levi enrols in the *liceo* (secondary school).

1935 She enters the university, in the *facoltà* (School) of Letters and Philosophy.

1938 The so-called 'racial' laws spelling out numerous anti-Semitic measures are promulgated by the Italian government headed by Mussolini. Natalia Levi marries Leone Ginzburg, a young but already distinguished scholar of Russian origin.

1940 Italy enters World War II. Leone Ginzburg is sent into confinement to a remote village in the Abruzzo region, near L'Aquila. Natalia Ginzburg joins him there with their two sons. A third child, a daughter, is born during this period of confinement.

1942 She publishes her first novel, *La strada che va in città*, under an assumed name, Alessandra Tornimparte.

1943 The family returns to Turin, then moves to Rome. Leone, involved in anti-Fascist activities, is arrested and imprisoned.

1944 Leone Ginzburg dies after being tortured. Natalia Ginzburg remains briefly in Rome, then moves to Florence. She begins her lifelong association with the Einaudi publishing house.

1945 She returns to Turin, home of the Einaudi publishers.

1947 Her novel *È stato così* is published.

1950 Natalia Ginzburg marries Gabriele Baldini, professor of English literature at the University of Trieste.

1952 She moves to Rome, where her husband has a position with the university. Publication of the novel *Tutti i nostri ieri*.

1960 Ginzburg begins a two-year stay in London, where Gabriele Baldini has been named director of the Italian Cultural Institute.

1961 Publication of the novel *Le voci della sera*.

1962 Natalia Ginzburg returns to Rome. She publishes a collection of essays entitled *Le piccole virtù*.

1963 She publishes the novel *Lessico famigliare*.

1965 She writes her first comedy, *Ti ho sposato per allegria*, which is successfully produced. The title is also given to a collection of several comedies, published in 1966.

1969 Death of Gabriele Baldini.

1970 Publication of the collection of essays entitled *Mai devi domandarmi*.

1973 Ginzburg publishes a second collection of comedies, entitled *Paese di mare*, and a novel, *Caro Michele*.

1974 Publication of the collection of essays entitled *Vita immaginaria.*

1977 Publication of two novellas with the title *Famiglia.*

1983 She publishes a volume entitled *La famiglia Manzoni,* a documentary narrative concerning the family of the nineteenth-century novelist Alessandro Manzoni. She is elected to the Chamber of Representatives (Camera dei deputati) as an Independent of the Left.

1984 Publication of the novel *La città e la casa.*

1991 Natalia Ginzburg dies in Rome.

Contributors

SERENA ANDERLINI-D'ONOFRIO is Assistant Professor in the Humanities and Italian at the University of Puerto Rico, Mayagüez. She is the author of *The 'Weak' Subject: On Modernity, Eros and Women's Playwriting*, a theory of gender, representation, and subjectivity from a feminist bisexual perspective (New York: Associated University Presses, 1998). She has contributed to *Feminine Feminists: Cultural Practices in Italy* (1994) and has co-translated Adriana Cavarero's *In Spite of Plato: A Feminist Rereading of Ancient Philosophy* (1995). Her latest works have appeared in *Via: Voices in Italian Americana* and the *Journal of Gender Studies*.

PEG BOYERS is Executive Director of *Salmagundi* magazine and author of a forthcoming book of poems written in the voice of Natalia Ginzburg entitled *Your Ash, Natalia*. Many of the poems from the book have appeared in magazines, including *Partisan Review, Raritan, Paris Review, The New Criterion, Ontario Review, New England Review, Notre Dame Review, Southern Review, Boston Phoenix Literary Supplement, Michigan Quarterly Review*, and *The New Republic*.

LUIGI FONTANELLA is Professor of Italian at the State University of New York in Stony Brook. He is a poet, novelist, and literary critic. His most recent books are *Round Trip* (1991; poems, Ragusa Prize); *Ceres* (1996; poems, Orazio Caputo Prize); *Storia di Bontempelli* (1997; criticism); *Hot Dog* (1998; novel; translated by J. Vitiello); *The Transparent Life and Other Poems* (2000; bilingual edition, translated by M. Palma). Fontanella is the editor of *Gradiva* and the president of IPSA (Italian Poetry Society of America).

ANGELA M. JEANNET is Charles A. Dana Professor of Romance Languages Emerita at Franklin and Marshall College. Her publications include *New World Journeys. Contemporary Writers and the Myth of America*, edited and translated with Louise K. Barnett (1977); *Parliamo dell'Italia* (1984); and a monograph on Calvino entitled *Under the Radiant Sun and the Crescent Moon: Italo Calvino's Storytelling* (2000). Her articles have appeared in *Annali d'Italianistica, Italian Americana, Italica, Italian Culture, Italian Quarterly, Stanford Italian Review, Studi novecenteschi, Symposium, Il Veltro*, and in various collective volumes.

GIULIANA SANGUINETTI KATZ is Associate Professor of Italian at the University of Toronto in Mississauga. She has published a study on *The Uses of Myth in Ippolito Nievo* (1981), a language manual on *Dialogues for Practice in Idiomatic Italian* (1988), and has co-edited two books on Pirandello: *Pirandello and the Modern Theatre* (1992), with A. Alessio and D. Pietropaolo; and *Le fonti di Pirandello* (1996), with A. Alessio. She is now co-editing *Theatre and the Visual Arts* with Domenico Pietropaolo. She has written articles on a variety of authors, from Boccaccio to Marta Morazzoni.

JUDITH LAURENCE PASTORE is Professor of English Emerita at the University of Massachusetts-Lowell. She is editor of *Confronting AIDS through Literature: The Responsibilities of Representation* (1993). Pastore's field is eighteenth-century English literature, but her interests range from women's studies to technology and values. Her publications include essays on Don DeLillo and on Natalia Ginzburg in *Italian Culture*.

EUGENIA PAULICELLI is Associate Professor of Italian in the Department of European Languages and Literatures at Queens College and in the Department of Comparative Literature in the Graduate Center of the City University of New York. She is author of *Parola e immagine: Sentieri della scrittura in Leonardo, Marino, Foscolo, Calvino* (1996) and a collection of poems entitled *Dimore* (1996). In addition, she has published extensively on literary semiotics, fashion theory, feminism, and Italian novelists and poets. She is currently working on a study entitled *Fashion Narratives: Constructing Gendered and National Identities*.

DAVID WARD is Associate Professor in the Department of Italian at Wellesley College. He is the author of *A Poetics of Resistance: Narrative and the Writings of Pier Paolo Pasolini* (1995), and *Antifascisms: Cultural*

Politics in Italy, 1943–1946. Benedetto Croce and the Liberals, Carlo Levi and the 'Actionists' (1996). He is currently working on a study of the writings of Piero Gobetti.

REBECCA WEST is Professor of Italian and Cinema/Media Studies at the University of Chicago. Selected publications include *Eugenio Montale: Poet on the Edge* (1981; Marraro Prize, 1982) and *Gianni Celati: The Craft of Everyday Storytelling* (2000). She co-edited 'Women's Voices in Italian Literature,' *Annali d'Italianistica* (1989) with Dino S. Cervigni, and *The Cambridge Companion to Modern Italian Culture* (2000) with Z. Baranski. She has written numerous articles on a variety of writers, film directors, and topics ranging from Dante and Calvino to Martin Scorsese and Italian feminism.

JEN WIENSTEIN is Faculty Lecturer in the Department of Italian at McGill University. Her publications on Natalia Ginzburg include essays in *Quaderni d'Italianistica, Atti del XII Convegno AISLLI, Donna: Women in Italian Culture* (1989), and *Atti del XV Convegno AISLLI.*

NATALIA GINZBURG

A Voice of the Twentieth Century

Introduction

REBECCA WEST

Natalia Ginzburg – using the name metonymically in order to mean her status in Italian literary culture, her writings themselves, and her being as a woman – gives us the opportunity to consider the significance of a volume such as this one. Although there now exist in English several collections of essays dedicated to Italian women writers and to Italian feminist thought, few are given over to the evaluation of a single woman writer. Ginzburg is certainly one of the most prominent among Italian women writers of this century, at least in her native country, and this fact alone may be sufficient to account for the choice that underlies this project. Yet it is also a fact that Ginzburg had an ambivalent and uneasy relation to feminism, and that she herself might well have felt uncomfortable with the feminist critical spirit animating the majority of the contributors to this collection. Like other women more or less of her generation who wished to write (Elsa Morante, Anna Maria Ortese, Alba De Céspedes, Maria Luisa Spaziani), she did not welcome the label 'woman writer,' preferring instead to make her way in the primarily male literary universe as a 'writer' *tout court*. When asked by Mary Gordon, in an interview published in *The New York Times Magazine* of 25 March 1990, with the title 'Surviving History,' if her friendship with Morante was different from that with other writers because they were both women, Ginzburg replied: 'Of course not. A writer is a writer. You care about writing. It isn't men or women. I find these feminists very annoying, putting together anthologies of women writers. As if there were a difference.' This desire, fully understandable in her time, to embrace and to be embraced by the 'universal neuter' that prevailed as a space ostensibly open to all talent and blind to the 'limitations' of a gendered conception and evaluation of art, was nonetheless a partially self-defeating desire and, more important, a completely impossible one, given the ways in which critical judgments were made and cultural productions described, qualified, and taxonomized within the boundaries of Italian intellectual and academic society during the years of Ginzburg's 'coming of age.' Although she enjoyed success, both critical and popular, the writer was always a 'woman writer,' and her work was judged according to tacit, and not so tacit, criteria applicable to the realm of *letteratura femminile.* Today, many critics and theorists have sought and continue to seek to endow the adjective 'feminine' with a boldly positive resonance, but until quite recently that resonance was muted or even utterly silenced by assumptions of inferiority, minorness, and/or negative particularity. In Ginzburg's case, it was the emphasis in her writing on autobiographical elements, on the family circle, and on quotidian detail that made her even more susceptible to the label of 'woman writer,' with all that this designation entailed. On the other hand, she had the status conferred upon her by her association with the Einaudi publishing house, and with the male intellectuals and writers who were her colleagues there. In this sense, she could be 'one of the boys,' at least in cultural terms; furthermore, she could enjoy the material and practical benefits of this association, among which was the assurance that she would not have to suffer the marginalization vis-à-vis the mainstream world of publishing that was the more common fate of many Italian women with a writing vocation in the thirties, forties, and fifties. In sum, then, it could be said that Ginzburg had certain guarantees of insertion into the 'universal neuter,' with the concomitant possibility of becoming a 'successful writer' in the eyes of the establishment, yet she also bore a certain portion of the burden that any 'woman writer' of her generation had to bear precisely because they were women – that is, critical and definitional strategies that were not 'neutral' and that did not endow the space of women-produced art with the same attributes as that of men. 'Difference,' until quite recently, and with a shift due in great part to the work of feminist critics and theoreticians, did not signify positively; nor did supposed 'equality' or ostensibly gender-blind criteria of judgment and evaluation succeed in 'forgetting' Ginzburg's 'natural' feminine attachment to the intimate, the quotidian, and the detailed.

Oppositional binaries, such as male/female, equal/different, and major/minor have been questioned by a variety of discourses both within and without the academy, with the result that more flexible conceptualizations are beginning to emerge regarding, for example, the role of gender in literary creativity. Few critics wish to embrace fully a separatist ethos when dealing with literature produced by women, and yet there is still a strong sense that certain aspects of the entire aesthetic realm are in fact categorizable as 'feminine,' even if that term is deployed purely metaphorically. In short, 'difference' is not the dirty word it once was, and alikeness or equality is not a quality dearly to be wished or dominantly to be imposed as a starting point for critical investigations into artistic activity.

In her study *Reading in Detail: Aesthetics and the Feminine*, Naomi Schor seeks to uncover the political dimension underlying our thinking about the quotidian, the trivial, the particular. In her tracing of the history of the detail in art and literature over the last two hundred years, Schor argues that interest in the detail as an aesthetic category is linked to the decline of classicism and the rise of realism; further, such a category is revealed as having been aligned with the feminine throughout the historical trajectory she follows. Schor writes: 'To focus on the detail and more particularly on the *detail as negativity* is to become aware, as I discovered, of its participation in a larger semantic network, bounded on the one side by the *ornamental*, with its traditional connotations of effeminacy and decadence, and on the other, by the *everyday*, whose "prosiness" is rooted in the domestic sphere of social life presided over by women' (4). Furthermore, because women have always tended to be identified with matter and nature rather than with abstractions and mind, art produced by them is historically seen as incapable of transcending realism in favour of more nonrepresentational and spiritually resonant genres and forms. Women can embellish and beautify, or they can directly represent material, quotidian reality, therefore; but more often than not throughout Western history they are seen as congenitally unfit for truly major artistic achievement.

Of the two semantic spheres designated here – the ornamental and the everyday – it is the latter in which much of Ginzburg's work can be placed, for it is indeed from the domestic and familial sphere that her writing most typically draws its sustenance. That this aspect of Ginzburg's production has had negative connotations for certain sectors of the patriarchal cultural, critical, and literary network is made clear in many characterizations of her works as they have been expounded over the years in the manuals, histories, and literary biobibliographical sourcebooks so prevalent in Italian culture. Although she is undoubtedly seen as an important writer, it is often the case that the 'domesticity' of her thematics is excused rather than extolled, almost as if it were a quality to be 'swept under the rug' (to use a 'womanly' turn of phrase). One of the most openly hostile (if ostensibly humorous) indictments of her personal and intimate art is found in writer Luigi Malerba's witty book entitled *Le galline pensierose* (*The Pensive Hens*), a collection of short pieces about anthropomorphic hens, of which Calvino wrote: 'si librano tra lo humour sospeso nel vuoto del "nonsense" e la vertigine metafisica degli apologhi "Zen"' ('they are suspended in the void of nonsense and the metaphysical vertigo of Zen fables') (cover blurb). Malerba describes Ginzburg in the following way:

> Una gallina di nome Natalia aveva deciso di scrivere un romanzo, ma non le vennero in mente né la trama, né i personaggi, né il titolo, né lo stile della scrittura. Fu cosí che quella gallina velleitaria scrisse invece i suoi ricordi di infanzia ed ebbe molto successo fra le oche.
>
> A hen named Natalia had decided to write a novel, but neither the plot nor the characters nor the title nor the style of writing came to her mind. It was thus that that vainly ambitious hen instead wrote her childhood memories and had a great deal of success among the geese. (115)

To be fair, this is the only *ad hominem* (or should we say *ad feminam*?) attack in the book, and it may well be that Malerba had his own personal reasons for including it; yet it is significant, I believe, that it is the writing of her childhood memories that is held up to ridicule, presumably because such writing is not 'real' literature with a plot, characters, and style. Nor is such writing reflective of important, 'real' history with its currents, directions, vast meanings, and generalizable, universally applicable lessons. As the unnamed author of the entry on Ginzburg included in the biobibliographical volume *Narratori italiani del secondo Novecento* writes: 'Tutti i suoi personaggi testimoniano la rinunzia a penetrare le complesse strutture della storia, ripiegando sugli ingranaggi minuti dell'esistenza individuale' ('All her characters are witness to a renunciation of penetrating into the complex structures of history, [instead] withdrawing into the minute workings of individual existence'). Minutiae; the detail; the personal; concrete experience: all of these substantives long represented the negative aspects of feminine art, especially when they held centre stage and were not folded into the 'complex structures of history.'

As we are all well aware, a shift in thinking has occurred over the last few decades of this century, a shift that has put into radical question many of the critical and methodological paradigms through which we have sought to understand the meaning of history, art, and individual experience alike. Feminists (and others) declared that the personal is political; social theorists rethought the private and the public spheres; historians and anthropologists challenged the apparent ineluctability of their 'objective' criteria; and psychologists and psychoanalytically minded critics put into vigorous discussion the assumptions underlying a neutered, overarchingly 'human' subjectivity. Both literature itself and literary criticism and theory have reflected the changes in perspectives, and perhaps nowhere more forcefully than in the realm of writing by women. What was once a less than desirable attachment to the domestic, the 'minor,' or the quotidian in women's writing is now investigated from critical perspectives that validate these areas, not only in and of themselves but also as they are imbricated in greater historical and ideological abstractions. Many of the pieces included in this volume analyse aspects of Ginzburg's writings that resonate with these revisionist views. For example, David Ward writes of the author's attitudes toward Fascism as expressed in an article written after the war, in which '[Fascism] is for Natalia located at a local level within the family,' and 'the burden of Ginzburg's article is to place responsibility for the construction of a robust anti-Fascist culture at the micro-level of radical change in the way parents relate to and bring up their children.' Angela Jeannet's entire piece is dedicated to arguing that Ginzburg's emphasis on the quotidian and the particular is not antithetical to a serious engagement with the question of history's meaning, and that Ginzburg's 'everyday' people and events in fact *live* history even if dimly understanding its whys and wherefores. Eugenia Paulicelli asserts that Ginzburg 'helps us to see the fragility of definitions of social and historical phenomena that we tend to take for granted'; and some of the contributors to this volume (Fontanella, Pastore) particularly emphasize the central role of personal memory (as contrasted with collective history) in Ginzburg's fiction. The writer does not impose an interpretive grid onto the events she narrates, yet the events are there; history is there, remembered and explored.

I have so far discussed thematics in Ginzburg's work, and I should like to conclude with some remarks about her style. Themes and style are, of course, intertwined, and just as her fictions are most often about everyday, unspectacular people and happenings, so too her language is characteristically defined as 'neutral,' the speech of quotidian reality. Pavese described her narrative voice as 'una lagna,' a sort of uninterrupted 'whine' or understated 'lament.' Ginzburg's style does not draw attention to itself as style; it avoids self-display, spectacle, elaborate rhetorical effects. In her essay, Jen Wienstein reminds us that Ginzburg feared being seen as a 'sickeningly sweet' or 'sentimental' female writer, and shunned effusion perhaps in great part because of this fear. The fear of being thought a woman writer – with all of the negative presumptions this label brought with it – was much greater in the early years of Ginzburg's career than when she was established and had enjoyed significant success. It is difficult, probably impossible, to know to what extent this fear, and the effects it had on her style, ultimately shaped what we think of as the typical Ginzburgian voice: perhaps not to any great extent. For, as Paulicelli argues in her essay, the mystery of creativity and of the forms it takes is very much at the heart of Ginzburg's deceptively 'clear' style, the clarity of which is often only superficial and permeated throughout by shadows and subtle colorations. As Ward rightly states: 'Clarity is one of the more elusive and misunderstood concepts in Ginzburg's entire body of work. For one thing, clarity and simplicity are not overlapping categories: what is seemingly clear not being necessarily simple.' To use an analogy from the realm of cinematic art, it might be said that Ginzburg's style is like film noir, in that light or clarity in both underscores the dark mystery that can be intermittently illuminated but never entirely dispelled or explained. Human actions, feelings, and motivations are written about in lucid, economic language, but the deep unknowability of others and ourselves is revealed. A supreme example of this is to be found in Ginzburg's portrait of Pavese in *Lessico famigliare*. That his decision to take his own life was based on his deep belief in reason, which decidedly did not rule the confused, complex world of 1950, is both a wonderfully clear and extraordinarily mysterious assertion on Ginzburg's part, for it captures and yet far from explains the complicated mechanisms at work not only in the mind of her friend Pavese but by extension, and in infinite forms, in the minds and hearts of those whom we believe to know best.

Natalia Ginzburg's life spanned the troubled years of Fascist rule, postwar reconstruction, the economic boom, and the technologized, postmodern contemporary scene. Her writing did not undergo radical shifts but rather absorbed into itself the complexities and challenges of everyday reality, which continued and continues to have at its core familial relationships, friendships, love, and all of the webs woven by human interaction. Upon her death, many wrote of her ethical commitment, her quiet strength, her absolute dedication to the craft of writing, in which she felt most herself. The essays in this volume explore the landscape of Ginzburg's literary territory with care, thought, and conviction, and the result is a book that does honour to her not eulogistically or uncritically, but with the seriousness due to her as a writer – a writer who was a woman, yes, but who need not have worried that women writers would always be marginalized or treated paternalistically. This volume is proof of that.

REFERENCES

Ginzburg, Natalia. *Lessico famigliare*. Turin: Einaudi, 1963.

Gordon, Mary. 'Surviving History.' *New York Times Magazine* (25 March 1990): 42–3.

Malerba, Luigi. *Le galline pensierose*. Turin: Einaudi, 1989.

Narratori italiani del secondo Novecento. Edited by Giorgio Luti. Roma: La Nuova Italia Scientifica, 1985.

Schor, Naomi, *Reading in Detail: Aesthetics and the Feminine*. New York: Methuen, 1987.

An Interview with Natalia Ginzburg

PEG BOYERS

PB I'm eager to learn about the Italian literary scene, to know, for example, whether writers think of themselves as belonging to movements or regional groups. Do you consider yourself a Piedmontese writer, for example – having grown up in Torino – or by now do you identify yourself as a Roman writer?

NG I don't know. I never felt origins were important or at all interesting. But I admit it was tremendously liberating to write frankly as a Torinese when I wrote *Family Sayings* ... But that doesn't answer your question. Groups? Movements? I don't really think these groups exist. I don't think in Italy there even are such things as *currrents* or *trends*. The whole scene is really much too chaotic for such groups to form and stay together as separate entities.

PB In the U.S. there have always been groups, although writers are frequently reluctant to admit their affiliations. Literary historians devote studies to 'The Southern Agrarians' or the 'Beats' or 'The Harlem Renaissance.'

NG Here there was a great deal more of that in the literary scene during the Fascist era. There were the Ermetici (Hermetics) and those who were not Ermetici. And later, in the postwar years there was the neorealist group and the group who opposed the neorealists. But then later all this seemed to have died out. There was a brief period when a group called 'Il Gruppo '63' formed, but since then it seems like everyone just writes according to his or her own beliefs and interests. But then I'm a bit outside the scene and perhaps am not the most reliable witness. It does seem to me that these discrete currents or groups simply do not exist in Italy. There really isn't any real literary society in Italy any more. There was at one time, but no longer. For a while a group formed around Pasolini. I'd say if there are groups now that they are of a more casual, personal nature: friends who know each other and read each other's work. But that's all. This is my impression, anyway.

PB Those of us who observe or follow Italian literature from abroad sometimes imagine that there must be movements associated with major figures like Calvino, on the one hand, and very different writers – modern realists, if you like – such as you and Moravia.

NG I know so little about certain kinds of postmodern literature that I can't even talk about it. And besides, these categories really interest me very little. As for Calvino, I have to say honestly that I love especially his earlier work, his stories, his fiction up to and including *Invisible Cities* – a very beautiful book which I adore. I love less what came after *Invisible Cities*. The more recent work seems to me too cerebral. But then, that's just my personal preference, and it is hard to convince readers about what is most authentic in someone's work. Recently a book by Calvino was published posthumously, a book called *La strada di San Giovanni*. In this book there is a beautiful story – the title story, in fact – which is a sort of memoir written in 1965 or so – which he never thought to publish. And there are other wonderful pieces in that collection.

PB And Moravia? You've written about what an important model he was for you in your youth.

NG We were good friends. The news of his recent death hit me hard. I still feel the pain of his loss. And of course I remember how I responded to his early writing. When I was very young *Gli indifferenti* was of crucial importance as I formed my first views about writing. I'd have to say that for me Moravia's earlier work was also his strongest. I love the work up to and including *Roman Stories*. I think he thought they were perhaps too popular, too much in the mode of a sort of national narrative. Whereas for me the stories in this collection are extraordinary. He managed in that book to depersonalize himself in a masterful way.

PB Depersonalize?

NG Yes, by that I mean that he re-created himself in the form of many different characters in such a convincing way. His gift for getting inside the personality of characters so totally different from himself was truly remarkable. This was a gift comparable to that of Pascin, a writer who managed to get inside many diverse characters at a time, so as to paint a complete fresco of the France of his period, of the life of the peasants, of the servants, of the city, and of the provinces. He was a really great writer who is absolutely forgotten now. I would like somehow to bring him back.

PG Is his work translated into Italian?

NG Yes, but now it is totally ignored. There is a work of his I particularly love, a novel called *A Life*, which I'm in the process of translating now.

PG From the French?

NG Yes. I find it very easy and even pleasurable to read and translate French.

PG How about English? Do you read much in English? You refer more than once to English and American authors in your essays – Ivy Compton Burnett, for example.

NG Ah, yes, La Grande Signorina! There was a time when I had an appetite to read her novels. I read them all as they appeared and loved them very much in the original. But I confess I'm very bad at reading in English so I don't really do it much any more. The truth is I'm lazy and reading in English is work for me. The English and American writers I love I read mostly in translation. Sometimes I receive in the mail reviews of the English-language editions of my books and I can't even tell for sure whether they are favourable or not. And I'm too embarrassed to ask for help.

PB Sometimes one is better off avoiding one's reviews. But from what I've seen of the reception of your work in the United States, at least, the reviews would not much distress you.

NG Perhaps. As I said, I've not been terribly confident of my comprehension of the reviews. Maybe it's just as well not to understand. I admit, though, that when I'm stumped by a certain word here or there I suddenly want very much to know whether I am considered boring or whether the reviewer likes me.

PG Are there other English-language writers who mean a lot to you?

NG Well, of course, Shakespeare. And I love George Eliot as well. I've read the major authors, but in Italian, not English. Perhaps my favourite English novelist is Jane Austen. I hardly know contemporary American literature. The two American authors I love most, who are by now dead, alas, are Carson McCullers and Flannery O'Connor. And then I love Fitzgerald and Hemingway – especially the Hemingway of the stories.

PG Yes, it makes sense that Hemingway's clear, direct style would appeal to you, although the sensibility of Hemingway is so at odds with that of your own work.

NG I wasn't alone in being influenced by Hemingway. He had a great impact, I think, on modern Italian writing. When Edgar Lee Masters's *Spoon River Anthology* came out in Italian, suddenly there was widespread interest in North American writing. But even before that, Pavese was busy introducing us all to the great American writers.

PB Is that when Einaudi began pursuing Hemingway?

NG Well, of course, the war intervened around then. By 1946 one book – I forget which – by Hemingway came out, and by 1947 Einaudi had published three others.

PB I saw some correspondence between you and Hemingway in a recent exhibition of Einaudi letters. They were fairly business-like. Was your correspondence with him ever more personal? Was he interested in your ideas about his work? Were you friends?

NG Hardly. I was his Italian editor *e basta*. He was a prickly character and rather exacting about financial matters in a way I found tiresome.

PB I'm wondering if Hemingway translates well into Italian. Your own work, I think, has been very successfully translated into English, perhaps because your Italian is so accessible to foreigners.

NG Yes, I know that my books are easy for foreigners to read in Italian and I'm very glad about this. As for Hemingway, I don't know if his works are well translated or not, since my English is so deficient. Nor can I judge how well my own books have been translated into English for the same reason. I have a feeling that *Lessico famigliare*, or *Family Sayings*, is not well translated, however. This may have to do with the fact that some of it is in dialect and dialect is really impossible to translate adequately. As for my other works, I'm not sure that the fact that they are simple matters. Sometimes I feel I'm too bound by subtle details of style or tone in my work and that this is a liability.

PB But isn't this a problem all writers face in one degree or another?

NG Yes. You're right. It's a needless – even stupid – pretention to say otherwise. In fact I have been lucky both in English and in German. But translating is always so limited ...

PB And yet, you say you enjoy translating from the French?

NG I do. But I know that while I'm doing it I'm missing so much. At least I don't translate poetry.

PB I remember reading an early poem which you wrote right after the war, in memory of Leone Ginzburg, who had died in prison. It was terribly sad, as I recall, in your characteristically understated way, but very evocative of what must have been the mood for so many people who had lost their loved ones in the war. Did you write other poems after that?

NG Very few – not enough to collect. I'm not really a poet. It's only once in a while that what I have to say seems to find its best expression in a poem. But I do read a number of poets – Montale, Sandro Penna, Saba.

PB Besides the English writers whom you named earlier, there must have been other writers whom you regarded as models.

NG In my adolescence, the Russians were tremendously important to me. More than anyone, Chekhov. Of the Italians, Svevo, the Moravia of *Gli indifferenti.* When I started writing, these were the writers I kept before me.

PB Did you ever feel these influences interfered with your writing?

NG Well, I don't know. I think it's important for a young writer to keep certain models in mind, and to read a tremendous amount. One remains very attached to the formative figures, but at the same time, little by little, one finds one's own voice through them. At a certain point one understands how one wants to go about writing and emerges with some sort of personal style. But this is a slow process of maturation, not a fast one. What I find among young writers is that they read very little. They skip over that very important and necessary stage, that kind of passionate, visceral reading one does during the formative years. It happens that I still read a lot of manuscripts so I see what young writers are up to, and usually I'm disappointed.

PB You read for Einaudi?

NG I'm not a formal consultant for them anymore, but nevertheless I receive many manuscripts. I get the impression sometimes that these young writers haven't read many books, that they write in order to pass the time. They don't have a good literary background on which to build. Style is not something that can be improvised: one has to construct it, to make it.

PB Do you feel that this lack you find in young writers is a function of the Italian educational system? Is it the case in Italy as it is in the United States that the young are not *required* to read much?

NG Alas, yes. Literature is simply not given to them. The schools in general are very weak in this sense. Students are not asked to read whole books. The anthologies that are used as textbooks in the schools contain tiny excerpts of larger works. This is not reading.

Once a friend of mine and I put together an anthology for the schools using complete works of literature, but it did terribly.

PB Wasn't it adopted by the schools?

NG Only by a few, and then it died out. Our goal was to provide the students with real readings of some length. We included short stories that were complete works despite their relative shortness – eight pages or so. But the anthology was not successful. The current anthologies sometimes provide students with as few as twenty lines of an author and call that 'reading.'

PB The idea that a voice or a style is not *improvised* but rather *made* or constructed interests me. Did you deliberately 'make' your own style, fashioning it one way rather than another? Your characteristic avoidance of the third person, for example – is this a deliberate element in what you regard as a chosen style?

NG It's hard to say what is chosen and what is – fate. Look at the third person! I simply can't seem to make it work for me. When I've tried, it just hasn't come out right. I've attempted it here and there. I do use it occasionally, referring to 'him' or 'he' or 'she' but only with a single passing gesture. What I can't get is the panoramic view of things. I've tried to get around this problem in various ways – for example, by writing plays and by writing a long epistolary novel in which I was able to employ many voices. In this way through the use of characters in plays and by means of letters in my epistolary novel *The City and the House,* I am able to get inside more 'I's.' In this way I arrive at a sort of panoramic view by using a variety of first persons. I'm sure this was my main purpose in writing the plays and also in writing the epistolary novel: the desire to explore more 'I's' who were different from myself. Have you read the plays?

PB Yes, but only last week, I confess, since they are unavailable in the United States. In fact, after reading the first play in your recent collection, *Teatro,* about the young journalist who makes three different appointments to interview a famous writer and who is repeatedly stood up, I admit I was a little nervous about the prospect of travelling from Florence to Rome to interview you. I very much hoped that the particular 'I' who eludes the interviewer in that play was a totally different 'I' from Natalia Ginzburg.

NG Well, you see, you needn't have worried!

PB In the preface to the plays you speak of your friendship with Elsa Morante and of the way you depended upon her to give you an honest – even if overly harsh – reaction to your work. Besides being a great friend to you, was Elsa Morante a writer whose work you admired and do admire still?

NG I still feel the tremendous loss of Elsa Morante. It was not only a personal loss to her friends, but a great loss to the world. She was, I believe, the greatest writer of our time. I don't know how much her work is valued in your country, but here while she had great success she was also rejected by a number of people. And this rejection caused her much suffering. There were those who believed her works to be of a texture deliberately designed for consumption.

PB Accessibility is not always a virtue, I suppose, and it's a real problem when it's achieved at the expense of other literary virtues. But I read – in English – Morante's novel *History*, and I can't imagine what the Italian critics would have objected to in that work. It's quite a demanding novel, a novel of great textural and thematic range.

NG I'm glad these qualities come through in the English version.

PB Do you read Italian literary magazines much? Are there important magazines in which one would look to read the work of new authors?

NG There's the magazine *Nuovi Argomenti* and there's *Paragone*. Both are good and contain fiction by new writers. *Paragone* is edited by Cesare Garboli and is really excellent, but it is badly distributed. *Nuovi Argomenti* is the one that Alberto Moravia started and which is now edited by Francesca Sanvitale. This is much more famous and well distributed. It's a shame that we really only have these two literary magazines. One feels the need for others. Perhaps there are other small circulation journals which have escaped my notice, but if they exist their marginality says something about our literary culture as well.

PB Have you ever been tempted to run a magazine of your own?

NG I wouldn't know where to begin. It's really not my sort of thing.

PB How about poetry? Is the situation more or less the same with regard to magazines for poetry?

NG Perhaps even worse. There's one magazine, *Prato Pagano*, for poems, but to tell you the truth, I don't see it often. There are so many poets, you know, and so few places which publish them. Most publishers would rather not publish poetry, so it falls upon poets themselves to finance editions of their own work.

PB The situation is much the same in the United States, where very few firms have poetry lists.

NG Here the publishing houses have a hard time selling the books they do publish. Garzanti has a very substantial poetry list, but it's strictly a place where established poets are published. Einaudi has a small but very good poetry line as well. But it's very small.

PB What poets do you read besides the three you already named?

NG I love poetry written in dialect. The poems of Tonino Guerra are among my favourites. He's from Sant'Arcangelo di Romagna and his poems in dialect are very beautiful. A collection of his called *I bu, I buoi* is a particular favourite of mine.

PB I know his name, but from the movies.

NG Yes, that's right. He's more famous as a film person. But in fact he's a better poet. I first discovered his work years ago when I worked for Einaudi in Torino. He had sent in a fiction manuscript which I didn't care for much, but which I felt Vittorini might like, so I passed it on. Later Vittorini published it and other stories as well. He's gone on to publish two novels, which resemble the sort of thing everyone today is writing.

PB When you say that Guerra's fiction is like everyone else's today, what do you mean?

NG It seems to me that people don't write about what is authentic in their experience any more. Tonino Guerra, who comes from Sant'Arcangelo di Romagna, comes disguised as something entirely different in his prose. He has taken up the task of depicting a world that is squalid, and he does this in a way that goes against his past, against everything that he has been or is. It's false. His poems have nothing to do with that; they are honest and natural, full of details which make a vivid, brilliant poetry.

PB Do you speak Romagnolo?

NG Not really. When I read Guerra's poems in Romagnolo dialect I have to read them in editions with facing translations. The dialect is very difficult. Pasolini also wrote wonderful poems in dialect and put together a great anthology of dialect poems.

PB Have you ever wanted to write for the movies?

NG I've made many attempts, but I've never succeeded in it.

PB When I read the plays it occurred to me that film might be a medium you'd want to try some day.

NG In fact I'd like to be able to but I just don't know how to go about doing it. I love going to the movies, much more than I enjoy going to the theatre, actually. I think perhaps I don't have enough of a visual imagination to write for films. I *see* what I invent, but in a very private, probably incommunicable way. It's hard to explain ...

PB In some writers the visual imagination doesn't seem to count for much. But then there is Henry James, or Proust.

NG Yes, in Proust one sees everything. But I hope that in my own work – not that I want to compare myself to Proust in any way – there's an important sense of the visual, of the visualized. I see it all so vividly. It's not that I don't see what I imagine. If I don't see it then I can't write anything. What I mean to say is that I don't have a very *detailed* vision, and perhaps that's what is needed to write well for the cinema. Tonino Guerra has that kind of vision in his poems and at his best it comes through in the movies he makes. But I really don't have what it takes to write film scripts.

PB You were close to Pasolini, and I recall that you even appeared in at least one of his films. Did you learn any of the practical side of movie making at that time?

NG No, I never learned any of that. I did know Pasolini well, yes. But the technical aspect of film never interested me. I do go to the movies all the time, though. I love Fellini. And Bergman is a great master. I just read his autobiography, *The Magic Lantern*, and enjoyed it tremendously. It's such an honest book, I feel. And one understands so much more about the art by reading about the man in this case: his boyhood, his father. So many great films he made. *Scenes from a Marriage* is a masterpiece. *Shame* is another.

PB That's a hard one to take. Possibly the most painfully revealing film I've ever seen.

NG Yes, painful and very hard. The hardest. Desperate. He is a great, great director. Only Fellini in my country seems to me a comparably great figure. Others are interesting in their own way, but usually without the poetry. I know that it is customary to say that Fellini *is* poetry, but it's *true*, as it is true that others lack that quality.

PB Forgive me if I shift rather abruptly to another matter I'd like to discuss with you – namely, your Jewish identity. There aren't many Jewish characters in your work – the rather unattractive Polish doctor in *La strada che va in città* and Franz in *Tutti i nostri ieri* are the only two that come to mind. Has your Jewish identity been important to you?

NG My Jewish identity became extremely important to me from the moment the Jews began to be persecuted. At that point I became aware of myself as a Jew. But I came from a mixed marriage – my father was Jewish, my mother Catholic. My parents were atheists and therefore chose not to give us, the children, any religious instruction. They were totally nonobservant. You might say that a Hebrew spirit dominated the household in the sense that my father had a very strong, very authoritarian character. And I suppose it's true that many of the family friends were Jews, but many were not. So, while I did not have any sort of formal Jewish upbringing, I nevertheless felt my Jewishness very acutely during the war years (my first husband, Leone Ginzburg, was a Jew) and after the war, when it became known what had been done to the Jews in the camps by the Nazis. Suddenly my Jewishness became very important to me.

PB In your essay on the Jews, written after the massacre at the Munich Olympic Games in 1972, you speak of an involuntary identification with Jews despite your inveterate resistance to the idea that they or any other people are unique. And yet the essay develops a harshly anti-Zionist position.

NG My criticism extends to the terrorists and fanatics on both sides. It's a terrrible world we live in. But of course one can say that without being able to do anything about the sort of involuntary identification you mention. Others, for a variety of reasons, feel the identification in a very different, perhaps more powerful way.

PB Surely that was true of Primo Levi.

NG Yes, yes. He was another sort altogether. His death was a terrible blow for all of us. We never thought he would kill himself. He was a kind of reference point for us, a model of great serenity and balance. After he killed himself I realized that of course the memory of the camps can never be effaced in any survivor. So many of our great witnesses to that horror have committed suicide. But for every suicide there are always undoubtedly countless factors which must be appreciated. These are never simple matters. But I'm sure that the memory of the camps makes it impossible for one to completely accept life afterwards. And yet he was a person, as I remember him, who was extremely serene and ironic. In the end, though, the torment of his experience in the camps was intolerable.

PB Would you say that in Italy he was chiefly appreciated for his writings on the Holocaust?

NG No, not only for those, but in general. He was recognized as an extremely important figure. He hated the word 'holocaust,' though, and so do I. In Italian, at least, it has the distinct effect of ennobling something which cannot be ennobled. I feel 'genocide' is a better, more accurately descriptive word. But, yes, he was recognized and respected in every imaginable sense.

PB What are your feelings about suicide in general?

NG I think that one can't judge it as something good or bad. I think that suicide, in general, comes as a result of so many tiny matters and so many large matters which together make life intolerable. I don't think it can be called an act of courage or an act of humility or cowardice. It's really beyond the realm of judgment. So many survivors of the camps have killed themselves: Bettelheim, Améry, Celan, and Primo Levi. But each case is different, involving a variety of personal motives. The case of Pavese, for example, although he was not a concentration camp survivor, is one which was discussed a lot after his death. Pavese had a propensity for, an attraction to the idea of suicide all his life, from the time when he was a young man. But since he talked about it all the time we all thought that he would never go ahead with it. And even in his case there were so many different motives. Eventually they all added up and he must have felt there was no other escape.

PB When Primo Levi died, one person who wrote about him in *The New York Times* said – I still find it hard to believe – that Levi's act was a great disappointment to us all and that this act of cowardice inevitably forced us to re-evaluate all of his work.

NG But these are the words of a cretin! Also in Italy there were idiotic things written at the time.

PB I wanted to ask you about your public life. Would you tell me about the elected government position you occupy?

NG Well, I'm a member of the 'Camera dei Deputati' – the Italian equivalent, I think, of your House of Representatives. I was elected by the Party of the Independent Left and now I'm serving my second and last term.

PB How did you become involved in politics?

NG Well, when I was asked to run for office I immediately said 'No, I'm not a political person. I could never do such a thing because I don't have the necessary qualities one would need to perform well in office.' But they persisted, saying that I should try anyway, so I agreed to it with the understanding that I would be useless. But it turns out that despite the fact that I have no head for politics, I have become very passionately involved in my role as representative. By being a member of the Camera I come to learn about certain areas where much needs to be done in order for justice to prevail. It's not that I intervene all the time. In fact, I intervene seldom since I detest speaking in public. Furthermore, I know my limitations and there are certain issues about which I know nothing and to which I am incapable of responding intelligently. But I've learned a great deal, and this knowledge has enabled me to write certain articles which I couldn't have written before without having had this sort of profound understanding of certain matters. Of course I'm more passionate about some issues than others. The issue of adoption in this country, for example, has been very much at the centre of my concerns for the last several years. I wrote a book about this problem, *Serena Cruz*,[1] because I felt that in this case there was an important battle to fight. And the battle must be fought.

PB Did you first hear about the Serena Cruz case in the Camera?

NG Yes, first and most forcefully in the Camera, but then it became such a famous case that I read and heard about it everywhere. The general response when the first interrogations regarding the case were made before the House was absolute silence. Even the president tried to intervene on behalf of the adoptive parents because she felt an injustice had taken place. But it was all for naught. Nothing could be done.

The terrible thing is that cases like this continue to come up. I hear about them because ever since I wrote the book on Serena Cruz people write to me about their troubles. Desperate parents whose children have been taken away from them send me letters. Many of them are child-mothers whose babies are taken away from them simply for the reason that the mothers are poor. And this is wrong.

PB I still don't understand how the agency has the power to do this. The Giubergia, for example, Serena Cruz's first adoptive parents, were never proved guilty. Isn't that so?

NG Whether they were guilty or not we still don't know. Probably some illegality was committed. But, my God, punish the parents, not the child for the illegality! Even the father begged to be put in jail in order to spare the child. He was ready to serve a jail sentence.

PB But how is it that legally the judges were able to take away the child?

NG Because they are terribly powerful. And it's right that they should be. It's right that one should not be able to interfere with the decisions of judges. But the law should allow for the possibility of judging cases one at a time so as not to make children suffer.

PB Do you know where Serena Cruz ended up or how she is doing?

NG It seems that she was given to another adoptive family and that she's happily relocated to this other set of parents. Let's hope for her sake that this is true. But the trauma she's suffered is there and there's no denying it. And these poor unlucky people who first saved her from the orphanage in the Philippines where she had been sexually abused, half-starved, and allowed to remain so filthy that ear mites infested her ears, these people who did their best to nurse her back to good health have no recourse. This is not justice.

PB The subtitle of your book is 'The Real Justice,' and certainly you succeeded in persuading this reader at least about what the outcome of the case should have been. But I've spoken to some Italian friends of mine who feel very strongly that, in fact, justice *was* done, that the judge acted correctly.

NG In my opinion justice was not done, and yet I've been savagely attacked for taking this position. There's no doubt that somehow the Giubergia made a mistake. These are not sophisticated people; nor could they afford good lawyers. If they had received better advice, both initially when arranging to bring the child to Italy, and later when the investigation began, perhaps they would have fared better. But for a mistake, my God, you don't make a child suffer! And the little boy, Serena's foster brother, has in a sense been punished, too, since it was his sister that was taken away. Since then he has been terrified the same fate might befall him and refuses to go to school. I'm in touch with the family and they say that only now he is beginning to come around. To lose one's little sister in such a brutal way is a serious matter.

PB In your book you speak harshly about Italy. You say Italy has become a *tepid* country.

NG Yes, but I also mention that there were people, as well, who tried to intervene. Even the minister of justice tried to intervene on her behalf. A great many people tried to save Serena, but we all failed. There was nothing we could do.

PB Have you had the urge to write on behalf of other such cases?

NG I write articles about this and that, but this case took me over in a special way. And it has had at least one good effect. An association for the protection of children is starting to get organized.

PB But wasn't the whole Serena Cruz horror the result of a so-called effort to 'save children' on the part of the Agency to Protect Minors?

NG Ironically, yes. But the association that is being formed now is a private organization of parents of adopted children. It's important to have such groups to work outside the official system, free from the judicial system. It must be noted, by the way, that there were judges who were absolutely opposed to the decision of the judges who decided the Serena Cruz case. But, unfortunately, a great number of judges and social workers are rigidly unable to judge cases in a humane way. I've just heard of a case of a child-mother of nineteen with a seven-month-old baby. The mother was too poor to afford regular housing. When she received an eviction notice she applied to the housing authorities for free housing and instead of helping her they told her she was not entitled to have custody of her child because she could not afford to support it. They were about to put her child up for adoption. The girl is now in hiding, terrified that her baby will be taken away. Instead of trying to help her they thought it more efficient to take her baby. And there are plenty of such cases. The prevailing mentality sees that the solution of such cases lies in taking the child away from its parents without the consent of the parents. And this is unacceptable. You can't take a child away from its parents unless there's a serious reason – child abuse, for example. A civilized society should be able to offer such people help in the form of housing, stable employment, and so on.

PB In your book you talked about how a certain kind of forward-thinking Italian ridicules the Italy of tears, of obsessive idealization of the mother, and so on.

NG Yes, the people who made a fuss about the loss suffered by the Giubergia family and so on were considered regressive in this sense, overly sentimental. And so now, instead of a society which values familial feeling, we have a cold society which is embarrassed by it.

PB Your work has always turned on the subject of the family, almost as if you were always deliberately rethinking family life, meditating on this or that aspect of marriage, friendship, and infidelity and seeing how these affect families.

NG Yes, I believe the family to be terribly important, even when it is obsessive or repressive or full of insidious germs which can pollute life. But it's a necessary institution, a way in which children become adults, for which there's no substitute.

PB It's certainly a great literary subject that has served authors for a long time. Have you ever thought of writing a family novel à la Tolstoy, for example, with lots of families?

NG I'm no Tolstoy, that's for certain! I'm a minor writer.

PB Well, Chekhov was a major writer and he didn't feel called upon to write huge Tolstoyan novels.

NG I don't know if I could write such a book. Every time I sit down to write a book I feel that I have to start from zero, that I have to relearn how to write. Society is different now. By now the family is so disintegrated and so isolated. In the 1800s it made more sense to write novels about large, interconnected families. Perhaps this is another reason I don't write such novels. Values have changed so much.

PB So you feel that the only way to write about the family now is by writing short works about very particular situations?

NG At least that's my solution.

PB When you wrote the book on the Manzoni family did you think first of writing it as a novel?

NG Not at all. I wanted to plunge into a different kind of work altogether, to write something based entirely on fact, on research. I was not only intrigued with Manzoni himself, but with the whole family. The family's story is what strikes me as more meaningful, painful, even tragic. I had to consult documents, read letters, and so on. I didn't invent anything in that book. I tried to refrain from commenting on the facts as much as I could because I wanted to present an accurate portrait of this unfortunate family. This family, and Manzoni himself, too, was truly unlucky. Many of his children died at an early age; others gave him cause for unhappiness in other ways. He had two wives; the second one turned him against the children of the first marriage. She only loved her own child, who, by the way, was not without his own qualities. In short, I wanted to create a sort of fresco of the whole family, a family biography.

PB When I read the Manzoni book the project reminded me in ways of the sort of thing your son, Carlo Ginzburg, might have undertaken. Not that he's a biographer, or that you are a historian. But do you think you were aware of undertaking something more or less within the realm of your son's work?

NG Yes, it could be that I thought of Carlo and that his work influenced me. I'm very taken with the books he's written.

PB Have you ever been tempted to write a historical novel?

NG No, I've never even used historical references in my novels. I was a terrible student of history in school. I'm not a good scholar. And I've always had a sort of inferiority complex about history. In writing *The Manzoni Family* I wanted to try something new and I really enjoyed myself doing it.

PB For readers of my generation a book like *All My Yesterdays* reads like a historical novel, although for you it was something different.

NG Of course. For me it was simply writing about the things I had known and experienced. It's history now, but for me it was really a matter of dealing with my own time.

PB You wrote your essay 'The Little Virtues' a long time ago, really in another age. A number of American readers are very much taken with the piece while finding it a direct challenge to their familiar assumptions. Would you still offer parents the same advice with regard to the upbringing of their children or have your thoughts changed?

NG I'm sure that I would write exactly the same thing; even in these difficult times one should only teach the big virtues, generosity more than anything else. The rest can be learned later on.

PB Have you written about the virtue of generosity as a component of adult relationships? I think I can infer a good deal on this score from your writings on friendship, but I don't recall that generosity is itself a theme of your essays.

NG As you know, generosity is a complex idea, and I've thought about it mostly in connection with particular relationships or issues. Because I have known so many different writers I have often thought about what generosity means in a writer. Sometimes, as with other people you meet, you can tell about a writer at once. Though I only met her on one occasion I knew immediately that Nadine Gordimer was an enormously likeable, generous, and admirable person, and that is what I felt over many years reading her work. On the other hand, I am not fond of Aleksandr Solzhenitsyn.

PB Do you mean you're not fond of him as a person or that you don't care for his work?

NG No, not as a person and not as the author of the absurd declarations he's made recently, criticizing Gorbachev and advancing irresponsible proposals. They haven't convinced me one bit. I really wish that no one would interfere with Gorbachev in any way or try to place obstacles in his way. I feel that Gorbachev is a political genius and should be given more time to work out solutions that will keep his country viable. Solzhenitsyn's anticommunism is a visceral thing and one can almost understand it. But the things he says about Russia are often absurd. And they don't help matters. Sometimes one has a first reaction to a person which turns out to have been mistaken. But I have never liked Solzhenitsyn, and recent events don't persuade me to revise my estimate.

But there is a Russian whom I've read recently with great pleasure and that is Tsvetaeva. I've just read her two volumes of letters straight through. What a horrible life; my God, what suffering! Now *there's* a suicide that doesn't surprise me. Who could go on with such a life? And the additional posthumous blow: she asked a writer to care for her son after her death and then he didn't lift a finger to help the child. A truly atrocious life. During the Revolution her life was horrendous, and afterwards, in exile as well. And then when her friends turned their backs on her, she was so alone. Terrible! Serena Vitali has translated her into Italian exceptionally well and the notes are very helpful and informative.

PB Do you like to read biography?

NG I adore biographies. But only *true* biographies: 'So and so was born on such and such a day and died on such and such a day.' I don't like embellished biographies.

PB Do you wonder what your biographer will say about you eventually, how your story will be 'embellished'?

NG No, never. I honestly never think about such things.

PB Often in the United States readers come to feel that they know something about writers by watching them in action at public events. Can you tell me a bit about the relationship between writers in Italy and the university? Do writers frequently get invited to universities to read their work or to give lectures?

NG Not much. It's not really done in general. For some reason, however, I've been invited many times, but I've always refused.

PB Why?

NG Because I prefer not to. I detest speaking in public. A few times I've gone to the schools to speak with students. And while I don't love this either, I do it occasionally. Once I'm there answering their questions, engaging in a discussion with them, I'm fine. But it's a strain for me and if I can avoid such occasions, I do. A journalist recently said in the newspapers that writers should keep their mouths shut as much as possible and I think he was probably right. Better to write than to speak.

PB Do you feel it is a responsibility of the writer to write for the newspapers or in other ways to respond to contemporary events?

NG I feel the need to do so. But I don't feel it's necessarily something all writers should do. Before writing the book *Serena Cruz*, for example, I first wrote several articles on the subject for the newspapers. Every once in a while I feel compelled in this way to respond.

PB When you are angered by something?

NG Yes, I'm afraid these articles are usually born out of a sense of anger. When I hear in the Camera about something that enrages me I feel a responsibility to write about it in the newspapers.

PB How long will you continue to serve in the Camera?

NG After this term, I quit. I've served two terms already, which for a person like me, with no head for politics, is a lot.

PB Can we hope to see anything new of yours in the bookstores before too long?

NG Over a year ago I completed a translation from the French of a short book by Saul Friedlander, *When Memory Comes*, which I love very much. It should be coming out pretty soon. I wasn't sure how to translate the title, however. In Italian the literal translation – *Quando viene il ricordo* – didn't sound right. At first I thought to use *Conoscenza e ricordo*, but it sounded too much like a collection of essays. Finally I settled on *Poco a poco, la memoria*. In Italian that sounds much better: *Little by Little, Memory*.

PB I'm happy to know that you are translating what is one of my most treasured books.

NG I saw the *Salmagundi* symposium on kitsch built around another book by Saul Friedlander. He seems an enormously kind and interesting man. I look forward to meeting him when he's in Italy in December.

PB He's exactly as you imagine him from the book you've translated.

NG I only hope the book will be out by then. I'm afraid I'm responsible for the most recent delay in its publication, however. The publisher had chosen a really hideous cover for the book and I complained so much they agreed to change it. Now the cover will be a wonderful painting by Egon Schiele of a little boy with another, smaller, more ghostly image of a boy next to him. That image represents for me an imaginary figure, or perhaps a memory. I'm actually a little nervous about the translation; I hope it came out well. Sometimes I think that French and Italian resemble each other *too* much, so that the obvious translation is sometimes misleading.

PB I've wondered why, after you translated *Swann's Way*, you didn't go on to translate the whole of *Remembrance of Things Past*?

NG Well, when I undertook to translate Proust I was very young. In 1937 Giulio Einaudi and Leone Ginzburg (whom I married in 1938) proposed the project to me. It was crazy of them to propose that I do it and crazy for me to accept; nevertheless, I did. It was a crazy time and one projected crazy things. Leone, who was already a professor at the university, promised to help me. In fact the first sixty pages or so were done under his supervision. But then he became very busy with his resistance activities and he didn't have time to oversee the work. And then, of course, he died and I had to carry on by myself. Anyway, I never went beyond the two Gallimard volumes of *Swann's Way*. After that I gave up and others finished the job.

PB So you were translating Proust all during the war?

NG Well, I was supposed to be. The contract I signed in 1937 with Einaudi promised to deliver the entire manuscript by 1947 But I did other things as well during the war. My children were small and we had to move about quite a bit. While Leone was confined in the Abruzzi – in a little town called Pizzoli – in 1940, I managed to get through a large portion of the translation. I had brought with me the first two Gallimard volumes and felt that if I ever got through them it would be a miracle. I must have understood at some level that I wouldn't go on after that, even then. Besides, I hadn't been paid anything (the press was very poor then) and this gave me a certain freedom, I felt, to quit when I wanted.

PB But you said you enjoy translating.

NG I do, but I'm not a natural at it. And then I was just a beginner in every sense. Leone was really a gifted translator, but I knew from the start that I wasn't. When I handed him my original draft of the first two pages he turned them back to me saying they were not very good. He told me that I should look up every single word, even those I felt I knew, just to be sure I had the best translation possible. I took his advice very literally and looked up every single word, even *maison*, from then on. I understood, finally, what a job of ants and horses translation is.

PB Ants and horses?

NG One has to be as exact and industrious as an ant and have the impetus, the strength, of a horse to pull ahead. But I was in love with Proust and this really carried me through the job.

PB Is that the handsome edition of the book over there which I noticed when I came in?

NG No, no. That was given to me in 1938, when Leone and I were married, by Santorre Debenedetti. But I didn't dare carry anything so splendid with me to Abruzzo. I used a raggedy edition which I felt free to mark up.

PB So you carried the Gallimard books and your translation around with you, even when you went to the Abruzzi?

NG Yes, that and the Ghiotti dictionary.

PB And when you had to leave Pizzoli in a hurry?

NG Well, that's another story.

PB Go ahead. Tell me.

NG Well, as I said, I had managed to translate quite a bit while we were in confinement. Then suddenly Mussolini fell and we were not constrained to remain in Pizzoli. Immediately Hitler took advantage of the unstable situation and invaded Italy. Leone went to Rome to continue his clandestine political activities and I stayed behind with the children. But I soon received word that the Germans were headed in my direction and Leone said that I should join him in Rome. I left the house in a hurry with the children and moved to the local *pensione* until I could make the next move. Of course, I took very little with me, certainly no books. The Germans arrived shortly thereafter, but my hosts at the *pensione* told them I was a Neapolitan cousin of theirs whose house and possessions – including, of course, all identity papers – had been destroyed by a bomb. They said I needed to get to Rome and asked the Germans to give me a lift. So I was taken to Rome with my children in a German military truck!

PB And what happened to the manuscript?

NG A neighbour went to the house right before the Germans ransacked it and took my books and papers and saved them for me until after the war. She hid them all that time under a sack of flour.

Meanwhile, I hardly thought about those papers, and when I did I thought of them as lost like so much that was precious to me during that period.

PB So when did your translation of the first two volumes appear?

NG In 1946. And although I was greatly relieved, I was also disappointed. Certain mistakes had been corrected, but I wasn't consulted about the corrections. There were many changes of which I didn't approve.

PB Like what?

NG Oh, small matters, but nevertheless important. I had called the famous *madeleine* a 'maddalenina,' which is really not at all ugly. But the editors decided to keep that word in French. Why, I don't know. But last year Einaudi came out with my original translation, in which only the *mistakes* have been corrected. So I'm happy.

PB You've translated Flaubert, too, haven't you?

NG Yes, in 1983 I translated *Madame Bovary* for an Einaudi series called 'Writers Translated by Writers.' It was a wonderful project. Primo Levi translated Kafka's *The Trial*, Calvino did Raymond Queneau's *The Blue Flowers*.

PB What are you working on now?

NG Oh, small projects, introductions to new books or new editions of old books that I feel it's important to endorse somehow. Things like that.

PB Can we hope for more works of fiction?

NG Yes, let's hope ...

NOTE

1 Serena Cruz is a Filipino girl whose Italian adoptive father claimed that she was his illegitimate daughter conceived on an earlier trip to the Philippines during the Marcos era, when he had adopted Serena's older foster brother. The Italian railroad employee had, after her third birthday, returned to the Philippines to claim her and sign paternity papers. Since there was no adoption, per se, of the child, there were no adoption documents. When the Italian Agency to Protect Minors heard there was a Philippine child in their country and found there were no adoption papers, they prosecuted the father for illegal adoption and took the child away from the family. It was never established whether the father was indeed her legitimate father or whether this had just been a ruse to circumvent the very cumbersome and

costly adoption laws in both Italy and the Philippines. For example, since Corazon Aquino was elected to office in the Philippines, it has been the law that adopting parents must reside in the Philippines at least six months – hardly a possibility for most working people – after adopting a child before taking the child out of the country.

Natalia Ginzburg between Fiction and Memory: A Reading of *Le voci della sera* and *Lessico famigliare*

LUIGI FONTANELLA

Allow me on such an occasion, and for a writer such as Natalia Ginzburg, whose biography has so often crossed the models of literary invention, to begin my critical discourse with a few personal memories, whose purpose here will serve as a friendly homage and intimate testimonial to this writer whom we have recently lost.

I shall begin by going *à rebours*, to the day of her funeral, held on a tepid autumn morning of 1991. I attended the ceremony with Achille Millo, whom I had met only a few months before, and who subsequently (and very quickly) became my friend and kindred spirit.

I had learned of Natalia Ginzburg's demise quite unexpectedly and by accident two days before from a television news report. Among several newscasts, there, appearing suddenly on the screen, almost shattering it, was an image of Ginzburg's sombre, absorbed countenance and, immediately following, the announcer's indifferent voice saying: 'Natalia Ginzburg died this morning at her home in Rome,' etc. etc. I couldn't help but stare dumbfounded upon that stony and 'columbian' face. Suddenly I was no longer listening to that neutral voice which, as in a double-image, continued to recite its own script. Now, as I write these lines, I cannot help but think of Ennio Flaiano, who gave death a scorching definition: Death is like that woman who, while you're speaking at a public telephone, passes you by, and beckons.

The interior of San Lorenzo church, which rises in the homonymous square at the end of Via dei Giubbonari (for me, one of the most glorious little streets in the old part of Rome – before it was to become ruined by throngs of parvenus), was jammed with people. Among the crowd: Giulio Einaudi, her affectionate publisher, Enzo Golino, Raffaele

La Capria, Enzo Siciliano, Aldo De Jaco, Gian Luigi Piccioli, Giulio Ferroni, Vittorio Foa (one of the Ginzburg family's dearest friends and confrères), and many other writers, young ones as well, whom I would not have expected to find in such great numbers. A few paces away stood Cesare Garboli, perhaps the most keen exegete of Ginzburg's works. It suddenly occurs to me now that it was together with Garboli that I last saw Natalia about ten years ago. It was on the occasion of the editing of one of my essays, precisely in her house, used by Garboli as a *point de chute* for his periodical stops in Rome. Actually it was on this very occasion that I had appealed to Cesare's extraordinary ability to know how to 'drain' a critical text. Ginzburg, gentle and discreet, received us in the ample living room where, a decade before, I – a timid, 'green' writer – had made my awkward entrance. My memory of that first meeting, twenty years ago now, is vivid and bright. I was teaching Italian literature at Visconti in Rome and carrying on research at the university, where I was among the many 'precarious ones' in the Department of Italian. Giacomo Debenedetti, with whom I had studied up to the threshold of my 'Laurea,' and to whom I owe almost everything as regards my critical formation, had died a few years before. Thus, I had lost, in addition to his affectionate, nervous, and illuminating guidance, every practical means of being helped with my academic career (being ignorant of the perfidious academic war that raged against 'Giacomino,' who, now that I think about it, could not have done anything for me in that Italo-morass, considering the obstacles he himself had to face).

In my class there was a certain Silvia Ginzburg: brilliant and lively, by far the most intelligent and sharp-tongued student. It was in fact through her, Natalia's niece, that Ginzburg was able to read my first short stories. She liked them. She wanted to meet me. And there I am on a November afternoon in 1974, passing through the main gate of that austere palace on Piazza Campo Marzio 3. She received me with a quiet grace while I did everything possible to hide my emotion, which was no more than an extreme sense of modesty. We spoke (she mostly) of modern narrative, of Elio Vittorini, of Cesare Pavese, of other writers. Then, at one point, she abruptly changed the subject and began a commentary on my three short stories, entering into narrative details and mechanisms: a commentary that to me, a novice writer, appeared as manna from heaven. Then she bluntly asked me what my plans were for the future. I dared to tell her that I wanted to be a writer and a literary critic, that I was already engaged in these activities, but that somehow I wished to do so full time. She immediately advised me that to leave teaching would be a mistake. In her pedagogical manner, she quoted several of Pavese's words (which I no longer remember verbatim), not only emphasizing the importance of teaching, but also how it would not contrast with the aspirations of a writer; as a matter of fact, it could actually serve as a basic area of ferment. Years later, in some passage of *Le piccole virtù*, I would rediscover that advice intact. And who knows if, thanks also to those words, that is the reason why I have remained for so many years in the teaching field. She also gave me some practical suggestions on narrative writing, such as how to avoid descriptions that were not absolutely pertinent and how to organize dialogues. It is incredible how, as in days long past, while I reread several of Ginzburg's main works, the above annotations were ringing in my mind and in my ears (one must remember that by 1974, Ginzburg had already published the central body of her major narrative).

I never tired of listening to this wise and pensive woman, whose writing, even though I respected it, was very distant from my tastes and from the rages that were fermenting in me at that period of time: I loved surrealism, and I had recently discovered writers like Antonio Delfini, Tommaso Landolfi, and Alberto Savinio, taking a passionate fancy to them. I'm not mentioning Italo Svevo, to whom Debenedetti had years prior introduced me, and whom I would routinely reread: theirs was a 'crazed,' nervous writing, much different from Ginzburg's sensible, tidy, and delicate writing. It was because of this fundamental difference in style between Ginzburg and myself that when, two years later, I sent her the manuscript of my first novel, she wrote me a long letter in a rather critical vein. But despite that, I never ceased to admire and respect her. Among other things, the dedication of one of my poems in *La vita trasparente* (1978), a poem for which Natalia wrote me a flattering note of praise and affection, bears testimony to this admiration.

Subsequently, our communication dissipated, because shortly thereafter I relocated to Harvard, where I had received an important scholarship. At that time, I must confess, I would never have imagined that I would have stayed so long in this country.

For me, Natalia Ginzburg remains a great teacher of life. Books like *Le voci della sera* (1961) and *Lessico famigliare* (1963) are already among the classics of the late twentieth century. Even today, although admitting that my literary tastes lie in other narrative forms, I must acknowledge that the clarity and moral force of her writing, the balanced doses of fantasy and memory, the understated tones of her melancholic cheerfulness, make Ginzburg one of the most original and discreet narrators of this century.

I cannot be less than satisfied that, finally, even American audiences have begun to appreciate her worth and that translations of her books are becoming more and more frequent. I am therefore most pleased that this occasion has 'demanded' that I reread many Ginzburghian pages and that I reflect with greater critical composure, as well as biographical distance, upon their main stylistic features.

My attention turns particularly to *Le voci della sera* and to *Lessico famigliare*, hereafter referred to as *VS* and *LF*. All textual references are taken from the first volume of Ginzburg's *Opere*, Mondadori's *ne varietur* edition of 1986 (translations of all Ginzburg's passages in this essay are mine).

Preliminarily, the persistent use of the imperfect and past perfect in these books must be underlined. The tenses are often combined together on the same page. A good example could be on page 708. The first tense (the imperfect), used frequently, proves effective in punctuating the psychological or projective dynamic, even though it is inserted in a *present* situation, whether concomitant to the real time of the event or of its relative transcription, or whether as a purely imaginative phase. One example is the tense that children use when they play in the context of a figurative present, where the action is transposed into a kind of 'past' that can be codified – habitual, so to speak, by representing exactly the nonreal. The hypothetical conversation between two children who are playing with their doll Sbrodolina – 'You *used to buy* the things and you *used to bring* them to me. You *used to cook* and then we *fed* Sbrodolina' – exactly signifies: 'You *are pretending* to buy the things and you *are pretending* to bring them to me; I *am pretending* I'm cooking,' etc.

The other tense (past perfect) indicates, instead, a completed thought or, actually, an event already framed in its temporal dimension: a matter of fact upon which one can embroider mentally (or conjecture) upon what could have been if it hadn't been as it then turned out to be. The following extract demonstrates the two tenses in question:

> Aveva, quando andava al torrente nell'estate, un vestito azzurro, con una striscia bianca sul fondo dalla sottana. Aveva un fazzoletto a palle bianche ed azzurre, che si cingeva attorno ai capelli. Aveva, d'inverno quando andava a sciare, un maglione bianco, col collo rivoltato. Metteva sulle

> spalle, nelle sere fresche dell'autunno, quando sedeva in giardino, uno scialletto nero da povera. Aveva sposato il Vincenzino senz'amore. Ma aveva pensato che era tanto buono, un po' malinconico, e che doveva essere così intelligente. Aveva anche pensato che lui aveva tanti soldi, e che lei non ne aveva. (708)
>
> She had, when she used to go to the stream in summer, a blue dress with a white stripe on the skirt. She had a blue and white polka-dotted handkerchief that she used to tie around her hair. She had, in winter when she used to go skiing, a white sweater with an upturned collar. She would place on her shoulders, in the cool evenings of autumn when she would sit in the garden, a beggar's black shawl. She had married Vincenzino without love. But she had reasoned that he was so good, a little melancholic, and should have been so intelligent. She had also thought that he had a lot of money, and that she had none.

Meantime, singular or rare terms appear, belonging to the narrator's affective memory. We shall find them again, in large measure and in the sphere of family relationships, in *LF*, to demonstrate, precisely, a lexicon that belongs to a specific *group* of persons dealing with one another, and who therefore *can recognize* it. Some examples: *Ciula* (short for 'fanciulla' > 'ciulla' > 'ciula'), that is, an inexperienced young woman, a person who is a bit rash; *Purillo* (literally: the small cotton tassel that is found on the tip of the Basque beret; by extension the beret itself); *Marzuppia* (slang term for 'madam').

Cesare Garboli, in the preface to Ginzburg's *Opus*, has happily defined *VS* and *LF* as 'tribal novels,' that is, novels wherein one can register a physiological relationship with the world. To that same relationship, Garboli states, refers the inexhaustible chatter of the girls whom Ginzburg makes, in her comedies, speak and monologize with one voice, which is a function of the body. Furthermore, this relationship is defined by the centrality of the primitive, carnal, 'physiologic' (by definition) theme in which the central concern is living together, eating together – in other words, being part of a tribe.

If it is true that these are Ginzburg's characteristic aims in *VS* and *LF*, it would appear natural and as a consequence (naturally, consequently) that the innate language of this group be exclusive, and, therefore, immediately recognizable *only* by the group.

From this springs the iteration of several narrative mechanisms, even of gestures, moody reactions, witticisms, which, though they appear wearisome at first, reveal, in reality, the ancestral nature they bear. And corresponding, paradoxically, to a narrative technique that is rather static and repetitive, an extraordinary narrative mobility is found. The lesson of Cesare Pavese, which Natalia profitably treasured, is here evident. The Pavesian influence is especially apparent where the narrative proceeds rapidly via abrupt cuts, quick situational mutations, and vertiginous changes of scene (examples of this phenomenon are at pp. 256ff. and 717ff.). This is an expansion technique, typical of the best of Ginzburg: a kind of accumulative narrating (and narrating to oneself) in which words-thoughts-situations amass casually on the page, leaning one against the other, one inside the other, without solution of continuity. This is a smooth and effective technique that reminds one of Robert Bresson's early cinematographic technique with its sudden chiaroscuros of prodigious expressive force.

To the lesson of Pavese, a very mobile narrator, I would also add the dialogical lesson of Elio Vittorini in *Conversazione in Sicilia*, and of *Il Sempione strizza l'occhio al Frejus*: a dialogue that so obsessively unravels itself with the same modalities ('says – said – says – says – said – said – said') so as to seem, in stretches, a kind of continued monologue. At the end of this tangle of whispered idle chatter, of which *VS* is substantially interwoven, the character of Elsa reappears, and the narration, suddenly, reacquires its own unitary compactness after the preceding irregular dissipation, and becomes filtered through the 'I' of the feminine character with the relative transition from the third to first person.

This narrative mechanism, which for the sake of convenience I might characterize as horizontal, where everything occurs via minimal albeit profound moves, is evident also in *LF*, 'un romanzo,' in the words of the author herself, 'di pura, nuda, scoperta e dichiarata memoria ... il solo libro che io abbia scritto in stato di assoluta libertà (1133) ('a novel' of pure, naked, discovered and declared memory ... the only book that I have written in a state of absolute freedom').

So, while in *VS* places and characters were fictitious yet always filtered through Ginzburg's biography, here in *LF* they become equipped with their own names. The whole contributes to form a narrative orchestration permeated by *nostalgia and fiction*: the binomial that is at the root of Ginzburg's narrative canon in these texts.

In an early passage of *LF*, it is Natalia herself who underscores this bipolarity by speculation and reciprocal effects:

> Cullandomi nella nostalgia, o in una finzione di nostalgia, feci la prima poesia della mia vita. (924)

> Lulling myself in nostalgia, or in a pretense of nostalgia, I wrote the first poem of my life.

And here I cannot help but quote a passage by Garboli that, recapturing some notations of Montale and of Pampaloni (although Silvio Benco in the distant 1940s had already spoken about the 'real and the fantastic' in *Il Piccolo*, 30 July 1942), placed in exhaustive relief this nodal aspect concerning the particular state of 'narrative nostalgia' or of Ginzburg's memory and fiction in *LF*.

> Tradotta in termini letterari, quest'approssimazione è la nostalgia (l'immagine) che un poeta ha del romanzo, il sogno di far cadere sul vissuto, su se stessi, quelle luci magiche, di esporre se stessi a quelle luci come per un'abbronzatura: e dov'è più vicina a realizzarsi, a toccare il fantasma del romanzo e ad afferrarlo, l'approssimazione all'Ineffabile, se non a qualche centimetro da ciò che è realmente accaduto? Quando la Ginzburg scrisse *Lessico famigliare*, abbandonando le storie immaginarie per i ricordi, fu visitata da una rivelazione: i romanzi sono già scritti; per farli esistere, per dare loro la forma, il corpo, bisogna 'strumentarli'; fare uscire la musica dall'aria (la forma dal blocco), e sottrarre, sottrarre, non finire mai di sottrarre, togliendo al vissuto la farina, il fior fiore, la vocalità, il brusío, il rumore della vita che cammina ... Ma di chi sono i 'ricordi'? *Lessico famigliare* non è scritto da un adulto che rivisiti il passato per amore del passato, e non è scritto da un adulto (come Proust) che interroghi il Tempo per incontrare se stesso; è scritto da un bambino che ha già visto tutto: i ricordi della Ginzburg sono una finzione, ricordi 'in prestito,' utilizzabili per un investimento nell'immaginario. (xxxiii–xxxv)

> Explained in literary terms, this approximation is the nostalgia (the image) that a poet has of the novel, the dream of letting those magical beams fall on what is lived, on oneself ... the desire to expose oneself to that light as if one were suntanning. This approximation to the Ineffable is closer to its realization, to touching and seizing the phantom of the novel, when it is distant only a few centimetres from that which has really happened. When Ginzburg wrote *Lessico famigliare*, abandoning imaginary stories for memories, she was visited by a revelation: novels pre-exist their writers; in order to bring them to life, to give them a shape – the body – one must

'set them to music,' make music from the air (a form from the block), and subtract, subtract, never stop subtracting. One must take from one's past experiences the flour, the cream, the vocality, the humming, the noise of life going on ... But to whom do the 'memories' belong? *Lessico famigliare* is not written by an adult who revisits the past out of love for the past, and it is not written by an adult (like Proust) who questions Time so as to meet himself; it is written by a child who has already seen everything: Ginzburg's already seen everything: Ginzburg's memories are a fiction: they are memories 'on loan,' that can be used for an investment in the imaginary.

As is well known, the memories of *LF* are primarily of the gloomy twenty-year Fascist period that, as Giansiro Ferrata wrote while reviewing the book in *Rinascita*, 'serves as an insistent and dramatic backdrop' (27 April 1963). But it must be immediately stressed that Ginzburg, although facing such a suffocating political climate whose tragic and closest victim would be her husband Leone, never lets herself be led by the hand, and keeps intact the *plaisir* of the narration. One of her assiduous readers has noted that even if reality is meagre, 'that which follows her, life, is full of significant mysteries and awesome marvels' (Geno Pampaloni, *Il Corriere della Sera*, 29 November 1970).

In *LF* the presence of idiomatic words, or jargon, belonging to Ginzburg's linguistic-familiar memory, becomes more massive. Here some examples (the terms in question are in italics).

Non fate *sbrodeghezzi*! Non fate *potacci*! (901, for things of bad taste)

Non fate *negrigure*! (901, inappropriate acts or gestures)

Sono andate via tutte quelle *babe*? Non ti sei stufata di *babare*? = Non ti sei stufata di *ciaciare*? (911, 'babare' to become stupid if together with other stupid people; 'ciaciare' = to babble, to gossip)

Ti te vedet quel pan lì? L'è tutta *barite*. (915, barium sulphate; by extension: something heavy)

Era una *baslettona*! (950, for a person who has a protruding jaw)

Cos'ha Terni con Mario e Paola da *ciuciottare*? (952, for whispering gossips, probably from the French *chuchoter*)

Cosa sono tutti quei *fufignezzi*? (952, for secret mix-ups and gossips)

Sgarabazzi! (953, for scribbles)

Alberto, lui è un *manfano*! (984, for cleaver)

Ho la *catramonaccia*. (1017, a mixture of gloominess and a sense of loneliness)

It is interesting to note that all these locutions were used by Natalia's relatives. She exhumes them tranquilly in her memorialized pages, at times asking her deepest self their significance. Several of these locutions have such *representative* force that, by synecdoche, they end up signifying the same character to which that locution was attributed. It had already occurred in *VS* with terms like *Ciula* and *Purillo*.

While on the subject of linguistic analysis, one must also note the frequent and idiosyncratic syntactic constructions used by Ginzburg: subject, direct object, and repetition of the latter via the pronoun ('I, Salgari's novels, had read and forgotten them'); or, even more frequently, the anticipation (the advance placement) of the direct object before the subject, at times doubling the direct object with the pronoun ('Our sweaters, my mother used to purchase them at Neuburg'; 'Milk, I hated it'; 'The caramels, my mother used to buy them only so as to teach me arithmetic').

Other variants include the subject used twice, with risk of anacoluthon since the first remains dangling in space, but efficacious, nonetheless, because it serves as a kind of bell that immediately announces the event that concerns it, but expressed by the other subject ('Leone, his true passion was politics'; 'Chiaromonte, his wife died at the hospital exactly during those days'); or the anticipation of the subject's verb ('[She] had been, in the past, quite rich, my grand-mother'; [They] moaned, my brothers and my mother at times'; '[Those] were, the first years in Turin, difficult years for my mother'; '[He] was, my father, always ready to invite people to supper').

Another interesting variant is the doubling of the subject, or the subject immediately fortified by the personal pronoun ('Gino, he didn't write poems'; 'My father, he smoked like a Turk'; 'Vittorio, he was not arrested').

These syntactic systems tend to stress the aura and the mnemonic *allure* of the story, mostly segmented by the imperfect: a constant priority *incipit* to the memorial flux. No other tense could lend itself to the same expressive effectiveness, or obtain the same 'mediumistic' results. On the whole, a private and public *retablo* springs from it, an epocal fresco wherein sentimental truth (never sentimentalistic) and 'falsehood' or invention (in a literal sense) intermingle and finally blend into themselves.

> Perché l'ospedale non mi facesse impressione, mia madre mi aveva dato ad intendere che l'ospedale era la casa del dottore; e che gli altri malati nelle stanze erano tutti i figli, cugini, e nipoti del dottore. Io, per obbedienza, credetti; e tuttavia, allo stesso tempo sapevo che si trattava d'un ospedale; e quella volta come anche più tardi, la verità e la menzogna si mescolarono in me. (974)

> So that the hospital would not alarm me, my mother had me believe that the hospital was the doctor's house, and that the other patients in the rooms were all children, cousins, nieces, and nephews of the doctor. I, out of obedience, believed it; yet, at the same time, I knew that it had to do with a hospital; and that time, as some time later, truth and falsehood were mixed up in me.

The characters of this theatre of memory are not only familiar countenances, but clearly the very same characters that have culturally represented an era: from Turati to Kuliscioff, to Salvatorelli, Carlo Rosselli, Carlo Levi, Giulio Einaudi, Lussu, Chiaromonte, Paietta, Foa, Balbo, and obviously the never-to-be-forgotten Cesare Pavese and Leone Ginzburg. Here, then, the remembered story becomes (Hi)story with a capital 'H,' while the small 'h' is reserved for all the private little streams of which it is composed. We will therefore forgive Ginzburg for the almost obsessive repetition of certain expressive attitudes or for those not so rare notations almost listed with nonchalance or a distracted 'negligence' for which a poet-friend like Pasolini, who at times was too severe, would chide her.

The uninterrupted flow of life (and of History) occurs without any obstacles, and Ginzburg, with her *reticent truth*, is capable of softening (like the painter Morandi) the more exacerbated peaks yet readily allowing the objects and events (capital events even) that make up the public and the private of her own story to appear before the reader's eyes – events such as the slaughter of the Rosselli brothers, the frequent passport confiscations, the arrest and tragic demise of her husband,

Leone, and, in sum, all the dark and violent Fascist outbreaks. Ginzburg's reticence extends itself to the narration via the effective use of *aposiopesis*, which permits the reader some self-reflection on those things recalled or only suggested. The author uses this allusive silence as a kind of veil that makes it difficult to distinguish pity from decency, or modesty, or a persistent discretion.

I will concur with Montale that, as it transpires in many pages of *VS*, the story becomes 'cloudy,' opaque, 'so that the grey becomes so vivid that it appears luminous once the eyes become accustomed to that particular uniformity of colour' (in *Il Corriere della Sera*, 20 June 1961). Even the atrocious death of the person most dear to her, her husband, Leone, is conveyed directly, in an almost casual manner, 'listlessly.' Can one believe this obstinately extinguished tone, even as she speaks of the life and death of a person who was fundamental to her life? It would be objectively difficult to believe if one did not frame Ginzburg's attitude in a personal and comprehensive stoicism as regards life's sufferings. As we already have verified, one of Ginzburg's principal characteristics is to announce the event (no matter how tragic) without intermediate frills and then, further along, *à rebours*, to circle around it, embroider upon it, to reflect upon it. Such is the case regarding her long editorial experience at Einaudi. In these important pages, Ginzburg vividly recaptures the socio-literary ambiance in Italy immediately following the war:

> Era necessario tornare a scegliere le parole, a scrutarle per sentire se erano false o vere, se avevano o no vere radici in noi, o se avevano soltanto le effimere radici della comune illusione. Era dunque necessario, se uno scriveva, tornare ad assumere il proprio mestiere che aveva, nella generale ubriachezza, dimenticato. E il tempo che seguí fu come il tempo che segue all'ubriachezza, e che è di nausea, di languore, di tedio; e tutti si sentirono, in un modo o nell'altro, ingannati e traditi: sia quelli che abitavano la realtà, sia quelli che possedevano, o credevano di possedere, i mezzi per raccontarla. (1066)

> It was important to go back, and select words, to scrutinize them, to hear if they were true or false. If they were or were not deeply rooted in us, or if they had only the ephemeral roots of the common illusion. Therefore it was necessary, if one wrote, to return and to be employed at the same profession that one had before, in the general drunkenness, forgotten. And the period that followed was like the period that follows drunkenness,

> that is, of nausea, languor, tediousness; and everyone felt, in one way or another, betrayed or cheated: whether or not they lived reality, whether or not they possessed, or thought to possess, the means of recounting it.

In the latter part of this passage she echoes, allusively but with real suffering, the pain felt by those who, like Pavese, would not survive that state of deception and of tediousness – what Montale would define as *il male di vivere* ('sickness of living'). A year before the publication of *LF,* in *Le piccole virtù,* Natalia would cut the most poetic and vibrant portrait that we have of the author of *La bella estate,* her dear friend, Cesare Pavese.

In summary, *LF* consists of a constant and arresting, diffused hum of lives that intertwine continuously with each other; thus, the entire book appears as a small curtain that opens onto an ideally personal stage where Ginzburg permits *her own characters* (friends and relatives) to recite in a truthful manner so that we can follow them with a detached fondness and with Manzonian, clear reserve. It was not happenstance that in the last years of her life, Ginzburg dedicated a book, the fruit of a long historical-epistolary research, to the Manzoni family. Also, it is significant, in mentioning terms like 'small curtain' and 'private stage,' that soon after *LF* Natalia would find the expressive canon of the theatre to be equally congenial to her narrative dialogical art. The comedy *Ti ho sposato per allegria* (1964) was pratically written under *LF*'s wing, and in the subsequent three years the following plays appeared in succession: *L'inserzione, Fragola e panna,* and *La segretaria.* Guido Fink's valid comments on Natalia's theatre are, in large part, also applicable to *VS* and *LF*, especially to those pages where vivid and figurative dialogues thicken:

> Non c'è più una vera differenza fra chi sta sulla scena e chi viene solo nominato, fra il parlar d'altro e il seguire le fila di un discorso rigorosamente conseguente. (*Il Mondo,* 1 novembre 1973)

> There is no longer a true difference between who is on stage and who is only mentioned, between talking about something else or following a topic of conversation that is rigorously self-consistent.

The conclusion of the 'novel' (as well as that of my essay) cannot help but be *in medias res,* just as it was at the beginning. Ginzburg doesn't feel the need for a rounded conclusion, for a 'finale': there cannot be a finale to a story that tells about one's life still progressing. Ginzburg is simply aware that the narrative and memorialized 'distance' has already peaked. *LF*, in fact, closes with her transfer from Turin to Rome. Here then, those years, those episodes, those characters quickly acquire a fabled, 'antique' taste, tender and bitter-sweet. Again, one is reminded of a passage from Montale: 'Men and things are more similar to a fable than to a memory. The world has no weight for Natalia' (in *Il Corriere della Sera*, 20 June 1961).

LF and *VS* do not have a novel's size or dimension, nor its breadth, nor its organic structure. The two books (particularly *LF*) are an uninterrupted flux of moments that *synchronically* interact on the page with continuous comings and goings of memory, a memory which is fictional narrative and touching yet retained evocation at the same time. Garboli said it well in his preface to Ginzburg's *Opere*: 'Dall'immaginario all'autobiografico, e di nuovo all'immaginario, l'arco ha il suo zenith nei trionfali ricordi torinesi di *Lessico famigliare* (xxviii–xxix) ('From the imaginary, to the autobiographical, and again from the autobiographical to the imaginary, the arc reaches its zenith in the triumphal *torinese* memories of *LF*). This novel is a free recollection and is therefore totally disconnected from structural shackles; free to roam at pleasure in its own *Erlebnis*, as well as in the folds of the souls of others, but always with respect and indulgence.

Postscript

Some works by and about Ginzburg were published after the completion of this essay. I take the opportunity to refer to them in this postscript, which thus brings up-to-date and further expands my reading of *VS* and *LF*.

Cinque romanzi brevi e altri racconti (Torino: Einaudi, 1993) contains an important introduction by Cesare Garboli which provides an exhaustive examination of Ginzburg's early works, especially in relation to her later irregular production as writer-essayist. As far as my analysis is concerned, Garboli's emphasis on the crucial moment of Ginzburg's evolution as a prose writer, characterized for years by the narratological dilemmas of 'how to write' and of the 'point of view' of the narrator, seems particularly relevant (Garboli's choice of glossing Ginzburg's own prefatory note to the first edition of *Cinque romanzi brevi*, 1964, is appropriate). The dilemmas are clarified and solved 'nel momento in cui la prima persona della Ginzburg diventa anagrafica (*Lessico famigliare*), e il punto di vista del Narratore va a coincidere con l'io di Natalia Ginzburg in carne ed ossa, il nesso tra immaginazione e realtà si snebbia quasi per miracolo, e la confusione diventa chiarezza' (vi) 'once Ginzburg's first person becomes self-referential (*Lessico famigliare*) and the point of view of the Narrator comes to coincide with the I of the real Natalia Ginzburg; almost miraculously, the connection between imagination and reality is revealed, and the confusion becomes clarity.'

Garboli then considers two novels which, though important, do not fit within the scope of my essay, namely *La strada che va in città* and *È stato così*. In these works, which are in specular relation to each other, Ginzburg articulates, in two stylistically different ways, the theme of the impact of the world upon the Girl and the ensuing end of childhood. Garboli considers *La strada* one of Natalia's most beautiful books 'un libro senza rughe: non perde mai di freschezza, e mantiene intatta, a ogni rilettura, attraverso gli anni, la sua ruvidezza selvatica e adolescente (viii) ('a book without wrinkles: it never loses its freshness, and each reading, over the years, conveys the same untamed adolescent roughness'). The other novel, *È stato così*, reminds the scholar of an old and forgotten short story, 'Estate,' which, before being collected in this new edition of *Cinque romanzi*, first appeared in *Darsena nuova* (March 1946). To this early period belongs also the poem 'Stagioni,' published in *Darsena Nuova* in May 1946. Both 'Stagioni' and 'Estate,' along with Ginzburg's letters to Silvio Micheli, the editor of *Darsena Nuova*, were later collected by Garboli, who published them, with an introductory note, in *Paragone* 508–10 (June-August 1992, but issued in October 1993). This material sheds much light on the period that precedes and follows *È stato così*, a period of dejected bitterness and spiritual malaise (and let us not forget that her husband Leone had been tortured to death just two years before in the Regina Coeli prison), to which the story 'Estate,' 'nella forma di un adagio disperato' (Garboli) ('in the form of a desperate adagio') (Garboli), dramatically bears witness. Reading this text is a profoundly emotional experience; the same is true of the poem 'Stagioni,' which seems to me to support further what I argue in my essay regarding Ginzburg's poetic apprenticeship and its propaedeutic role for *VS*.

Natalia Ginzburg's Early Writings in *L'Italia libera*

DAVID WARD

Rome's Traforo, the tunnel which connects via del Tritone and via Nazionale, is not usually considered one of the consecrated sites of Italian political life. Yet, for Natalia Ginzburg and her close friend Carlo Levi, it has a significant if highly personal history. For both, the Traforo has intimate connections with their years of militancy in the Partito d'azione (Action Party), the short-lived Liberal-Socialist Party co-founded by Leone Ginzburg, Natalia's first husband. As did many other young Italians, both Levi and Natalia Ginzburg equate the brief life of the party with the equally brief period of optimism about Italy's future that pervaded the whole country following the fall of fascism and the end of World War II. After more than twenty years of a Fascist regime and a traumatic, divisive war which had not only pitted Italian against Italian, but had also seen Italy invaded twice and reduced to a battleground in someone else's war, many Italians were convinced that out of the ruins of history a unique opportunity had been offered them to refound their country along dramatically new lines. The vast dislocation that all aspects of Italian life and culture had suffered during the war and under occupation had the paradoxically beneficial effect of clearing the ground on which a new culture and society could be built. As Italo Calvino put it, writing of the atmosphere of those years in the Preface to the 1964 edition of his *Il sentiero dei nidi di ragno* (*The Path to the Nest of Spiders*), this was indeed a time when anything seemed possible, when one could 'ricominciare da zero' (start again from zero).[1]

For Carlo Levi, who became the first post-Liberation editor of the Action Party newspaper *L'Italia libera* (*Free Italy*), before resigning in January 1946 after the fall of the provisional government headed by the party's leader Ferruccio Parri, the Traforo is the setting for one of the most important dialogues in *L'orologio* (*The Watch*), his fictionalized account of the days in and around November 1945 when the Parri government was brought down to make way for the first of many Christian Democrat administrations.[2] In the tunnel, presented as a Plato-like cavern of echoes and shadows, three of the novel's protagonists discuss how in the wake of Parri's demise it had been possible for the old regime to reassert itself. Distinguishing between *luigini* (the ruling class) and *contadini* (the peasants), Levi analyses why the post-war hopes and aspirations for radical change in a post-Fascist Italy that the Action Party militants had lodged in the Parri government were thwarted. By *luigini* Levi means the proponents of a deeply rooted Gattopardesque political culture, known as *trasformismo*, which prizes continuity with the past over the instances of rupture that the *contadini*, the militants of the Action Party, proposed. Aiming to bring the ideals and values of the Resistance experience to bear on the construction of a new post-Fascist Italy, the *contadini*, or, as Levi also calls them, the *poeti* (poets), were the new protagonists on the political scene whose ambitious, sometimes ingenuous projects were gradually stifled by the tenacity of the stubborn, conservative political culture of the *luigini*.[3]

For a time at least, Natalia Ginzburg recognized herself in Levi's definition of *contadini* and shared the aspirations toward rupture with the history, habits, and culture of Italy's past that the Action Party embraced. Indeed, in the writings she published in the final years of the war and in the years immediately following it we find an optimism that readers only familiar with her later work might find surprising. Ginzburg returns to these important years in her short 1971 newspaper article entitled 'Il traforo,' now available in the collection *Vita immaginaria* (*Imaginary Life*).[4] Whether or not she had the passage from Levi's novel in mind, the Traforo itself, more than twenty years after that experience, still reminds Ginzburg of her militancy in the Action Party. Whenever she walks through the tunnel, she writes, 'incontro e saluto la sua memoria' ('I meet and greet its memory') (140). Her period of militancy in the Action Party is no matter of simple nostalgia, however. For Ginzburg, the Action Party stands in her memory as a monument to a tangled web of emotions whose effects were still felt by an entire generation even twenty years after the event. Writing of the pervasive optimism of the period, she says: at that time 'il mondo appariva chiaro, lineare, semplice' (the world seemed to be a clear, straightforward, simple place), (140), in which she had 'la certezza assoluta di poter scrivere e parlare di qualunque cosa' ('the absolute certainty to be able to write and speak about anything'), (141), and her future seemed to be laid out irresistibly in front of her.

As the essay continues, however, her harsh words immediately alert us to the damning critique she reserved in later years for what she came to see as the disastrous effects the unfounded optimism of those years had had on an entire generation. In no uncertain terms she writes of the repulsion she and others of her generation feel when they look back on the 'rovine e le ceneri' ('ruins and ashes') of a world in which they had invested their 'orgoglio, vanità e amore' ('pride, vanity and love)' (141). Not only was the optimism that underpinned the plans for large-scale national renewal of those years unfounded, but the failure to implement their plans also greatly conditioned that generation's future choices. Having seen their original ambitious plans come to nothing, this generation is now wary about making any plans at all. From the one extreme in which limits seemed to exist only to be swept away, the negative experience of the postwar years had pushed an entire generation to the other extreme, where limits take on the reassuring and familiar contours of a safe haven: 'Avendo noi sbagliato tanto in giovinezza ci sembra di salvarci dagli sbagli muovendoci ora pochissimo e pronunciando un numero assai esiguo e cauto di parole' ('As we have made so many mistakes in our youth, it seems to us that we can save ourselves from mistakes by doing as little as possible and expressing a very limited number of cautious words') (142).

Yet, at the same time, this generation is also haunted by the idealism of those years now long gone. The dilemma and tragedy of this generation lie not only in the retrenchment their early negative experiences have provoked, but also in the fond memory they still have for the postwar world they imagined. The memory of that imagined world stays with those who imagined it, rendering them always nostalgic for a world that in any case would never have been feasible, but which still exists as a mirage in their consciousness. Feeling repulsion for 'quel volto, quel passo imprudente, quelle parole incaute e quei pensieri incauti e quelle illusioni' ('that face, that imprudent step, those reckless words and those reckless thoughts and those illusions') (143), Ginzburg looks back on a youthful image she holds dear and on indestructible memories that still today move her. Even though they turned out to be bogus, the sense of clarity and unity of purpose that characterized the postwar years are still desired as an antidote to today's incomprehensible world. But attractive as that image of their former selves might be, it is also the source of the bitter and confused relationship with the past with which that generation has been unable to come to terms. Overcome by self-doubt and self-imposed silence, Natalia's generation is haunted by a continuing desire for that long gone sense of freedom and plenitude that they know, but refuse to admit, is also the cause of their present crisis.

The same article supplies an example of the confusion inherent in today's world. Aiming to go to a left-wing demonstration, Ginzburg achieves the opposite: she unwittingly and distractedly enters a nearby movie theatre where a neofascist group is holding a meeting on the 'Role of Women in Contemporary Society' (146). Disturbed by the idea of such ideologically opposed groups holding meetings in the same street at the same time, and by the fact that the neofascists are discussing a topic dear to the left, Natalia seems to hark back to those former times when such confusion, she thinks, would not have been possible.

The left-wing political meeting she eventually went to also supplies another tangible sign of her generation's crisis. This time it takes the form of the failure to express outrage in the face of intolerable events, exemplified here by the case of Pietro Valpreda, the anarchist wrongly accused of and jailed for planting the bomb in Milan's Piazza Fontana, which marked the beginning of that murky period in recent Italian history known as the *strategia della tensione* (strategy of tension). Despite her attendance at the meeting, she realizes that her commitment is half-hearted. Although she knows it is intolerable to entertain the idea that an innocent person should go to jail, nonetheless, she writes, 'io la tolleravo e avrei continuato a tollerarla' ('I tolerated it and I would continue to tolerate it') (144). Later that afternoon, she tells us, she would continue to lead her life of Sunday phone calls and cigarettes.

The tone of 'Il traforo' recalls the equally damning analysis of the same period that Natalia had written eight years earlier in *Lessico famigliare* (*Family Sayings*). Here one of the mistakes of which she writes in 'Il traforo' is exemplified: namely, that of being ingenuous enough to believe that political change could be brought about by cultural activity; in other words, that the confines which separate poetry from politics had been collapsed. This, she writes, was the common error, 'credere che tutto si potesse trasformare in poesia e parole' ('to believe that everything could be turned into poetry and words'). And when the ingenuousness of believing the world to be a simple place was unmasked by the realization that reality was 'complessa, segreta, indecifrabile e oscura' ('complex, secret, indecipherable and dark'), a nauseous and long-lasting hangover took the place of the lightheadedness that had gripped an entire generation (166).[5] And her other novel which deals head-on with the Resistance experience, *Tutti i nostri ieri* (*All Our Yesterdays*), published in 1952, concludes with this sentence, which deflates any lingering last hopes the reader may have had about the possibility of postwar renewal: 'E risero un poco ed erano molto amici loro tre insieme Anna, Emanuele e Giustino, ed erano contenti d'essere loro tre insieme a pensare a tutti quelli che erano morti, e alla lunga guerra e al dolore e al clamore e alla lunga vita difficile che si trovavano adesso davanti e che era piena di tutte le cose che non sapevano fare' ('And the three of them together, Anna, Emanuele, and Giustino laughed a bit and were very friendly and happy to be together and to think about all the others who were dead, and the long war and the pain and the chaos and the long difficult life that they had in front of them which was full of things they had no idea how to do') (321).

The harshness of this retrospective glance twenty years later should not induce us into forgetting that these words are also addressed to Ginzburg herself. Part of the clear, linear, and simple world she had imagined in the years in and around the end of World War II was Ginzburg's conviction that she herself would write political articles in newspapers ('Il traforo,' 140) and thereby contribute, perhaps, to the new Italy the Action Party project foresaw. And for a while she did. Indeed, reading the articles she wrote in the mid-1940s, one is surprised to find exactly the same idealistic proposals and ideas that she was to attack so sharply a few years later. The articles in question are 'I nostri figli' ('Our Children'), 'Chiarezza' ('Clarity'), and 'Cronaca di un paese' ('Chronicle of a Village'), all published in *L'Italia libera* on, respectively, 22 November 1944, 31 December 1944, and 9 January 1945. To the best of my knowledge none of these writings has been republished elsewhere, and certainly not in any of the major collections of Ginzburg's writings. Echoes of some of the themes contained in the articles, however, recur in Ginzburg's other published works. A few lines from 'Chiarezza' can be found in *Tutti i nostri ieri*, and, as we shall see, 'I nostri figli' has, thematically at least, a great deal in common with the article 'Il figlio dell'uomo' ('The Son of Man'), written about a year later. 'Cronaca di un paese' recounts the same experience Ginzburg had described in 'Inverno in Abruzzo' ('Winter in the Abruzzo'), written in the autumn of 1944, originally published in *Aretusa*, and now the opening essay in *Le piccole virtù* (*The Small Virtues*).[5] Both texts share a similar structure based on micro-narrative accounts of the events and inhabitants of the village where Leone, Natalia, and their children were exiled. Their experience in Abruzzo, in fact, was very similar to Carlo Levi's earlier one in Lucania. Indeed, both the micro-narrative format of 'Cronaca di un paese' and the themes it brings up bear a striking resemblance to Levi's *Cristo si è fermato a Eboli* (*Christ Stopped at Eboli*), which he wrote between December 1943 and July 1944 in hiding in Florence.[6] Both texts tell of a village divided between the *signori*, the degraded and corrupt local bourgeoisie and the peasants; of the ineptitude of local doctors; and of the villagers' widespread habit of writing anonymous letters to denounce their fellow villagers.

Although both texts were presumably written at about the same time, 'Cronaca di un paese' is far less confessional in tone than 'Inverno in Abruzzo.' The latter, in fact, acts as a reminder that the seeds of the later critical stance Ginzburg was to take on the events and atmosphere of those years were present even as they were taking place. Already, in fact, in the autumn of 1944, under the shadow of Leone's death in prison, Ginzburg reflected on the damage that broken dreams inflict on the self. Dreams never come true and 'appena li vediamo spezzati, comprendiamo a un tratto che le gioie maggiori della nostra vita sono fuori della realtà ('as soon as we see them broken, we understand immediately that the greatest joys in our life are outside reality') (18). Yet the nostalgia for a time when those dreams 'fervevano in noi' ('welled up in us') (18) continues. The time of dreams that had not yet come untrue, she writes, taking up a theme she was to broach in later texts, was the time when 'avevo fede in un avvenire facile e lieto, ricco di desideri appagati, di esperienze e di comuni imprese' ('I had faith in an easy and happy future, full of satisfied desires, experiences and common aims'). This was 'il tempo migliore della mia vita e solo adesso che m'è sfuggito per sempre, solo adesso lo so' ('the best time of my life, and only now it has escaped me for ever, only now do I know that') (18–19).

Yet, written at approximately the same time, a few months after Leone's death, which left Ginzburg a young widow with three small children to raise, her other articles for *L'Italia libera* reflect the unbounded optimism of the period. 'I nostri figli,' like many of her later works, takes the form of a reflection on the institution of the family and on parenthood. As even the most cursory of readings reveals, Ginzburg's fiction flows over with characters, usually women, for whom contact with these institutions, along with marriage, has led to disastrous personal consequences. Either through the weakness of individuals, the pull of the institution itself, the incompetency of parents or parent figures, or a combination of all three, Ginzburg's often helpless young women fall into a world of life-denying conventions for which their adolescence and family upbringing has done nothing to prepare them in advance.

Delia in *La strada che va in città* (*The Road to the City*), the never-named protagonist of *È stato così* (*That's the Way It Was*), and Elsa in *Le voci della sera* (*Voices in the Evening*) all fall into loveless marriages, and retreat from what could be professional careers and some degree of personal gratification into drudgery, boredom, and full-time child-rearing. Pressure to conform to institutional conventions also overcomes ideological barricades: Raffaella, who had fought in the anti-fascist Resistance movement, ends up by marrying an unreconstructed fascist, as does Concettina, who was brought up in an anti-fascist family in *Tutti i nostri ieri*. Again, parents or parent figures like Maria in *Tutti i nostri ieri* or Matilde in *Le voci della sera*, whether well-meaning but misguided, or completely unsuited to bringing up children, remain blind to the needs and aspirations of their daughters. One of the constant themes to which Ginzburg returns is the unbridgeable gap which separates the hopes, needs, and aspirations of a prewar generation from those of a postwar generation. Spurred on by the dislocation and turmoil experienced in all sectors of civil life during World War II, the rate at which the postwar generation had developed needs different from those of the prewar generation had accelerated enormously. That swift rate of change, however, had neither been understood by parents nor matched by developments in the institutions and conventions which govern daily life. The younger generations grow up in and into institutions like family and marriage made for previous generations whose needs are no longer shared by their children. Although aware of their new needs, the postwar generation had failed to either rid itself of the old institutions which were central to their parents' lives or to elaborate new ones.

Offering new parents advice on how to bring up their children, the article 'I nostri figli' strikes a far more optimistic tone insofar as it indicates the path to be followed if the institutions of marriage and family are to be reformed from within. At her most utilitarian, Ginzburg sketches the guidelines for parents to bring up their children in such a way that, as she writes in the article's concluding words, the 'speranze di un tempo più saggio e felice' ('hopes for a wiser and happier time'), which had been raised by the heady experience of the Resistance, are not extinguished.[7]

The essay itself focuses on the passage in adult life from the relative freedom and ease of a pre-parenthood stage to the difficulties encountered in the post-parenthood stage. If, in the former stage, courage, sacrifice, enthusiasm, universal love, energy, and so on, are all qualities it is relatively simple to find in oneself, in the latter we are faced with new complications which change us radically, throw us violently into the adult world, and bring us closer to the 'espressioni ed atteggiamenti' ('expressions and attitudes') we associate with our parents. In the place of a universal concern, we take on a necessarily narrower viewpoint, which can lead to what Ginzburg calls an 'egoismo famigliare' ('family egoism'). In such a state, our thoughts no longer go out to the world as a whole, but are concentrated on the daily problems connected with our children: 'Che cosa mangerà il nostro bambino? Con che cosa si baloccherà? Come vestirlo? Come fare perché sia sempre sano, forte, felice?' ('What will our child eat? What will he play with? How to dress him? What to do to make sure he's always healthy, strong, happy?')

For Ginzburg, this passage is a crucial stage in adult life and signals, in the worst of cases, a watershed between the previously held hopes for a wiser, happier world and the dashing of those hopes. It is for this reason that parents must negotiate this passage with the utmost care. At issue, however, is not only the question of bringing up one's children so that they don't become spoiled little brats; going further, Ginzburg pushes the question into the realm of the political. The danger she sees is that spoiled little brats may become little fascist brats. In an early indication that the personal is always political, she locates in 'egoismo famigliare' a fertile terrain in which a fascist culture can find cannon fodder and sink its roots: 'Se gettiamo uno sguardo sul passato, possiamo facilmente constatare come l'egoismo famigliare ... sia stato la caratteristica principale, forse anche la prima sorgente di quegli anni oscuri, privi di ogni interesse politico e d'ogni carità umana, che si chiamarono l'era fascista' ('If we glance back at the past we can easily see how the family egoism I am speaking about has been the main characteristic, perhaps even the primary source of those dark years, devoid of any political interest and human charity, that were called the fascist era').

Fascism, then, far from being a phenomenon external to Italian institutional life, or a parenthesis in the course of history, or the invasion of a barbarian tribe, or a virus which has infected an otherwise healthy body, as Benedetto Croce and many other anti-Fascists from a variety of ideological standpoints had argued, is for Ginzburg located at a local level within the family. As such, Ginzburg's analysis of Fascism and its origins is very much in line with that of the Action Party. For the likes of Carlo Rosselli and Piero Gobetti, the intellectual mentors of the party, as well as Leone Ginzburg and Carlo Levi, Fascism was an entirely Italian phenomenon which sprang from the limits of pre-Fascist liberal society. Fascism, then, was not an aberration from the norm; rather it was a consequence of a set of flawed premises. Or, as Piero Gobetti put it, Fascism was Italy's autobiography.[8]

But if Fascism is located at a local level in the family, it is also at the same level that an effective anti-Fascist culture can, and indeed must, be put into practice. Herein lies the crucial role of parents. The thrust of 'I nostri figli' is to indicate what changes in family *costume* anti-Fascist parents need to make to ensure that their children do not grow up into little fascists. In order to do this, writes Ginzburg, parents must, first, stop being conventional parents, and continue to be the young, enthusiastic, and lively companions they were previously; second, learn how to deprive their children of a thing or two so that they do not grow up spoilt; and third, remind them that there are also other, less fortunate children with similar and more pressing needs in the world.

The burden of Ginzburg's article is to place responsibility for the construction of a robust anti-Fascist culture at the micro-level of radical change in the way parents relate to and bring up their children. Not only can we read 'I nostri figli' as a thinly veiled criticism of her own family headed by an anti-Fascist yet determinedly patriarchal and intolerant father, but also as an alternative to the ineffective anti-Fascism practised by the characters in *Tutti i nostri ieri*: the father, for example, whose anti-Fascism consists of a memoir which is never finished, let alone sees the light of day; and the children, whose daydreamings of heroic anti-Fascist actions are completely severed from the everyday reality of the struggle.

The text which 'I nostri figli' most closely resembles for both tone and content is 'Il figlio dell'uomo,' first published in the Italian Communist Party newspaper *L'unità* (*Unity*) in 1946, and republished in *Le piccole virtù*.[9] As we shall see, this text acts as a bridge between 'I nostri figli' and the second of her *L'Italia libera* articles, 'Chiarezza.' In 'Il figlio dell'uomo,' the accent once again falls on the gap which separates the present generation of parents from past generations. The experience of Fascism and the war has produced a new generation of young people, now become parents, whose hopes, aspirations, and fears have little in common with those of their parents. No longer able to follow the time-honoured directives on how to bring up children, they refuse to tell their children the lies their parents had told them. There is, writes Ginzburg, 'un abisso incolmabile fra noi e le generazioni di prima' ('an unbridgeable gap between us and earlier generations') (72).

Her generation, she goes on, is both unlucky and privileged: unlucky because, having experienced the fear of arrest, exile, deportation to the death camps, persecution, and having stared reality square 'nel suo volto più tetro' ('in its darkest face') (70), they know they will never forget or recover from that trauma: 'Non guariremo più di questa guerra ... non saremo mai più gente tranquilla' (We will never get over this war ... we will never again be tranquil folk') (70). But at the same time, this generation is also privileged. The same experiences which have brought them face to face with the bare essence of things in all their brutality – 'vicini alle cose nella loro sostanza' ('close to things in their essence') (70) – have complicated their lives, but also brought them a degree of unprecedented existential wealth. As Ginzburg writes in the essay's concluding sentence, the 'anxiety' felt by the members of this generation, which cuts to the very heart of their being, is the source of their happiness: 'noi siamo legati a questa nostra angoscia e in fondo lieti del nostro destino di uomini' (we are tied to our anxiety and we are ultimately happy about our human destiny') (72).

This happiness derives from the clarity of vision that the war generation's specific experiences have made possible. Their privilege, in fact, is to have been exposed directly to reality without the customary mediations. Having shared the horror of war with their children, and having seen beyond the 'veli e le menzogne' ('veils and lies') with which their parents had hidden from them 'la realtà nella sua vera sostanza' ('reality in its true essence') (72), the present generation can no longer tell their own children the same mystifying stories of storks, cabbage patches, little trees and rabbits which had constructed their own worlds. The present generation's clarity of vision, as well as contrasting with the previous generation's, also contrasts strongly with the false clarity and over-simplification characteristic of the Fascist era, which is the subject of 'Chiarezza,' the second of the articles she wrote for *L'Italia libera*. The Fascist era, she writes, is guilty of not having had the intellectual or moral courage to admit that the world was a complicated place of contradiction and doubt. There were, for example, no suicides reported under Fascism, only accidental shootings; no poor people, only those who received the providential benefit of Fascist charity. In this climate of 'perenne ottimismo' ('permanent optimism'), there was no place for the 'malcontenti, 'dubbiosi' or 'tormentati' ('the unhappy, the doubters, the tormented'). Indeed, it was the false optimism of the Fascist era, she continues, which created in many the need to rediscover a dimension to life which was more complicated, 'intima e tormentata' ('intimate and tormented'). But that refuge into the self also had negative consequences which led literature to decouple itself from a direct engagement with reality: 'fu appunto quella semplificazione a renderci tutti più complessi e difficili, più involuti in ogni nostra espressione ed azione, a negarci ogni possibilità di una vera chiarezza' ('it was that simplification that made us more complex and difficult, more introspective in our every expression and act, and denied us the possibility of true clarity').[10]

But if now in the post-Fascist era the time has come for 'un ritorno alla chiarezza' ('a return to clarity'), the question still remains of how to shake off the bad habits of the recent past. Given that for an entire generation 'il fascismo ... è penetrato nella nostra anima e l'ha avvelenata' ('Fascism ... penetrated our soul and poisoned it'), the foremost task of the new era is to go back once again to the 'forme più elementari e spontanee nella parola, nei rapporti umani, nei pensieri e nei sentimenti' ('most elementary and spontaneous forms in words, in human relationships, in thought and in feelings').

The article ends with the suggestion that clarity, far from being a crystal-clear vision of self-evident, free-standing facts, is itself contingent on an act of self-examination: 'credo che il primo atto da compiere sia questo, ritrovare se stessi' ('I believe that the first thing to do is this, find ourselves again'). But the major error of the postwar generation, as Ginzburg reminds us in 'Il traforo,' was to have bought into exactly the same kind of over-simplified false clarity of vision that had characterized Fascism. Clearly, for Ginzburg, clarity is not a crystal-clear given.

Indeed, clarity is one of the more elusive and misunderstood concepts in Ginzburg's entire body of work. For one thing, clarity and simplicity are not overlapping categories: what is seemingly clear is not necessarily simple. Although Ginzburg is renowned for a pared-down, economic style, her writing itself is far from simple. 'Lui e io' ('He and I') may be a clearly expressed exposition of her relationship with her second husband Gabriele Baldini, but it is far from being a simple relationship;[11] and 'Il traforo,' her look back on her militancy in the Action Party, though similarly expressed in her habitual limpid prose style, reveals a knot of still unresolved tensions.

Clarity is not so much a question of seeing the sharp contours of reality pared down to its bare essence, as being ready to admit that even at its clearest the essence of reality is a tangled web of conflicting and changing emotions, a microcosm of which is her own experience then and now with the Action Party. In an interview given to Delia Lennie in 1971, Ginzburg ties the question of clarity to an 'awareness of one's own limitations.'[12] And a year later in another interview, she speaks of the choice of language a writer makes as more a question of moral than of aesthetic choice.[13] More than an index of perfect vision, clarity is an ethical index of an individual's willingness to recognize the finitude of the human self as well as the limitations this places on our standing in and relationship with the world. Our relationship to reality is less one in which we dig deep to discover its immutable truths, than one in which we consider reality as an unresolved, evolving project which will stretch beyond the span of any single individual's lifetime. Devoid of the intellectual and moral courage necessary to acknowledge these limitations, Fascism, for example, contented itself with offering the kind of superficial clarity that the Ginzburg of her postwar phase decidedly rejects.

We may also consider Ginzburg's experiments in impersonal narration, which characterize a good many of her works, in this light. If the individual does not hold the keys with which to unlock the eternal secrets of reality, then, any pretence to do so is an act of moral dishonesty. Many of Ginzburg's texts can be seen as attempts to reconcile two almost contradictory demands: first, to stare reality in the face and tell its story in narrative form; and second, to maintain an attitude of humility before that reality. We can follow the tension between these two demands in Ginzburg's experiments in narrative voice. In fact, many of her works can be seen as mini-laboratories in which she attempts to develop a narrative voice which, on the one hand, satisfies the first ethical demand by telling the story of the world while, on the other, it satisfies the second by avoiding the imposing, organizing, and ultimately authoritarian voice of the omniscient narrator. Although *Lessico famigliare*, for example, is purportedly a semi-autobiographical account of the Levi family, Ginzburg, eclipsing herself almost entirely, never becomes the overt organizing presence around which more conventional historical or autobiographical texts revolve. Reducing to a minimum references even to the most joyous and tragic events of her life – marriage and widowhood with Leone Ginzburg, who died of a heart attack following torture in Rome's *Regina Coeli* prison in 1944 – Ginzburg, in *Lessico famigliare*, employs the kind of nonassertive narrative voice she later attempted to develop in her epistolary novels *Caro Michele* (*Dear Michael*), *La città e la casa* (*The City and the House*), and the historical reconstruction based on letters, *La famiglia Manzoni* (*The Manzoni Family*).

Yet, at the same time, there is space within the body of Ginzburg's writings for a forceful, indeed dogmatic, voice which seems to brook little argument. Both in 'I nostri figli' and in 'Il figlio dell'uomo,' she writes with great strength and conviction of an experience that is hers, but is also that of an entire generation. The confidently expressed 'we' of these pages is in no doubt at all about who she and her group are, where they have been together, what they have shared together, and what those experiences have done to them. If Ginzburg harbours doubts about the extent to which we can know or understand in any unequivocal way the knot of contradictory emotions that make up reality, she also believes that there are certain experiences that impress themselves so strongly on the human self that they can be narrated with conviction. The kind of narrative voice toward which Ginzburg is working is one which can express both the uncertainty she feels about the world as a whole, but also the certainty about the truth of those events which she has experienced, as it were, in the flesh. In her interview with Toscani, Ginzburg likens her position as narrator to that of 'a man contemplating the universe from a very small outcrop of rock, and all he can write about is what he can hold in his hands and see beneath his feet. He can have no certainty about anything else.'[14] Certainty, then, is circumscribed to what the writer experiences from his or her particular position. This, to be sure, gives certainty only a modest purview, but it is, despite its modesty, a certainty on which we can rely and which authorizes us to state that certainty in no uncertain terms.

The experiences about which we can be certain are not, then, to be found in the *longue durée* of history, but in the specificity and unicity of a particular event. To recover the particularity and certainty of that event it is necessary to sever it from its contiguity with the numerous other events which surround it and create its context. Ginzburg's fear is that, seen in the general context, the strong and unique contours of an event may be honed down and the event's particularity lost. To focus on that particularity we need to force ourselves perhaps to forget the historical context which surrounds the event. A positive mental effort, then, needs to be made if we are not to allow ourselves to be overwhelmed by a bigger picture of history which may offer alibis to individual outrages and temper our reactions by treating such outrages as, say, the spirit of the age, or justifying them as the consequence of contingent circumstances.

If we look all the time at the big picture of history, Ginzburg tells us in an interview apropos of Serena Cruz, an adopted child on whose behalf she organized a vast and vociferous campaign in the late 1980s, we risk seeing nothing, only perhaps a large confusing backdrop against which we are no longer able to distinguish the immensity of the small truth in all its particularity. What we must not do is 'to place the particular facts of this case within an anonymous and immense series of analogous facts that fill up the world and in so doing see absolutely nothing. The power and immensity of numbers crush and overpower the particulars of one single, solitary misfortune ... it is necessary ... that we preserve and keep alive in our memory that indignation ... or that offense, as though it were indestructible and unique.'[15]

But if this is a coping mechanism that allows Ginzburg to avoid a full-time engagement with the master discourse of history, while at the same time allowing her to, as it were, dip into it when her limits of tolerance have been reached, as in the case of Serena Cruz, it is still far from being a satisfactory answer. For one thing, it makes full-time militancy in a political party and adherence to a manifesto almost impossible. Despite her term of office in the Italian Parliament as a member of the Sinistra Indipendente (Independent Left) group, Ginzburg was always reticent to commit herself fully to an endorsement of any political party's program. This reluctance certainly derives from her negative experiences in the mid-1940s with the Action Party and the disappointment she and many of her generation felt as it became evident that the shape postwar, post-Fascist Italy was taking was very different from what they had hoped or imagined. For this generation, whose aspirations outstretched their abilities and which saw itself increasingly as the victim of history, an appropriate motto might be 'Once bitten, twice shy.'

The body of Ginzburg's writings are haunted by the presence of the person who came to exemplify most tragically the mistakes of that generation: her friend and fellow writer, Cesare Pavese, to whom she dedicates some of her most moving pages in both 'Ritratto di un amico' ('Portrait of a Friend'), originally written in 1957 and now in *Le piccole virtù*, and in *Lessico famigliare.*[16] In many ways, Pavese is constructed as the negative example against which Ginzburg defines and elaborates her own survival tactics. As Ginzburg describes it, Pavese's great mistake was to believe that the world was made to his measure and would unfold in the same logical, reasoned way he had imagined. If the errors of Ginzburg and her like were generated by 'impulso, imprudenza, stupidità e candore' ('impulse, recklessness, stupidity and candour'), Pavese's came 'dalla prudenza, dall'astuzia, dal calcolo, e dall'intelligenza' ('from prudence, cunning, calculation and intelligence') (*Lessico*, 198). And, adds Ginzburg, 'Nulla è pericoloso come questa sorta di errori' ('Nothing is more dangerous than this kind of mistake') (198). When he discovered that the world had gone in a direction different from the one he had calculated, the shock was so great that it pushed him to his suicide in 1950. Differently from Ginzburg and others like her, Pavese was unable to ascribe his errors to stupidity or inability or ingenuousness. Whereas others were able to use their own human frailty to account for the failure of their projects, Pavese was unable to do so. Pavese remained, then, a prisoner of what Ginzburg calls 'la voce amara della ragione' ('the bitter voice of reason') (199), whose roots stretched down so deeply into his consciousness as to deny him the life-saving freedom that Ginzburg's fragility and awareness of her own limits granted her. In Ginzburg's terms, Pavese saw things too clearly for his own good, and was unable to come to terms with an unclear, confused world which did not obey the logic by which he had imagined it to be governed. This is the danger Ginzburg sees in investing too much of ourselves in a commitment to a world that is believed to be a clear, linear, and simple place, as she thought it was in the mid-1940s. To learn and accept that we are not the measure of reality, that we do not hold its reins in our hands, is both to acknowledge our own limits – painful as that may be, especially if we compare ourselves to an earlier more idealistic phase – and to save our lives from the disappointment and tragedy which has haunted and continues to haunt Italy's postwar generation of which Ginzburg was a part.

NOTES

1 Italo Calvino, *Il sentiero dei nidi di ragno* (Turin: Einaudi, 1964), 7. Unless otherwise indicated, all translations from Italian are my own.
2 Carlo Levi, *L'orologio* (Turin: Einaudi, 1950).
3 For a longer account of the Action Party's defeat, see Vittorio Foa, *Il cavallo e la torre: Riflessioni su una vita* (Turin: Einaudi, 1991).
4 Natalia Ginzburg, 'Il traforo,' *Vita immaginaria* (Milan: Mondadori, 1974), 140–6. Further references will appear parenthetically within the text.

5 Ginzburg, 'Inverno in Abruzzo,' *Le piccole virtù* (Turin: Einaudi, 1962), 13–19. Further references will appear parenthetically in the text.
6 Carlo Levi, *Cristo si è fermato a Eboli* (Turin: Einaudi, 1945).
7 For the text and translation of 'I nostri figli' see pages 226–9 of this book.
8 Piero Gobetti, *La rivoluzione liberale: Saggio sulla lotta politica in Italia* (Turin: Einaudi, 1983), 165.
9 Ginzburg, 'Il figlio dell'uomo,' *Le piccole virtù*, 69–72. Further references will appear parenthetically in the text.
10 For the text and translation of 'Chiarezza' see pages 230–3 of this book.
11 Ginzburg, 'Lui e io,' *Le piccole virtù*, 53–65.
12 Delia Lennie, 'Una scrittrice: Natalia Ginzburg,' in *Posso presentarle* (London: Longman, 1971), p. 70. Cited in Alan Bullock, *Natalia Ginzburg* (New York/Oxford: Berg, 1991), 27.
13 C. Toscani, 'Incontro con Natalia Ginzburg,' *Il ragguaglio librario*, 39, no. 6 (1972): 210. Cited in Bullock, *Natalia Ginzburg*, 27.
14 Toscani, 'Interview with Natalia Ginzburg,' 211. Quoted in Bullock, *Natalia Ginzburg*, 42.
15 Ginzburg, quoted in Peggy Boyers, 'On Natalia Ginzburg,' *Salmagundi* 96 (Fall 1992): 58.
16 Ginzburg, 'Ritratto d'un amico,' *Le piccole virtù*, 25–34.

REFERENCES

Boyers, Peggy. 'On Natalia Ginzburg,' *Salmagundi* 96 (Fall 1992).
Calvino, Italo. *Il sentiero dei nidi di ragno*. Turin: Einaudi, 1964.
Foa, Vittorio. *Il cavallo e la torre: Riflessioni su una vita*. Turin: Einaudi, 1991.
Ginzburg, Natalia. 'I nostri figli.' *L'Italia libera* 2, no. 165 (11 December 1944).
– 'Chiarezza.' *L'Italia libera*, 2, no. 198 (31 December 1944).
– 'Cronaca di un paese.' *L'Italia libera* 3, no. 7 (9 January 1945).
– *Tutti i nostri ieri*. Turin: Einaudi, 1952.
– 'Inverno in Abruzzo.' *Le piccole virtù*, 13–19. Turin: Einaudi, 1962.
– 'Ritratto d'un amico.' *Le piccole virtù*, 25–34. Turin: Einaudi, 1962.
– 'Lui e io.' *Le piccole virtù*, 53–65. Turin: Einaudi, 1962.
– 'Il figlio dell'uomo.' *Le piccole virtù*, 69–72. Turin: Einaudi, 1962.
– *Lessico famigliare*. Turin: Einaudi, 1963.
– 'Il traforo.' *Vita immaginaria*, 140–6. Milan: Mondadori, 1974.
Gobetti, Piero. *La rivoluzione liberale: Saggio sulla lotta politica in Italia*. Turin: Einaudi, 1983.
Lennie, Delia. 'Una scrittrice: Natalia Ginzburg.' In *Posso presentarle*. London:

Longman, 1971. Cited in Bullock, Alan, *Natalia Ginzburg* (New York/Oxford: Berg, 1991.

Levi, Carlo. *Cristo si è fermato a Eboli*. Turin: Einaudi, 1945.

– *L'orologio*. Turin: Einaudi, 1950.

Toscani, C. 'Incontro con Natalia Ginzburg.' *Il ragguaglio librario* 39, no. 6 (1972): 210. Cited in Bullock, *Natalia Ginzburg* (New York/Oxford: Berg, 1991).

Natalia Ginzburg: Making a Story Out of History

ANGELA M. JEANNET

For a long time, Western culture was bound to a distinctive concept of history and practice of historiography that assumed humanity's progress from one stage to another, at times in a positive and at times in a negative direction, but always in a manner that satisfied the human need for intelligibility and belief in causality. Whether historians privileged 'great' public events, social phenomena, biography, major movements, or the gathering of empirical data, elaborating a coherent historical continuum was their pride, as innumerable texts of a narrative or documentary character tell us. Many generations grew up in symbiosis with that ideal construct whereby human experience found logical and chronological ordering; even novelists found it congenial. It is not surprising, then, that when new ways of perceiving and recording human experience appeared, the cry went up that History had come to an end. Actually, it's not history that is over. Human experience continues and will continue as long as human beings – however one defines us – will live. Rather, we have witnessed a challenge to the primacy of certain types of narratives of history, those that were moulded by and within a well-established tradition. The relationship of fiction to truth has been re-examined and redefined, as the re-elaboration of our experiences and perceptions has acquired less dogmatic contours, and the previously sealed boundaries between various forms of speaking about that experience have become blurred.

Scholars were perhaps slower than writers in acknowledging the subversion that had taken place in the perception of experience and the noncanonical ways by which human experience could be remembered and shared. At least since the turn of the twentieth century European writers have turned almost obsessively to exploring the ways we speak about 'our yesterdays,' and to undermining the conventional reconstructions of the past. The problematic task of recapturing 'facts,' the peculiar 'logic' of memory, with its lack of linearity and its connections with sensorial life, and the human yearning for finding permanence were the stuff of literature; and, in spite of doubts and misgivings, writers insisted that the written language could be the most powerful agent of memory retrieval, bearing the promise of a salvation that religious faiths were unable to provide anymore. Then, with the 1930s, the 'age of suspicion' began, so named by another Nathalie and major European writer, Nathalie Sarraute. All totalizing statements were discredited. Since there was no 'immense edifice' of the past to be retrieved, such as Proust had hypothesized, language could only aspire to unearth fragments of the universe of memory, and the literary text in particular was entrusted with the task of recording what was unspoken or hidden, the almost imperceptible movements of human consciousness. A new literary season had begun, of which Natalia Ginzburg is a major representative, in her own way.

A writer of world stature, she was not well known outside her own country until a few years ago, in part because she published in a language that is not widely known abroad, and in part because provincialism was fostered and enforced in Italy for years by various agencies: Fascism, an underdeveloped bourgeoisie, and the Roman Catholic Church. Many readers, even those who were usually more perceptive, were puzzled or frankly put off by her writing, and manifested their unease by loading their praises with condescension. Most criticism of Ginzburg's work was until recently found in book reviews, as a glance at the bibliographical material will show.[1] The agreement was that Ginzburg dealt with private, family matters, with the 'debris of domestic history,' as a reviewer said,[2] those trivial events of life that parallel the great historical events but seem removed from their flow, like passersby on the banks of a swollen river. Because of such apparent lack of focus on historical events, most critics underestimated the peculiarly unassuming diction of Ginzburg's fictional voice. One of her most attentive readers, though, Daniel Harris, mentioned the 'covert politics' of that author, particularly in *Tutti i nostri ieri* and *Le voci della sera*; and, more recently, Francesca Sanvitale has written fine pages on Ginzburg's personal way of addressing the thematics of history in her fiction.[3] Actually, Ginzburg is a consummate expert in language, an unblinking observer of historical events, and an uncompromising teller of stories. Today, half a century after the horrors of World War II, after Natalia

Ginzburg's death, when new horrors burst like a poisoned wound in the heart of Europe, we feel a new urgency to read her works and those of some of her contemporaries, such as Primo Levi, to understand the complex relationship that obtains between existential experience, historical narratives, and fictional constructs. Our task is to see how history is inscribed in Ginzburg's fiction, a history that is inescapably documentable, and caught the woman and the writer, with millions of others, in its mechanisms.

Far from being uneventful, Ginzburg's life, like the lives of those of her contemporaries who shared with her a certain location and situation, was immersed in historical events. From childhood, she lived in an environment that considered intellectual achievement and informed participation in life a matter of course. Her milieu also combined antifascism and Jewishness, even though those two components of identity may have been taken for granted, at first, by her and her family. In other words, she shared with a number of twentieth-century Italian writers an unspoken marginality and an awareness of difference that inevitably led to an alert political consciousness. It would be superfluous to review here the stages of Ginzburg's life: her childhood and adolescence in a tightly knit bourgeois family, her first novel published under an assumed name, her marriage to a young intellectual and political activist, the confinement she shared with her husband and their children, her husband's assassination and her life in hiding at the end of World War II; then, her employment at the Einaudi publishing house, her second marriage, her publications, her interest in the theatre, and finally her participation in Italian political life as a member of the Chamber of Representatives and of the European Parliament. In short, she fully experienced the tragic and exciting events of most of the twentieth century. However, one cannot rely on the characters in her novels, nor on her autobiographical writings, nor even on her essays, for an evaluation of all this biographical information. She hid behind her fiction, or better – like most writers – she constructed a persona that fit with her fictional universe. Conversely, the details of her life cannot be used to explain or justify her writing, as it is often done especially in the case of women writers. Rather, those details tell us that her persona is a rightful inhabitant of her fiction, and they are a sign of the intensity and integrity with which she constructed her fictional universe.

Like Italo Calvino, and unlike Primo Levi, Natalia Ginzburg repeatedly asserted that she mistrusted autobiography; like Italo Calvino, and because of a similar cultural background with stoic components, she was uneasy with the testimonial mode. But, with the same conviction as Primo Levi, she saw the writer's voice as the voice of memory, the witness of the past. It is therefore even more surprising that Ginzburg was not immediately placed among the protagonists of a European culture that was committed to the definition and recapture of memory. More important, and contrary to early evaluations of her work, her writing is precisely a sustained reflection on history, an interrogation on the nature of it, and an elaboration of the techniques needed to address the problematics of a narrative of history. It is this article's aim to move away from the early perspectives on her writings and to challenge the still-prevailing preconceptions and misconceptions that are caused by inattention to cultural factors and by sexist stereotypes.

Ginzburg published her major fictional works almost exactly at ten-year intervals: *Tutti i nostri ieri* (*All Our Yesterdays*) in 1952, *Le voci della sera* (*Voices in the Evening*) in 1961, *Caro Michele* (*Dear Michael*) in 1973, and *La città e la casa* (*The City, the House*) in 1984. A number of shorter works had preceded them. The first two novels are central in the author's production, chronologically and structurally, and will be exemplary texts for this analysis. In them, the author addresses the symbiotic relationship of history and fiction, with full awareness of the failures of traditional narratives. The 'logic' of events is in Ginzburg's view a construct of little interest to those who live those events. On the other hand, ordering the inescapable truth of historical events in a sequence that satisfies one's well-trained reason is an ideological construct that is of little interest to the writer, whose task it is to privilege faithfulness to human experience, to concreteness, directness, and simplicity. She pointedly avoids the historical frescoes in which novelists show their skill at evoking sweeping vistas, landscapes, mass movements, and the pathos of the psychology of individual heroes. The discrete moments of a hypothetical historical continuum are lived blindly by her characters while they struggle with their own lives, whose main characteristics are unawareness, desire, and loss. For Ginzburg's characters, history cannot be told in a sequential, lucid discourse; it causes stammerings, a series of flickers of recognition, and sudden bursts of action. Since they are to a large extent unintelligible to those caught in them, events loom like clouds above personal lives that are enveloped in a secrecy that consists of both emotional reserve vis-à-vis the outside world and bewilderment in the face of what is happening in it. Each character that survives the onslaught of a foreseen but capricious fury will continuously relive those events throughout a lifetime, mixed with personal losses and problematic gains. Such a perspective on history demands (or is the result of) the singular quality of Ginzburg's prose: paratactic, enunciated in short breaths and pauses, in an uninterrupted pattern of speech and silence, repetitions, and indirect discourse.

The setting of the novels is obviously Italy, an Italy at the same time recognizable and abstract, with its cities and villages and seasons, a place that she described (speaking of Elsa Morante's *La storia*) as 'il luogo che il caos ha scelto come luogo di sventura' (*Opere* II, 584) ('the place that chaos has chosen as the place of misfortune'). That place, with its familiar aura and total lack of the picturesque, serves as the perfect background for a fiction that refuses 'beauty.' Description is reduced to a minimum, and the local touches are strictly functional. The setting is what it is supposed to be, unobtrusive and vivid, a familiar home for the fictional characters.

The characters that people Ginzburg's fiction belong to a social class accustomed to silence, a middle class with its unheroic lives and an infinite number of small shames. The tragic mode does not become such characters. Not that the tragic dimension of life is forgotten, but it can only be honoured by understatement; only by insisting on discretion can the text avoid misrepresenting it. Ginzburg relies on an effective technique to convey her vision: the protagonists often do not speak, although they participate intensely in the story to the point of being the story's only voice and gaze. The characters whose voices we *do* hear through direct discourse are usually those of the lesser participants: old aunts and mothers, cautious men, sullen adolescents, servants and domestics, the powerless and bemused. Ginzburg's fiercely controlled writing tells of the protagonists' reluctance to communicate and to let themselves go, perhaps to the reader's disappointment. Far from being a realistic medium, or a 'lagna,' as one might be tempted to conclude with Cesare Pavese,[4] Ginzburg's prose is a tour de force of stylistic dominion that paradoxically empowers the lonely narrator, who is almost always female. Effusions are out. Emphasis is absent. Speech is suspect. But brief utterances freed from the bonds of cause and effect are crucial, and silence is full of meaning. Silence is a constructive element in Ginzburg's universe. It is the moment of observation in her texts, the moment when her protagonists focus with all their being on the barrage of a myriad events, great and small, and gauge the impact those events have on their universe. The protagonists cannot grasp, in the present, the relative importance of each event as it hurries by. They can only look with all their might, as Pirandello's characters once did. Then, as they look back, Ginzburg's characters do not put order on or fill gaps in the hopelessly jumbled, immense pile of rubble that is the past. They do not neatly sort out stories and history, and vice versa. Having saved and stored their observations and experiences, they remember single details of what happened, especially the ephemeral and mundane, with total immediacy and brightness, all those things we usually forget: the air of that moment, which is the most personal and intimate aspect of all occurrence, 'le morte stagioni' ('the bygone seasons') in Leopardi's words, a gesture, a word, a dress, a death, and the stupidity of incomprehension (an unmentionable failure), and the heartbreaking dailiness of courage and cowardice, of cruelty and sacrifice. *That* is the function of writing, for Ginzburg, and not indulging in supposed reconstructions of an intelligible past. By accepting its task of modestly acknowledging its own inevitable partiality, and by not presuming to speak for all and for ever, fiction covertly validates pain in its irrational and often unexplained reality, and validates also the egoism of the inevitable drive to happiness. And all this happens through language, because, like her contemporaries Calvino and Levi, and like the major part of the Italian tradition, Ginzburg *believed* in language, and because she was certain that 'la poesia ... è per sua natura amorosa anche quando è crudele' ('Il vizio assurdo,' in *Opere II*, 570) ('poetry ... is loving by its nature, even when it is cruel').

Events, then, cannot be listed, described, and analysed in crystalline, sinuously flowing prose. Their absurdity breaks the links they perhaps shared. Their expression can only be litany-like, unceasing, with neither 'real' beginning nor 'real' end, half dreamlike. It is the reader who must supply the energy to bind those events together and provide the compassion that is the hallmark of literature. And we know, then, why it has been possible for us and for the author to love the unlovable characters who are stranded in Ginzburg's universe, as in the case of Purillo in *Le voci della sera*:

> C'è per esempio un personaggio secondario che tutti considerano stupido e antipatico, per di più è fascista, fa sempre discorsi banali e stonati: eppure il lettore si rende conto che è una bravissima persona, onesto e generoso e infelice. L'autrice non ha fatto il minimo sforzo per suggerirci il nostro atteggiamento verso il personaggio: ci ha portato a giudicarlo cosí a poco a poco, come succede nella vita. (Calvino, 'Review,' 136)

> There is, for instance, a minor character whom everyone considers stupid and dislikable. He is even a fascist, and always says things that are banal and inappropriate. Yet, the reader realizes that he is actually a fine person, honest, generous, and unhappy. The author has not made the slightest effort to suggest what our attitude toward this character was supposed to be. She has led us to judge him as we did, little by little, as it happens in life.

Tutti i nostri ieri was Ginzburg's first major novel. The 'nostri' in its title boldly binds reader, narrator, and writer in the evocation of a common past: we – whoever *we* may be – are included by it. Then, upon opening the volume, we find in epigraph the quote that provided the titles for the Italian text of the novel (*Tutti i nostri ieri*) and its American translation (*All Our Yesterdays*), as well as for the British translation (*Light for Fools*): 'And *all our yesterdays* have *lighted fools* / The way to dusty death' (*Macbeth*, 5.5.22–3). Several strands are woven into the story, but they all involve directly or indirectly the central character, a girl who witnesses the turmoil that takes place in Italy during the thirties and forties. Her mother is dead, and her father is wrapped up in his own ineffectual brand of anti-Fascism. She falls in love with a boy her age, who is unable to face an unexpected paternity, and is left by him bewildered and pregnant. While war rages around her, she marries a friend of the family, and sees her husband murdered by the Nazis and relatives and friends decimated and dispersed. But she and her daughter survive to face a world where the pain for losing loved ones is accompanied by a sense of personal mutilation. The novel is placed under the sign of darkest tragedy, the atmosphere evoked is poetic, and the theme announced is one of loss, a loss made irreparable by death and more harrowing by the awareness of human folly. But tragedy has a different voice in the twentieth century than it did in the Elizabethan text, and the Shakespearean quote heightens the sense of incongruity that comes from mourning a loss not only of lives and hopes, but also of grace.

In the late forties, as entire populations, among which the Italian, attempted to remember and to forget at the same time, to witness and to honour with silence, to retell experiences that were unspeakable, and to find new words to bring about a livable future, many writers and artists asked themselves how one could tell the stories that asked to be told. Although that question is the fundamental one for any writer, it seemed impossible to that generation to look to the past for suggestions and enlightenment, and return to old storytelling patterns. The immediate past was too strange, fragmented, and irrational, while the future seemed incongruous in its novelty, immense and uncertain. Italo Calvino wrote important pages on the dilemmas and advantages of being a young writer after World War II, in his famous preface to the 1964 edition of *Il sentiero dei nidi di ragno.* In that same period, Elio Vittorini was writing his *Le donne di Messina* (1949; *Women of Messina,* 1973), a sprawling and intense account of life in a country of refugees, and Primo Levi was writing not only *Se questo è un uomo* (1947; *If This Is a Man,* 1959), but also *La tregua* (1958; *The Truce,* 1965). All the significant Italian texts of the postwar period have in common the importance given to everyday life experiences, the choral quality of the narrative, and the fact that the events affecting people's lives are placed in the background, a disjointed sequence of determinant and yet distant, basically incomprehensible, occurrences. Perhaps the best condensation of such elements of storytelling is found – more than in the early films by Rossellini and De Sica, where plot, sentimentality, and heroism still prevail – in the films directed by the brothers Taviani, where we hear an echo of that same collective experience, replayed in a more optimistic key.

Vittorini repeated the words of a medieval rhyme in the title of his *Le donne di Messina,* Primo Levi returned to Dantean images in *Se questo è un uomo,* and later the Tavianis, in *La notte di San Lorenzo,* returned to the *Iliad,* in an effort to link the events of recent history to the authors' cultural roots; by so doing, they underlined, perhaps unwittingly, the tenuous character of exactly those cultural links. Ginzburg returned to one of the major sources of heroic horror in Western culture, to Shakespeare. We are thus able to measure the distance that separates her characters' experience of the world from the world-view that once elicited the poet's eloquent lines. The horrors of our times inspire revulsion and desperate sorrow, rather than awe. Our losses are so thorough that only understatement can do them justice. And writers now acknowledge the fact that masses of ordinary people, traditionally silenced by History and Literature, perish and survive in the storm of historical events. For Ginzburg and her peers, the stories of history must be told by new voices. Her ambition is the same as that of the writers who are her contemporaries: to create a new textual artifact that neither separates neatly public and private, nor makes explicit their mutual impact.

Who is best suited to observe and retell what history has done and does to characters, fictional or not? Foreshadowing later feminist positions, Ginzburg privileges the perspective of a powerless human being as witness to 'what happens' (O'Healy, 21), weaving together historic and personal events, the sound of the indifferent march of time, and the mystery of an individual's entering adult life. A female child, as later in the Tavianis's film, provides the point of view in *Tutti i nostri ieri*. Some of her characteristics, and the events that form the background of her life, remind us of the characters seen in the works of other writers belonging to that same Italian generation. She is very observant, although she is very young and, as such, inexperienced, and she is oblivious to the root causes of things. Everything that happens around her is recorded by her without recourse to psychology or causality. She is the youngest child in a relatively well-to-do family. As she grows up, the world around her does not become any more comprehensible for her, it just becomes more familiar in its dailiness. Although tragic events surround her, they do not have a magnanimous quality. The novel confirms the Poet's words quoted at its beginning, and at the same time undermines them, as all the novel's voices, young, vulnerable, and unaware, stand in contrast to the kingly, male, and mature voice of the tragedy's protagonist. Many readers have commented on the technique Ginzburg uses to reduce in size even those characters who loom large on the stage of history so that they must rejoin the crowd of ordinary folk. Far from being a foreseeable peculiarity of a minor female writer, this downsizing is a calculated technique that allows the construction of a distinctive universe. Even the choices imposed on her characters by moral imperatives are immersed by Ginzburg in the mundane concerns of how to save one's life, find a haven, deal with responsibility, and face maturity, loneliness, and aging. Again, a novelist who was Ginzburg's contemporary clearly analysed the stance taken by some postwar writers, including himself: 'Il senso storico, la morale, il sentimento, erano presenti proprio perché li lasciavo impliciti, nascosti' (Calvino, 'Preface,' 19) ('The sense of history, ethics, and emotions were all present precisely because I left them implicit, hidden'). The writer's choice of a protagonist who had no active hold on the events served to undermine and personalize the traditional text of History: 'La storia in cui il mio punto di vista personale era bandito ritornava ad essere la *mia* storia' (Calvino, 'Preface,' 20; his italics) ('That story from which my personal perspective was removed truly became *my* history'). The ambiguity of the Italian term *storia*, which corresponds equally to 'story' and 'history,' underlines the writers' double concern, as Elsa Morante stressed by the very choice of title for her 1974 novel, *La storia*.

Historical events thus affect the lives of Ginzburg's characters in a capillary way, and every phenomenon in Italian culture as well as the writer's every personal experience is woven into her text: the decline of the upper bourgeoisie, Fascism and anti-Fascism, first love, the persecution of the Jews, family events, death and survival at the end of a world war, and suicide (Pavese killed himself in 1950, just before *Tutti i nostri ieri* was written). History is seen not as a flowing river impelled by the one-directional gravity of time and the purposeful cunning of politics, and not as a plot with orderly subplots. History is a mass of events great and small, a total presence in each and every human moment; it is an organic composite of the personal and the public, in which all threads tangle.

In a very economical way, the narrator tells us about the changes taking place in Italian society, through the actions and behaviour of an eccentric group of people, actions and behaviour that are announced, seemingly at random but in detail, in the first three pages. A portrait of Anna's mother, already dead at the onset of the story, presides over the economic decline of the family, 'con un cappello a piume e un lungo viso stanco e spaventato' *Opere I*, 268) ('wearing a plumed hat, and with a drawn face, tired and frightened'). Characteristically, we first learn about the country's political climate through the title of a would-be book that Anna's father is writing:

> Era intitolato: *Niente altro che la verità* e c'erano cose di fuoco sui fascisti e sul re. Il padre rideva e si stropicciava le mani a pensare che il re e Mussolini non ne sapevano niente, e in una piccola città dell'Italia un uomo scriveva pagine di fuoco su di loro. (*Opere I*, 270)

> Its title was *Nothing But the Truth* and it contained explosive information on the Fascists and the king. Father used to laugh and rub his hands happily when he thought that the king and Mussolini didn't know anything about it. And in some little town in Italy there was a man who was writing explosive things about them.

But the book ends up in the stove, unfinished, and its author dies immediately after, closing his tormented and confused life among his restless brood: 'Il suo viso adesso era molto bello, non più tremante e sudato, ma fermo e dolce' (*Opere I*, 282) ('His face now was very beautiful, not agitated and sweaty any more, but immobile and tranquil'). The father's passionate and ineffective form of resistance is matched by the petty but murderous violence of provincial Fascists. From the characters' perspective, the conflict between Fascism and anti-Fascism is either a continuation of ancient small-town rivalries and hatreds among leading families; or an occasion for adventure for the young people in Anna's circle, such as Ippolito, Emanuele, and Anna herself; or a homely but frightening phenomenon of triumphant *prepotenza*, for the Sbrancagna, Emilio and his father, who are Fascist sympathizers; or a terrible fate, for the peasants, among whom is the servant aptly called 'la Maschiona' ('Big She-Man') (*Opere I*, 468–71). Only later on, and not in Ginzburg's texts, Fascism and anti-Fascism will be presented as wilful creations of leaders and nations, or as a confrontation of good and evil.

Ginzburg calls upon all her skill when she evokes World War II. Instead of the monolithic entity that the name given to it by history manuals suggests, her war is elusive, made up of many events and innumerable emotions. It seeps into every life and becomes the daily companion of every character, as uncertainty and fear grow with an imperceptible crescendo. The reactions of the various characters are in keeping with their psychology and status in life. The politicized Emanuele rejoices over the losses suffered by the Germans and their Italian allies, even though he is disturbed by the contradiction in his own stance, as young Italian soldiers and hapless civilians must die in the firestorm of war. For Ippolito, the descent into despair is almost unnoticeable, until he makes his last gesture, which awakens disbelief and guilt in his young friends. For the protagonist, an adolescent love story, a pregnancy, and her marriage to a much older friend of the family are the events of primary importance, and yet they cannot be separated from the events of the larger community of human beings: ('Una sera Anna era a letto e allattava la bambina e d'un tratto Cenzo Rena venne da lei e le disse che la Germania faceva la guerra contro la Russia' (*Opere I*, 460) ('One evening, Anna was in bed nursing her daughter, and all of a sudden Cenzo Rena came into her room and told her that Germany was going to war against Russia'). As for the peasants, the war is described by them as an infinite tangle of crossroads in remote lands, a murderous maze, where the Italian mothers' sons get confused and lost forever. And perhaps neither the peasants nor the narrating voice realize the aptness and poetic power of their metaphor, those 'strade incrocicchiate' where 'era facile sperdersi' (*Opere I*, 468). ('crisscrossing roads' where 'it was easy to get lost'). The characters' astonishment at the consequences of the war's presence is the readers' astonishment, too. It is that bewildering presence that kills one character after the other: Ippolito, signora Maria, Franz, and Cenzo Rena, among many others.

The most demanding component of the novel, though, must have been the evocation of the persecution of the Jews. Nothing could have had greater intensity, in Ginzburg's consciousness, than the remembrance of the fate visited upon her people and her very own family. Yet, no sentimental or dramatic tones tempt this indomitable writer. The contrast between the depth of the persecutors' ferociousness and the shallowness of the hunt's ideological underpinnings is achieved in such a controlled way as to pass almost unnoticed, as a 'normal' event, and at times a comical one in its absurdity. The victims are not really likable people. Franz is litigious and rather cowardly, 'un povero salame' (*Opere I*, 307 and 498) ('a silly dolt'). A pitiable Turkish man ends up in confinement probably because he is mistaken for a Jew (*Opere I*, 458–9). The only other Jewish people sent into confinement in the southern village of Borgo San Costanzo are three frail old ladies who are quite poor, much to the villagers' initial disappointment, since Jews were rumoured to be rich. Ultimately, the old ladies are accepted in the community because they have useful talents and fit well in the general misery and bewilderment. Other works, by other authors, describe unspeakable horrors or celebrated deeds of resistance and survival; this novel remembers ordinary people and their suffering, when they found themselves thrown together in faraway, forgotten places, among other ordinary and suffering people, all because of someone's political madness.

The numerous characters in the novel are vividly drawn, but there are three whose development is most convincing and reveals the perceptive eye of the writer. Anna, the fourteen-year-old protagonist, and her sister Concettina are two complementary faces of young womanhood. The latter is fully the upper-bourgeois girl, dutifully committed to her university studies in spite of her relatively limited intellectual capacities. She loves comfort and elegance, is greatly concerned with her physical appearance, and has a number of suitors, whom she disdains in favour of a solid if uninspiring bourgeois marriage. She becomes the overprotective mother and conventional matron whom we often find, with a shock of recognition and some dislike, in Ginzburg's fiction. However, life being what it is, full of pain and mishaps,

Concettina turns out to be devoted to her unlucky friends and relatives, a loyal if impatient nurturer, limited and loving, her only passion being her commitment to her 'tribe.'

Anna, on the contrary, is passionate and dreamy. The fact that the text often refers to her – through the voice of her older husband – as 'un insetto' ('an insect'), who sits immobile on a leaf letting life go by, is a misleading clue that tempted many a critic into error. For instance, Piero Citati, in his otherwise perceptive review, erroneously asserts that 'Anna passa attraverso la guerra sempre eguale, chiusa nel suo "silenzio d'insetto," e gli avvenimenti la lasciano intatta, non incidono sulla sua coscienza' (Citati, 363) ('Anna lives through the war without changing, closed in silence like "an insect." The events do not touch her, they do not mark her consciousness'). Actually, she is far from unscathed by the events in which she is immersed. Her true life is so deeply buried in silence, her isolation as an adolescent female is so thorough, that no one can fathom her need for love, her yearning for action, and her sexual awakening. Her love, mixed up and imperfect, goes to an awkward and confused rich kid; her political ideas, unformed and baseless, wither on the vine; and her tentative physical involvement with her first love ends up in a pregnancy as surprising to her as it was inevitable, given the two children's ignorance and emotional need. Few writers have explored with greater compassion the confusion of a generation of women too young to understand the politics and the realities of life in a moment of epochal upheaval, and too old to be untouched by them. Everything in Anna's life – family and love, pregnancy and death, rebellion and ignorance, her entire condition of being a barely teenage female – is mixed up with the events she must live, as the world thrashes about in the agony of war, forgetting her. People die around her, people kill themselves, some are executed, and her memory falters, until a minute event brings back to her memory her buried past: 'Tutto ... tutto ritornava al suo cuore in un soffio forte e profondo') (*Opere I*, 445) ('Everything ... everything was coming back to her heart, in a powerful and deep gush').

No illusions cloud the consciousness of another central character, Danilo, the persistent and unsuitably working-class suitor of Concettina. He is a leftist political ideologue and underground conspirator who instructs his bourgeois friends in political theory. Ginzburg draws him without sentimentality, as a true political animal, a pragmatist who, upon returning from prison, surprises and saddens his friends and co-

conspirators, idealistic as they still are, with his transformation into a cold-eyed strategist:

> Emanuele ... gli spiegò che Concettina voleva sposarsi col signor Sbrancagna, un fascista. Danilo chiese cosa c'era di tragico, il fascista li avrebbe aiutati quando fossero stati nei pasticci. Poi prese subito a parlare d'altro, come se Concettina fosse stata una persona qualunque, e come se lui mai l'avesse aspettata dei pomeriggi intieri davanti al cancello. (*Opere I*, 339)

> Emanuele ... explained to him that Concettina wanted to marry Mr. Sbrancagna, who was a Fascist. Danilo asked what was so tragic about it, the Fascist was going to be helpful when they would be in trouble in the future. Then, he immediately started talking about something else, as if Concettina was just anybody, and as if he hadn't waited entire afternoons for her, in front of the iron gate.

Danilo will survive and continue his political career. Not so his friends, whom despair and disappointment will destroy, or diminish and silence.

New stories must be told using new techniques. As Calvino remembered, 'gli elementi extraletterari stavano lí tanto massicci e indiscutibili che parevano un dato di natura: tutto il problema ci sembrava che fosse di poetica, come trasformare in opera poetica quel mondo che era per noi *il* mondo' (Calvino, 9; his italics) ('The extraliterary elements were *there* in such a massive and peremptory manner that they looked like facts of nature. We felt as if the problem was one of poetics, how to transform into a creative work that world that for us was *the* world'). Whether Hemingway or Chekhov or Pavese presided over the development of Ginzburg's writing techniques, there are elements that become, in this novel for the first time, Ginzburg's hallmarks. I shall mention only three that are determinant and belong to different stylistic categories: a technical device, a narrative strategy, and a thematic element.

The entire novel is written in two tenses of the past: *imperfetto* and occasionally a *passato remoto.* The sequence of *imperfetti* gives the narration a sense of permanence that a more dynamic tense would not have. The *imperfetto* is the tense of remembrance and contemplation, and brings no closure. In Ginzburg's novel, everything in the past hovers between continuity and repetition. Moreover, the characters' statements in the *imperfetto* of indirect discourse become objective absolutes, as the narrator reports them, perpetuating them with her remembrance. And then, occasionally, a *passato remoto* bursts out, rending the fabric of narration with its suddenness and finality.

As for narrative strategies, the ending of *Tutti i nostri ieri* sounds like the conventional closure of 'women's' novels, so much so that Bettina Knapp curtly dismissed the novel's characters as superficial: 'Anna partí con la bambina ... tutti erano vivi e l'aspettavano ... e Anna rivide Giustino ... e Concettina e Emilio e il bambino di Concettina' (*Opere I*, 565) ('Anna left with her little daughter ... they were all alive and they were expecting her ... and Anna saw Giustino again ... and Concettina, and Emilio, and Concettina's little boy'). But Ginzburg skilfully inserts minimal reminders of the past, piercing like thorns in the characters' flesh. Giustino, 'che era stato Balestra' (*Opere I*, 566) ('who had been "Balestra"'), she says, alluding to his Resistance days, gone by now. Anna 'had begun to resemble her mother, as she looked in the portrait' ('aveva preso ad assomigliare alla madre nel ritratto'), and thus we are made to grasp, in the barely modified repetition of the novel's early sentence – 'i tratti stanchi e spaventati di quel viso' (*Opere I*, 567) ('the traits, tired and frightened, of that face') – the commonalities of women's experiences, hidden behind their silences, and revealed only in those unguarded moments that photos and portraits so poignantly preserve. And the ending, with its musical scanning, poetically tells us how the survivors, Anna and Emanuele and Giustino, are left to carry the burdens and duties of both past and future: 'Erano contenti d'essere loro tre insieme a pensare a tutti quelli che erano morti, e alla lunga guerra e al dolore/ e al clamore/ e alla lunga vita difficile/ che si trovavano adesso davanti' (*Opere I*, 574; the scansion into lines of 9, 4, 9, and 11 syllables is mine) ('They were glad to be together, they three, to think of all those who had died, and the long war and the sorrow and the fury, and the long, difficult life they now saw stretching before them').

Finally, there is Ginzburg's concern with 'family,' a theme so persistent that mentioning it has become commonplace. Yet, the term 'family' may be misleading, in this universe. Ginzburg's characters are not truly members of families. Ginzburg's 'families' are groups of people temporarily sheltered by houses; they are tribes in centrifugal movement that find brief moments of respite, then move on again, and end up decimated. Their various components – widowers, estranged spouses, surrogate mothers, old aunts, lovers, lovers' relatives, neighbours, children of various ages, and step-relatives – are very precariously and unconventionally linked. They cling ferociously to each other, but they are invariably poised to escape into solitude and distance, obsessed by their own unresolved, and perhaps unresolvable, problems. They become the idiosyncratic characters that find a permanent dwelling only in Ginzburg's world.

Ginzburg's second major novel, *Le voci della sera,* was published in 1961, nine years after *Tutti i nostri ieri.* By that time, the Italian peninsula had gone through an intense period of reconstruction, and was experiencing what came to be called an 'economic miracle,' whose secret lay in the low wages and backbreaking work of masses of Italians. As for the political climate, in spite of its novelties such as the rebirth of political parties, universal suffrage, and the demise of the Savoia monarchy, it was a disappointment to many who had hoped for a total break with the past. Literature fitfully attempted to explore the common store of experiences that the Italians had accumulated in those fateful years between 1940 and 1950, but only Vittorini, Carlo and Primo Levi, Fenoglio, Calvino, and Pavese produced a few significant works in that vein. Besides, by 1963, their names were cited with contempt by an emerging generation of writers who were above all interested in technical experimentation. Ginzburg, once again, was neither cited with admiration nor reviled, even though she achieved in her short novel perhaps the most successful blend of technical innovation and complexity of meanings.[5] Calvino, however, did say that 'la presenza di Natalia nella letteratura italiana ci appare sempre più unica e preziosa e ricca d'insegnamento' ('Natalia Ginzburg,' 134) ('Natalia's presence in Italian literature is, in our view, increasingly unique, invaluable, and exemplary').

In *Le voci della sera,* Ginzburg pursued her reflection on the narratives of history which she had begun in *Tutti i nostri ieri.* The story, again, is simple. Elsa, a middle-class girl who is the main character, is the lover of Tommasino, the youngest son of a prosperous family of small industrial entrepreneurs. They live in a provincial town, in the years following World War II. The memories of the past and a tight family circle are inescapable and oppressive realities which ultimately contribute to the demise of the young people's fragile love story. Ginzburg demonstrates an even keener technical skill than in her previous novel, due to her maturing and perhaps to the chronological distance from the events she evokes and her physical distance from Italy (she was then living in England with her second husband, Gabriele Baldini). Calvino said of the novel: 'Tutti gli elementi che erano nell'altro [romanzo] sono qui fusi con più rigore e compattezza e ironia e affetto, e un'ombra di tristezza che ci raggiunge senza cercare di soverchiarci' ('Natalia Ginzburg,' 136) ('All the elements that were present in the other [novel] are blended here with greater rigour, concision, irony, and compassion, and with a hint of sadness that touches us without trying to overcome us'). Quite clearly, as several readers have noted, *Le voci della sera* is the pivot between the first period of Ginzburg's writing, which was detached, more traditionally chronological, with frequent use of indirect discourse, and the second period, when first-person narration, free indirect discourse, greater reliance on dialogue, and more agile structures become the rule. In this novel, Ginzburg reaches a fearlessness that allows her to use fully her own voice. The fragmentation of remembered events is pushed to its maximum, with daring manipulation. The claustrophobic quality of family life imparts a sense of total closure to the text. The language is clean, spare, and exact. And, with admirable swiftness, her brief fictional text explores with finality the pain of living, which she perceives to be at the very same time historically and existentially determined.

The volume opens with a disclaimer: this is a story about nowhere, and the characters 'non vivono, né sono mai vissuti' (*Opere I*, 668) ('do not live, nor have ever lived'). But the writer's empathy is granted at the very moment that distance is created by that peremptory assertion, thanks to one of Ginzburg's favourite syntactical devices, the use of the gerund, cool and slightly archaic, in place of an explicitly causal clause: 'E mi dispiace dirlo, avendoli amati come fossero veri' (*Opere I*, 668). ('And I regret saying that, having loved them as if they were real').[6] Clearly, the author's disclaimer is in truth an assertion of total involvement and control. In a parallel way, the world of *Le voci della sera* is ruled by one gaze, that of the narrator, who is constantly present in the first person. Elsa is the narrator, even though she is silenced, since her voice is not heard and her name is not spoken until late in the novel, and then as if by chance, by another character. The paradox of the narrator's apparent absence is misleading, because her choices, of focus and language, are the story. First of all, narrative time is *her* time, the time of her remembering. It is both disjointed and fluid, going seamlessly back and forth, within a range of almost forty years, disanchored from conventional moorings. The story of each character, which she tells, is made up of moments that are completely reshuffled by her remembering, deaths being known before marriages, and present physical appearances being superseded by the blossoming of the characters' youthful selves. The protagonist lives as in a house of mirrors that reflect endlessly every instant she has witnessed, or vicariously experienced through other people. The rise of Fascism, the persecution of Socialists and Communists, the destruction due to the war, the *sfollamento* (a mass exodus from the cities that had become vulnerable to war actions and hunger), the years spent in prisoner camps, the Resistance, and then life in a world no longer at war but beset by profound dislocations – all those events return obsessively. They are seen, forever gone yet present, through the filter of the daily routine of a small group of people, as the protagonist goes about living her own story.

The beginning, placed in the late fifties, could not be more pedestrian, or more characteristic of Ginzburg's style. A daughter is returning, with her mother, from a visit to the doctor, where the older woman had a sore throat checked. The mother's stream of remarks and exclamations, occasioned by worries about her health and a lively interest in small-town gossip, is underscored by her daughter's silence. This dialogue manqué is mildly comical, and at first is disconcerting because of its triteness and because actually the silent woman is the all-knowing narrator. We soon realize that there is much suppressed energy in the protagonist's silence that accompanies the disjointed monologue of the secondary character. As the evening walk continues, various people cross the two women's path, and they are transformed into a gallery of vivid portraits. Neighbours and acquaintances are caught in various moments of their existence through image association, by the narrator's inflectionless voice that engages in its own parallel monologue, with no break in the text's continuity. All the senses contribute to the narrator's evocation of images from the previous half-century, as private experiences, political change, and family mythologies mingle inextricably:

> La fabbrica produce stoffe. Manda un odore che riempie le strade del paese ... Il vecchio Balotta era socialista. Rimase socialista sempre ... ma era diventato, negli ultimi tempi, di umore assai malinconico e torvo; e al mattino, quando si alzava, fiutava l'aria e diceva a sua moglie, la signora Cecilia: – Che puzzo, però ... La signora Cecilia diceva: – Non sopporti più l'odore della tua fabbrica? E lui diceva: – No, non lo sopporto più. E diceva: Non sopporto più di campare.' (*Opere I*, 674–5)

> The factory produces fabrics. It spreads a smell that fills the streets of the town ... Old Balotta [the benign owner of the factory] was a Socialist. He

> remained a Socialist, always ... but his mood, in the last few years, had become very melancholy and brooding. And getting up in the morning, he used to sniff the air and tell his wife, Signora Cecilia: 'It really smells ...' Signora Cecilia would say: 'You can't stand the smell of your own factory any more?' And he used to say: 'That's right, I can't stand it any more.' And he used to say: 'I can't bear to go on.'

Vittorini's 'stench' ('puzza'), (*Conversazione in Sicilia*, Part I, chap. 6), symbolic allusion to political rot, is here a concrete cause of nausea for a stricken man, whose political and family disappointments merge into one, and it becomes a perversely Proustian stimulus for the narrator's memory.

The narration proceeds by rapid flashbacks and short returns to the recent past through about fifty pages punctuated by recognizable temporal expressions, thrown like small anchors in the storm, to help us find our bearings: 'Venuto il fascismo ... Durante la guerra ... Poi venne la guerra ... Dopo la liberazione ... L'indomani ... Poi ... Dopo la guerra ... '). ('Fascism having arrived ... After the war ... Then came the war ... Now ... After the Liberation ... The following day ... then ... '). Thus, we piece together the story of two families, going back and forth over the terrain the narrator is painstakingly crossing and re-crossing. The De Francisci, who have five children, are the owners of a textile factory in a small northern Italian town. The narrator's father is the firm's business lawyer, and the head of the Bottiglia family is its administrator. The three couples, their children, their various relatives and acquaintances, and the townspeople, are shown in very brief episodes similar to snapshots, against their provincial backdrop. They live in continuous contact, so that actual and imagined events, eavesdropping, and gossip weave a suffocating network of relationships, while the Fascist regime is established, persecutions take place, the war arrives, then the Resistance, the end of the war, and finally the years of rising prosperity, when those who have not died survey in disheartened astonishment their changed world. We learn, by bits and pieces, that through the years some characters die; some are assassinated; some survive thanks to luck, their own cowardice, or opportunism; and the young people experience unhappy loves and loveless marriages. In a way, *Le voci della sera* is the true continuation of *Tutti i nostri ieri*, in content and atmosphere. The years have passed, and yet everything keeps returning as vividly as if it had never gone, so that, for the narrator, remembering is at the same time an obsessive recall and the sole life-affirming activity. The text supports her perspective with constant repetitions of words, phrases, constructions, bits of songs, and situations, achieving an effect of dynamic staticity, as in some of her unforgettable portraits. The one of Cate, the unsatisfied wife of one of Balotta's sons, is a love poem to female beauty, full of joy and regret:

> [Cate] era alta, bella, robusta, con una massa di capelli biondi che pettinava a volte in due trecce ... a volte in un casco molle e pesante, attorto e puntato in cima al capo.
>
> Aveva un viso pieno, dorato dal sole ...
>
> La ricordarono poi per molto tempo, al paese, quando tornava dal torrente dove andava a fare i bagni, col vento che le frustava la sottana sulle gambe nude, tornite, dorate dal sole, i capelli umidi e arruffati sulla fronte ...
>
> La ricordarono quando scendeva dalla collina ... grande, bella, bionda, coi suoi biondi bambini.
>
> Aveva, quando andava al torrente nell'estate, un abito azzurro ... aveva un fazzoletto ... che si cingeva intorno ai capelli ... Aveva, d'inverno, quando andava a sciare, un maglione bianco. (*Opere I*, 707–8)

> She was tall, beautiful, strong, with a mass of blond hair that she combed sometimes in two braids ... sometimes in a soft, heavy bunch, twisted and pinned high on her head. She had a wholesome face, made golden by the sun ... Later, they remembered her for a long time, in town, as she used to be when she returned from the stream where she used to go bathe, with her windswept skirt around her naked, shapely, suntanned legs, with her blond hair, wet and tangled on her forehead ... They remembered her when she used to come down from the hill ... tall, beautiful, blond, with her blond children. She wore, when she went to the stream in the summer, a blue dress ... She wore a blue and white hair band ... She wore, in winter, when she went skiing, a white sweater.

The past endures, for better and also for worse. It is in the lives of the youngest characters that the destruction wrought by historical events and the trite concerns of a stolid bourgeoisie is most obvious, conveyed by the text's controlled indirectness:

> 'Lui mi fa una carezza sul viso. Mi dice: –Povera Elsa!
> –Perché povera? –dico. –Perché ti sembro povera? –Perché sei capitata con me, che sono uno sciagurato ... *–Io, –dice, –io sono senza ideali. Rido, e gli dico: –Povero Tommasino.*
> *–Perché povero, che ho tutti quei soldi?* (*Opere I*, 739–40; my italics)

> He touches my face. He tells me: 'Poor Elsa!' 'Why poor,' – I say, – 'Why do you pity me?' 'Because you happened to meet me, and I am a wretched man.' *'I' he says, 'I have no ideals.' I laugh, and I tell him: 'Poor Tommasino.' 'Why poor, when I have all that money?'*

In the central part of the novel (*Opere I*, 732–40), suddenly, the narration has returned to the present tense. We are told of a new love, this one between the narrator and Tommasino, who are last in a line of mismatched lovers, and we learn also the name of the protagonist, Elsa. Their brief romance, 'qualcosa di molto leggero, di molto fragile, pronto a disfarsi al primo soffio di vento' (*Opere I*, 769) ('a very light, a very fragile thing, ready to be undone by the first breath of air'), is stranded in a world that is weighed down by unbearable burdens. Among a flurry of conventional visits, domestic squabbles, neighbours' inquiries, recipes, and reminiscing, an engagement is born, lasts for a few weeks, then dies, and we experience, as the protagonists do, the power of the claustrophobic environment created by the family and by the past. None of the characters in the novel has been able to escape that power. Tellingly, the return to the past tenses is immediate in the subsequent thirty-five pages. The dialogues become even more comical in their domestic triviality, and they are also chilling in their innocent cruelty, given what we have been able to surmise from the sparse words of the narrator, whose suppression we are witnessing. The latter part of the text vibrates with the characters' desire to escape and their revulsion for every aspect of the past and the present – desire and revulsion that are equally frustrated by their loyalty to the dead and a stubborn attachment to what has survived:

> –Al paese, –dice, –non mi sento libero. Mi pesa addosso tutto. –Cosa ti pesa? –Mi pesa, -dice, –tutto, il Purillo, la fabbrica, la Gemmina, e anche i morti. –Mi pesano, capisci, anche i morti. –Una volta o l'altra, –dice, –pianto lí e me ne vado. (*Opere I*, 740)

> 'In this town,' he says, 'I don't feel free. Everything weighs on me.' 'What weighs on you?' 'Everything,' he says, 'everything weighs on me, Purillo, the factory, Gemmina, and our dead, too. Even the dead, you know, weigh on me.' 'One of these days,' he says, 'I'll drop everything and leave.'

But Tommasino is unable to open himself up to passion and gamble. He will not leave the town. As he perceptively puts it: 'ho sempre come l'impressione che abbiano già vissuto abbastanza gli altri prima di me.

Che abbiano già consumato tutte le risorse, tutta la carica vitale che era disponibile' (*Opere I*, 771) 'I always have the impression that the others, those who came before me, have already lived enough; that they have already used up all the resources, all the life energy that was available'). And Elsa will remain unmarried, in spite of her passionate love for Tommasino, which she must bury under the silence of her humdrum life; she will remain hostage to her dwindling tribe. In the final pages, the narration has moved on by a year, only to continue as always – 'E' di nuovo ottobre' (*Opere I*, 776) ('It's October, once again') – and the voice of deadening domesticity goes on and on. That is how survival happens – the novel tells us – how it is fraught with pain and unspoken regrets, and also how human lives lose their vitality, how they are twisted and ultimately broken by a history that has become one with individual stories. The end of the novel tells us that the wounds caused by that intertwining bleed inside (*Opere I*, 771). No high-sounding statements proclaim that truth, which is instead entrusted to an unanswered question, asked by Cate, remembered by Vincenzino, and echoed by Elsa: 'Ma perché si è sciupato tutto, tutto?' (*Opere I*, 725, 731, 760) ('But why, why did everything get ruined?'). History is 'evil,' 'il male,' even if this writer does not linger on its vilest manifestations. Sorrow and joy are equally elusive, even as they touch deeply the characters' consciousness. 'Ora, di tanto odio, non restava più nulla: e anche questo era triste' (*Opere I*, 727) ('Now, nothing was left of so much hate. And this, too, was sad'). The characters' reflections on their losses must by necessity remain incomplete, fleeting, too profound and painful to be formulated according to the rules of logical discourse: ('La felicità –lui disse –sembra sempre niente, è come l'acqua, e si capisce solo quando è perduta ... E anche il male che noi facciamo, è cosí, sembra niente, sembra una sciocchezza, acqua fresca, mentre lo facciamo' (*Opere I*, 725) ('Happiness,' he said, 'always seems to be nothing, it's like water, and we understand it only when it's gone ... And the evil we do, also, is like that, it seems like nothing, it seems insipid, just like water, while we are doing it'). 'Acqua fresca' could be called – far from disparagingly – Natalia Ginzburg's prose.[7] In its depths, the horror of history is visible.

Stories and history are bound to one another, Ginzburg says, if we realize that we must abandon certain preconceptions about what history is, how one tells it, and how one constructs the actors in it.

Of the misconceptions that caused reductive readings of Ginzburg's works, some were due to insufficient awareness of what had happened in the Western world, in the early forties, in language and experience. The rhetoric of war that extolled heroic deaths and the sacredness of ends was not a superficial phenomenon, and was not limited to the countries that 'lost' World War II. Ginzburg's stories, by their linguistic plainness and contained passion, undercut the war rhetoric that to this day poisons the entire planet, misleads the young who thirst for adventure, and allows the wholesale devaluation of human life in the name of economics and ideologies. Cenzo Rena, one of the more complex and likable characters in *Tutti i nostri ieri*, warned young Anna, who dreamed of a not clearly defined 'rivoluzione': 'Quando il destino si annunciava con alti squilli di fanfara bisognava sempre stare un po' in sospetto. Gli squilli di fanfara di solito non annunciavano che cose piccole e futili ... invece le cose serie della vita coglievano di sorpresa, zampillavano a un tratto come l'acqua' *Opere I*, 420) ('When destiny announced itself with high trumpet sounds you had to keep a suspicious mind. Fanfares usually announced only small and futile things ... instead, life's serious matters caught you by surprise, they would spring up suddenly, like water'). Heroic historical narratives are dead, and that is perhaps not the last among the sorrows of the more naive characters. The young protagonists know it well by the end of Ginzburg's novels, and reveal their awareness with their sadness and resignation.

Some of the misconceptions that plagued the readings of Ginzburg's works were due to sexism.[8] Ginzburg challenged the prevailing stereotypes as to what female characters think and do and how female writers write. In these novels, the women of the various social classes are *participants* in historical events, confused, unaware, frustrated, hurt, yearning for serenity and happiness – just like the men. Women and men both are participants who are not told the 'meaning of History,' and cannot make sense out of the events. All of them worry about their own lives torn by war and massacre, and stumble through war times striving to care and live and die for those they love. As for the writers who are women, they do not pour words on the page as one more female excretion, but rather they fashion a difficult artifact; they do not write only about half of humankind; and, most importantly, they do not say about males what is stereotypically said, that they are either wonderful heroes or (at the other self-aggrandizing extreme) monsters of self-deception, in the Sartrean vein.

Natalia Ginzburg's originality was in her uncompromising way of speaking about the ordinariness of good and evil, of revolt and acquiescence. Her originality is also evident in her conclusion, that not even lucidity and suffering foster awareness in human beings, who merely endure, stunned by pain and loss, in 'a world that has turned to ashes' ('un mondo caduto in cenere') ('Cuore,' *Opere II*, 103). In spite of their generosity and humanness and courage, the marginal people who do not speak but *live* history, and the voice that tells about the *attualità* of historical events, have no heroic tales or great wisdom to transmit: even their best deeds are somewhat flawed by inconsistencies, chance, and imperfect understanding. It is a confirmation of our desire to delude ourselves that the person who spoke in a new way about being totally immersed in history was believed to be a modest writer, a *crepuscolare*, evasive about the great events of history, and all in all rather tiresome. She was, instead, exacting in style and compassionate in vision. For her, life and cruelty and politics and fear and the elimination of people are terrible everyday things, dimly understood, dull and petty and unfathomable in their horror and stupidity. She said that survival also is a daily thing that overcomes, but does not erase, the immense pain and sorrow of our yesterdays, as the massacres of this century, from Auschwitz to Bosnia, unfortunately should have taught us.

NOTES

1 See the bibliographies included in *Opere* (Milan: Mondadori, 1986), 1577–91, and in Bullock's *Natalia Ginzburg* (246–53). All the quotes from Ginzburg's works come from the two volumes of *Opere*. All the translations are mine.

2 The otherwise excellent piece by Giacinto Spagnoletti also insists on Natalia Ginzburg's detachment from politics (Spagnoletti, 41–2). For a different reading of this issue, see Italo Calvino's 'Natalia Ginzburg o le possibilità del romanzo borghese,' 136–7, and Donald Heiney's 'Natalia Ginzburg: The Fabric of Voices,' 92.

3 A volume on Italian women writers, which appeared after the writing of this article, contributes to a revision of Ginzburg's evaluation. The author, Sharon Wood, focuses on the complexity of Ginzburg's works and on her interest in the relationship between individuals and historical events (Wood, 135–51). Several essays in the volume *Natalia Ginzburg: La casa, la*

città, la storia also show greater keenness in analysing Ginzburg's fiction (see in particular the essays by Luigi Surdich and Jean-Philippe Bareil).

4 As quoted by Garboli in *Opere II*, 1579.

5 *Le voci della sera* was translated into English in 1963 for the Hogarth Press of London and E.P. Dutton of New York. The 1989 Little, Brown edition to which I had access actually divides Ginzburg's novel into sections! They are entitled:

I. Elsa and her Mother and Family
II. Old Balotta
III. Elsa and her Family
IV. Balotta's Children
V. Vincenzino and Caté
VI. Elsa and Tommasino
VII. The End of the Affair

6 Other examples of Ginzburg's frequent use of the gerund, all in *Le voci della sera* (*Opere I*) are: 'essendo stato minacciato di morte' (679) ('having been threatened with death'); 'avendo lui ... un'impresa laggiù' (684) ('since he had a business down there'); 'desiderando fare la signora' (694) ('as she desired to be "a lady"'); 'essendo totalmente incapace' (700) ('because he was totally incapable'); 'avendo ammobiliato le stanze' (704) ('having furnished the rooms'); 'essendosi conosciuti da bambini' (712) ('since they had been childhood friends'); 'essendosi spaventato' (721) ('having got frightened'); 'Avendo avuto in giovinezza un amico' (727) ('Since he had had a friend, when he was young'); 'avendolo visto piccolo' (732) ('as he had known him when he was little'); 'non avendo il Purillo ... nessuna personalità' (735) ('since Purillo had no personality'); 'essendosi lei litigata' (763) ('after she had a row'); 'vergognandosi della gente' (774) ('being bashful').

7 'Acqua fresca' (actually 'fresh, spring water') is a recurring image and metaphor in Ginzburg, since 1933 in 'L'assenza' (*Opere I*, 176), where 'acqua fresca, limpida' refers to the indifference manifested by Maurizio, the protagonist. A good metaphor, it avoids the stereotypically gendered references and images so common in critical texts about women authors (see Cesare Garboli's entire 'Prefazione' to Ginzburg's *Opere*, especially *I*, xlv).

8 See, for instance, the already mentioned preface to the volume of *Opere*, written by Garboli (*I*, xi–xlvi), and the expressions used by various reviewers cited in the section on Ginzburg's 'fortuna critica' (*Opere II*, 1577–91), for instance: 'affettuoso interesse' ('a loving interest') (1577); 'charme' (1577);

'parole affettuose' ('loving words') (1578), 'il candore di una psicologia femminile che si offre inerme ma, nella sua ingenuità, minacciosamente indifferente' ('the candour of a feminine psychology that offers itself unarmed, yet is threateningly indifferent in its naivety') (1578).

REFERENCES

Brunette, Peter. 'Natalia Ginzburg Defeated by Manzoni.' *Los Angeles Times Book Review* (27 December 1987): 13.

Bullock, Alan. *Natalia Ginzburg: Human Relationships in a Changing World.* Oxford: Berg, 1991.

Calvino, Italo. 'Natalia Ginzburg o le possibilità del romanzo borghese.' *Europa letteraria* 9–10 (June–August 1961): 132–8.

– 'Preface.' *Il sentiero dei nidi di ragno.* Turin: Einaudi, 1964.

Citati, Piero. Review of *Tutti i nostri ieri. Belfagor* 8 (May 1953): 363.

Ginzburg, Natalia. *Opere I* and *II.* Milan: Mondadori, 1986–7.

Harris, Daniel. 'To the Letter.' *The Nation* (5 December 1987): 686–8.

Heiney, Donald. 'Natalia Ginzburg: The Fabric of Voices.' *Iowa Review* (Fall 1970): 87–93.

Ioli, Giovanna, ed. *Natalia Ginzburg: La casa, la città, la storia.* San Salvatore Monferrato: Edizioni della Biennale 'Piemonte e letteratura,' 1995.

Knapp, Bettina L. 'Natalia Ginzburg's *All Our Yesterdays*: The Introverted Cocotte and the Insect.' In *Women in Twentieth-Century Literature: A Jungian View.* University Park: Pennsylvania State University Press, 1987.

Morante, Elsa. *La storia.* Turin: Einaudi, 1974.

O'Healy, Anne-Marie. 'Natalia Ginzburg and the Family.' *Canadian Journal of Italian Studies* 9, no. 32 (1986): 21–36.

Sanvitale, Francesca. 'I temi della narrativa di Natalia Ginzburg: Uno specchio della società italiana.' In *Natalia Ginzburg: La narratrice e i suoi testi* (Rome: La Nuova Italia Scientifica, 1986), 23–40.

Spagnoletti, Giacinto. 'Natalia Ginzburg.' *Belfagor* 39, no. 1 (31 January 1984): 41–54.

Taviani, Paolo and Vittorio. *La notte di San Lorenzo.* 1982.

Vittorini, Elio. *Conversazione in Sicilia.* Milan: Bompiani, 1941. Translated by Wilfrid David under the title *In Sicily* (New York: New Directions, 1949).

Wood, Sharon. *Italian Women's Writing: 1860–1994.* London: Athlone, 1995.

The Personal Is Political: Gender, Generation, and Memory in Natalia Ginzburg's *Caro Michele*

JUDITH LAURENCE PASTORE

> Tens of thousands of Italian women marched in the heart of Rome ... to protest unemployment and a campaign to tighten Italy's abortion law ... Many women at the rally expressed sympathy for women raped during the warfare in Bosnia-Herzegovina.
>
> 'Women Protest Abortion Law'

> In [Natalia Ginzburg's] fiction and out of it, if the true patriarch has died or disappeared, the vision of, or longing for, a matriarch has not supplanted him – and all the siblings appear to be having a damned hard time of it.
>
> Goldensohn, 'Natalia Ginzburg'

A central tenet of contemporary feminism is that the personal is political. The two opening citations indicate this fusion. The first appeared in a newspaper reporting events in Italy two days before International Women's Day in 1993. The second is from an article by Lorrie Goldensohn, 'Natalia Ginzburg: The Days and Houses of Her Art.' In many ways, Ginzburg's career personifies the fusion of political events with artistic concerns, a fusion found again and again in her writings.

Insistence that the personal is political is central to modern feminist theory because it provides a tool for penetrating the power dynamics in relationships. Understanding the hegemony of patriarchal institutions is crucial to understanding why through most of history the social and artistic contributions of women have been marginalized. The assumption that women's contributions have significance mainly in the personal realm has until very recently allowed patriarchal institutions to go unchallenged. Judaeo-Christian dogma in Western culture has been the major political force denying women power. In the past, family hierarchy mirrored the social order, with a strong father at the top, and mother and children subservient. Both Jewish tradition and Italian culture have been strongly patriarchal; consequently, the parallel centrality of the family in both has served to reinforce the veritable sanctity of male dominance.

Natalia Ginzburg's childhood, as recounted in *Lessico famigliare*, was spent in such a patriarchal household, where Giuseppe and Lidia Levi seemingly conformed to normative gender patterns of the period. Ginzburg summarized her family in an interview with Peggy Boyers:

> I came from a mixed marriage – my father was Jewish, my mother Catholic. My parents were atheists and therefore chose not to give us, the children, any religious instruction ... You might say that a Hebrew spirit dominated the household in the sense that my father had a very strong, very authoritarian character. (Boyers, 'Interview,' 141)

Giuseppe Levi was domineering, irascible, seemingly rational; his wife, as described by H. Stuart Hughes, 'forever worrying, forever gently complaining "povera Lidia"' (1992, 158). She comes across in *Lessico famigliare* as somewhat shallow and impulsive, but nevertheless practical. Both parents provided a deep sense of emotional security through their strong love for their five talented children. However, the portrait of the young female artist which emerges from *Lessico famigliare* is one of ambivalent feelings toward personal success. While Ginzburg's position as the youngest girl in a brilliant household made her doubtful of her own abilities, at the same time she longed for literary accomplishment. After she married Leone Ginzburg, the trauma of their forced exile to the Abruzzi, followed by his arrest, torture, and murder, brought home to her the merger of the personal with the political in ways no abstract feminist theorizing could. This awareness was intensified by the severe poverty she experienced as a widow at the close of the war. Then exigency forced her to realize that writing could function not simply as an expressive outlet, a pleasant way to escape reality, but as a crucial means of support.

Another result of Ginzburg's experience with the pain of loss was her abiding fear of political chaos. This fusion of the personal and the political creates in many, if not all, of her mature texts a longing for the remembered order and security associated with a dominant father figure.

Caro Michele, published in 1973, and entitled *No Way* in the English translation by Sheila Cudahy, responds to the social unrest experienced both in the United States and capitalist Europe at that time. Written partially in dialogue reminiscent of Ivy Comptom Burnett's narrative style, and partially in an epistolary mode which foreshadows *La città e la casa* of 1984, *Caro Michele* records a world where not only the strong father has vanished, but where men instead of women are fictionally marginalized. Instead of creating a utopian matriarchy, where feminine values create peace and harmony, the textual denial of male dominance in all of Ginzburg's writings produces a lonely, meaningless existence, where the older generation lives either on memories or the pursuit of wealth they do not enjoy, while the young live with no conception of the past and no purpose in the present. These people are not the lost, violent souls of Dante's world. They are passive Prufrocks allowing sheer contingency to dictate their actions.

Caro Michele revolves around the following characters: middle-aged, once beautiful Adriana, mother of four daughters and one son, divorced from her artist husband, and living alone with his sister Matilde; her son, Michele, a bisexual, hippie radical; Mara Castorelli, an irresponsible young hippie woman whose illegitimate baby may be Michele's son; and Oswald, who is married to the dynamic Ada, but who, like Michele, is also bisexual and was for a time Michele's lover. The plot contrasts these characters, as the older ones desperately search for someone or something to give their lonely lives meaning, while the younger ones drift from one meaningless relationship to another, unconcerned about the past or the future, totally committed to living in the now.

Ginzburg contextualizes generational contrasts in a variety of patterns: between genders, between generations, and within generations. For example, though both Michele and Oswald are bisexual, their lives are very different. And though Michele and Mara are both so-called hippies, as a man, Michele is free from the biological constraints of childbearing that Mara must deal with. None of the women, moreover, follows exactly the same pattern. Adriana's passivity is in marked contrast with the energetic efficiency of Oswald's wealthy wife, Ada, or Adriana's aggressive sister-in-law, Matilde, who is trying to promote the publication of her first novel, comically called *Polenta and Poison.* Ada, Adriana and Matilde are all approximately the same age, but they manifest distinctly unique characteristics. Adriana's inability to act seems to be less harmful than the unthinking activities of the two young characters, Michele and Mara, activities characteristic of those qualities in the younger generation that Ginzburg fears. Michele becomes casually involved with political terrorism both in Italy and abroad, actions which lead first to exile and ultimately to death. Mara sponges off everyone to support herself and her baby, but has no clear idea of what she wants to do other than live comfortably. Her inability to 'get her act together' puts her constantly in dependent roles, the responsibilities of which she refuses to accept.

For Ginzburg, bringing children into the world requires enormous personal sacrifice and a willingness to be responsible for them for many years. Throughout her fiction, those characters who thoughtlessly parent offspring and refuse to provide emotional as well as physical security for them are depicted as infantile. Adriana's former artist husband is such a father. As Adriana explains to Michele: 'Però a lui delle tue sorelle non gliene importa niente. La sua stella sei tu' (345) ('He could not care less about your sisters; you are the only one who counts' [6]). When he and Adriana divorce, he insists on taking Michele with him, a separation that permanently damages both mother and son, but he refuses to take the four girls. Here Ginzburg agrees with feminists in their criticism of male dominance. Patriarchy is no guarantee of female support because not all men live up to their responsibilities; many behave as selfish, unthinking children. However, she does not agree with those feminists who want to shift power to women instead of men. Throughout her texts, she criticizes members of both sexes who refuse to assume the responsibilities of adult life. Simply replacing selfish, unthinking men with women in positions of dominance would solve nothing, since there are just as many selfish, unthinking women.

Although Ginzburg longs for the lost order of traditional beliefs, an order founded on patriarchal values, she has no illusions about such beliefs. Instead, her view of the human condition is darkly pessimistic. In a 1991 third-person account she compiled for a biographical encyclopaedia, she wrote: 'She believes in God, albeit in a chaotic, tormented and discontinuous manner' (quoted in Boyers, 'An Introduction,' 79). Still significantly using the third-person masculine pronoun as late as 1991, in another essay entitled 'On Believing and Not Believing in God,' Ginzburg examines the nature of her religious convictions; her beliefs, like those of Søren Kierkegaard, reveal an ability to live simultaneously with faith and doubt. Unlike the complacent Non Believer, Ginzburg's

Believer is so tortured by unanswerable questions as to find little comfort. Whereas atheism produces intolerance and feelings of superiority, Ginzburg's belief in God is 'so doubting, so wavering, so ready to be snuffed out altogether that it is not in the least consoling and does very little to throw light on things' (quoted in Boyers, 'An Introduction,' 80).

Lack of certainty is central to her belief system, which sees militant religious attitudes as ultimately unacceptable to God. One must believe in God because 'the world without God would seem terrible,' but this does not entitle one to any assurance. 'The Believer's belief is so incredulous that it is very much like not believing' (Boyers, 'An Introduction,' 80). Acceptance of this dark vision opens one to awareness of the sacred and the mysterious, an awareness denied to both the atheist and the militant believer. Any generic religious idea such as of God as a father or personal friend is out of the question; the closest she can come to envisioning God is when she thinks about real people she has loved, whether they are dead or alive. An ardent admirer of Proust, Ginzburg makes memory central not only in her artistry but also in her religious outlook. Memories of loved ones bring her the closest to God she can get, and serve as a religious experience. Describing this emotion, again using the masculine third-person singular, she writes that those moments fill him with 'burning tears and ... a strange happiness, then for a moment he feels, trembling and fluttering, something that vanishes at once which, perhaps, was God' (quoted by Boyers, 'An Introduction,' 81).

This attitude toward memory determines many structural elements in *Caro Michele*, including its conclusion. The final letter narrates Oswald's ability to experience this approximation of a religious moment because he can maintain his relationship with Michele even in death through the power of memory. By placing this moment at the conclusion, Ginzburg underscores its contrast with the inability of the younger generation to form meaningful relationships. Reputed to be the dead Michele's lover, Oswald has gone to a house Michele and his wife Eileen rented in Leeds, where he can find 'Di Michele ... nulla, salvo una camiciola di lana usata come cencio da spolvero' (495) ('nothing of Michele's except for a woolen undershirt that had been used as a dust cloth') (160). He tries to learn something from Michele's friend Ermanno Giustiniani, who either does not know much or does not want to remember his dead friend. Ermanno's refusal to remember Michele prompts Oswald to lament the historical consciousness of modern youth: 'I ragazzi oggi non hanno memoria, e soprattutto non la coltivano' (495) ('They have no sense of the past and above all they make no effort to remember') (160–1). In contrast, he and Adriana nourish their memories of Michele. One of her responses to Michele's death is to write asking her former lover Philip to send her the words of an old Spanish anti-Fascist song she once hated because her artist husband sang it but one she now cherishes because Philip taught it to Michele. Though Oswald cannot bring himself to keep such a souvenir of Michele as the old undershirt, later it haunts his memories: 'Ci si consola con nulla quando non abbiamo più nulla, e perfino aver visto in quella cucina quella maglietta cenciosa che non ho raccolto, è stata una strana, gelida, desolata consolazione per me' (496) ('One comforts oneself with nothing when there is nothing else. Even the sight of that ragged shirt that I left in the kitchen gave me a strange, sad and icy consolation') (161).

Both the older man and woman experience a connectedness with the past produced by an item like Proust's *madeleine*, paltry in itself but capable of transcending the limitations of materiality and triggering a remembrance of a lost loved one. Until Michele dies, Mara experiences no such connectedness in either her thoughts or actions. The fact that she does not know who fathered her child symbolizes her refusal to become an adult. Like the flower children of the sixties, she deliberately rejects the responsibilities of middle-class adulthood. She takes it for granted that other people will help her care for her baby, leading her to act in ways guaranteed to make people want to avoid her at all costs. She borrows money and possessions she has no intention of returning, exploits others to suit her needs, and lies both to them and to herself about her actions. Ada finds her a position as a live-in maid with Oswald's shop assistant Mrs Schlitz and her mother, who finally ask her to leave:

> L'avremmo tenuta con noi tanto volentieri. Era anche una buona azione. Ma non ha buon senso. Ci svegliava la notte perché l'aiutassimo a cambiare il bambino. Diceva che le faceva tristezza cambiarlo da sola ... Faceva anche pena. Però non si capisce perché ha voluto avere quel bambino dato che le dà tanta angoscia di tirarlo su. (396–7)

> We would have been very glad to keep her with us and it would have been a kind thing to do but she has no sense at all. She used to wake us up at night to help her change the baby. She said it depressed her to do it alone ...

> We felt sorry for her. Still, one can't understand why she wanted to have that baby, when she finds it so painfully difficult to take care of him. (57)

Mara's relationship with Fabio, Ada's lover, is more complex. Mara is first motivated by spite and wants to take something away from Ada, who represents adult capability, but in the end she thinks she is in love with Fabio. He in contrast grows to hate her childish irresponsibility and lower-class manners. Here, Ginzburg's sympathies are divided. Alan Bullock sees Mara as 'a source of much comic relief in this novel' (*Natalia Ginzburg*, 156). However, I believe that if Ginzburg intended her to be merely a comic figure, she would not have emphasized throughout Mara's refusal to abandon her baby in the face of one rejection after another. Her refusal and her resiliency keep her from sinking into the passive lethargy which cripples Oswald and Adriana. Her resiliency of course also enables her to continue with her self-destructive behaviour pattern. For example, she returns Ada's help by stealing her lover Fabio. After Fabio demands that she and her baby leave his apartment, the same generous woman who befriended her when her baby was born agrees to have her come to Sicily as a maid/babysitter. Once there, Mara's careless conduct gets her thrown out when the couple discover her in their marriage bed with the husband's brother. In each instance – with Ada, the Sicilian couple, and Fabio – Mara is being used. The employment found for her in each case is in service, whether as maid or mistress. As live-in servants, the major occupation for women until World War II, women traditionally have been treated as sex objects. Like many single women with young children, Mara must accept live-in service to survive. Seen in this light, Fabio's treatment of both her and Ada is totally selfish. As an older, educated man, he should have some compassion for Mara, even if he feels no loyalty to Ada. Instead, he merely uses Mara sexually until he grows tired of her. His embarrassment with her when he takes her with him to Adriana's is both snobbish and self-centred. Although he has enjoyed having a childlike mistress, he also wants her to behave in a sophisticated manner when she is in polite company. This is really a variant on the frequent male fantasy of possessing a woman whose conduct is virginal in company and highly erotic in bed. Like Adriana's artist husband, Fabio's refusal to grow up harms others, while he remains untouched, insulated by his wealth from the demeaning aspects of existence, which Mara as a poor, unwed mother cannot escape.

Hampered as Mara is by having to care for her baby, she still never once thinks of abandoning it. With possibly the highest number of abortions of any Western industrialized nation, Italy – like America today – is going through a violent debate over 'pro-choice' versus 'right to life.' In the early 1970s, when Ginzburg was writing *Caro Michele*, an equally fierce debate raged over loosening the then existing total ban on abortions (Birnbaum, *Liberazione*, 87, 89). Consequently, Mara's decision to have and keep an illegitimate child has major contextual significance. Ginzburg is dramatizing, as only art can, the intricate fusion of the personal and the political. Her attitude on abortion reflects her highly complex religious views discussed earlier. In the essay she wrote in the early 1970s when Italy was undergoing a vigorous campaign to legalize abortion, she points out that the painful conflicting issues in the debate do not have easy answers, in spite of the slogans used by those who are 'pro choice' and those who are 'pro life.' Ginzburg wants women ultimately to have the right to choose whether to have a child. However, she also wants women to recognize that there can be no disputing that abortion is a denial of sacred life; the foetus, although not a fully developed human being, is 'the remote and pale blue-print of a person' (quoted in Boyers, 'An Introduction,' 59). When a woman has an abortion, she chooses, according to Ginzburg, 'to separate herself for good from a single, precise and real possibility of life' (quoted in Boyers, 'An Introduction,' 59).

> Logical reasonings, the light of usual moral considerations, don't apply and are of no help because there are no logical reasons or clarifications where everything is immersed in darkness. It is a choice in which the individual and her destiny face each other in the dark. (quoted in Boyers, 'An Introduction,' 59)

Mara was irresponsible to have a child when she was still a child herself; simply becoming a mother does not make an adult of her. It takes Michele's death to make her finally aware of her own vulnerable mortality. She remembers her time with Michele as part of childhood:

> Era per me un grande divertimento stare con lui e abbiamo passato insieme delle ore meravigliose, che per me non avevano niente da fare col vero amore ma rassomigliavano alle ore che passavo da bambina quando giocavo a palla incatenata con gli altri bambini sulla strada davanti a casa mia. Tutt'a un tratto ... mi sono messa a pensare a Michele e mi è venuto da

> piangere, e ho pensato che non mi riesce più di essere allegra a lungo e non mi riuscirà più, perché penso e mi ricordo sempre troppe cose. (484)

> I had a lot of fun with him and we had some marvellous times together, which had nothing to do with real love. They were like the hours I spent as a child playing tag with other children on the street. All of a sudden ... I began to think of Michael and to cry. Then I knew that I can't ever be happy for very long and I will never succeed in being happy for any length of time because I remember and think about too many things. (148–9)

Like Oswald and Adriana, Mara too discovers through Michele's death the significance of memory. Memory is the human soul, enabling us to transcend the limitations of material existence. The sorrows and joys which accompany it are what distinguish us as human beings and mark our passage from innocence to adult experience. In this sense, memory elides the distinctions between gender and generation, binding all of us together. Memory is the great democratic force, reminding us of the political mistakes of the past and revealing the shallowness of abstract ideologies of both left and right. The only ultimate distinction lies in whether we choose to face the truth of memory or run from it, back to the mindlessness of childhood. The degree to which the personal becomes political is contingent upon how much responsibility each individual is willing to take for his or her own conduct. Whether Mara's awakening will lead to greater maturity is left unresolved, primarily because Ginzburg is highly sceptical of solutions, particularly simple ones. Consequently, in both her writings and her political positions, she refuses to follow rigid party dictates whether Marxist or feminist. One cannot lose memory of the self in the safety of party politics any more than one can retreat to the innocence of childhood. Life demands ongoing individual responsibility, together with a willingness to analyse one's actions for oneself no matter how tempting it is to long for the absent, strong father. Mara's earlier actions do not offer much hope that she will reach this point. Unfortunately, when one does accept the burden of memory, as Oswald and Adriana do, the pain produced threatens the will to live. Without some kind of religious reverence for life itself, the pain of existence could not be endured. Oswald and Adriana cling to crumbs to sustain themselves – the lines of an old Spanish Civil War song, the tattered remains of a castoff undershirt. On such fragments are those who reach maturity in *Caro Michele* forced to survive. The true adult knows that personal pain is part of the human condition, which no political strategies, no matter how noble or grandiose, can obviate.

NOTE

1 All Italian quotations of *Caro Michele* are from *Opere*, and all English translations are by Cudahy.

REFERENCES

Birnbaum, Lucia Chiavola. *Liberazione della donna: Feminism in Italy*. Middletown, CT: Wesleyan Universitv Press, 1986.

Boyers, Peggy. 'An Interview with Natalia Ginzburg.' *Salmagundi* 96 (Fall 1992): 90ff. Reprinted on pages 10–31 of this book.

– 'An Introduction: Natalia Ginzburg in Her Essays.' *Salmagundi* 96 (Fall 1992): 54ff.

Bullock, Alan. *Natalia Ginzburg: Human Relationships in a Changing World*. New York: Berg Women's Series/St. Martin's, 1991.

Ginzburg, Natalia. *Lessico famigliare*. Translated by Beryl Stockman under the title *Family Sayings* (New York: Seaver/Henry Holt, 1988). Revised from the original translation by D.M. Low (Manchester: Carcanet, 1984).

– *Caro Michele*. In vol. 2, *Opere*. Milano: Mondadori, 1986–7. Translated by Sheila Cudahy under the title *No Way* (New York: Helen and Kurt Wolff/ Harcourt Brace Jovanovich, 1974).

Goldensohn, Lorrie. 'Natalia Ginzburg: The Days and Houses of Her Art.' *Salmagundi* 96 (Fall 1992): 96ff.

Hughes, H. Stuart. 'The Families of Natalia Ginzburg.' *Salmagundi* 96 (Fall 1992): 157ff.

'Women Protest Abortion Law.' *Vero Beach (Florida) Press Journal* (19 March 1993): 1SA.

Writing the Self: The Epistolary Novels of Natalia Ginzburg

PEG BOYERS

Letters can be the most candidly personal and revealing form of communication or they can serve as a handy medium for the self-conscious construction of personality. At their most interesting they serve both functions, revealing secrets the self never knew it had, inventing a candid personality not only previously unknown but fictitious. Using letters as opportunities for controlled relations with others, the disembodied self can freely don the mask of sincerity and intimacy without the uncomfortable threat of physical consequence. William James can flirt with his convalescent sister, Alice, without worrying about incest; Abelard and Heloise can pour out their hearts with passionate abandon while keeping their monastic vows. Epistolary relationships, even those of a professional nature – say, between authors and editors – can evolve to a fineness hard to match off the page, unfettered as they are by coarse reality. Indeed, some epistolary relationships become so satisfying in themselves that the infrequent occasions when the correspondents *do* meet are inevitably disappointing. How many of us have suffered through such meetings and felt the relative thinness of those flesh-and-blood encounters? Upon confronting one's paper interlocutor face to face, all seems strained and unnatural – starting from the moment of salutation. How distant are 'Hello' and 'How are you?' when compared with 'Dear' or 'My dear'! The pressure to be more true, more vivid, more intense and amusing (not to mention more beautiful) than the self imagined by one's correspondent paralyses the meeters, rendering them speechless. At a certain point attempts at real connection through substantial conversation are abandoned and the two find solace in anecdote and gossip. The visit is endured more or less gracefully on a superficial plane. Much warmth is dutifully expressed but not felt, and the two part, disillusioned with themselves and with each other, impatient to somehow pick up the thread of their correspondence again, to dispel the impression that fleshy reality has made, to re-establish the ideal self in the imagination of the other, the place of which, for the moment, has been usurped by the inferior stuff of actual presence.

Almost as great a pleasure as writing and receiving letters oneself is the perhaps ethically dubious practice of reading the letters of others. Until recently it was only possible to snoop around in the correspondence of dead strangers. Nowadays, however, many of the wily famous have given up their privacy and sold their letters pre-humously, as it were, for fantastic sums. Some of the *less* wily but *as* famous find, to their chagrin, their letters exposed in these collections for the simple reason that they were at one time so imprudent as to correspond with the *more* wily. And this can be a very embarrassing state of affairs, indeed. But whether by the wily or by the not-so-wily, the letters of the famous are ever of interest and we are grateful to enterprising archivists and meticulous editors for their assemblage.

Reading the letters of famous people – artists and public figures – we seek to understand more deeply the work or the deeds with which we are already familiar. We read the letters in the context of the work in order to be surprised or confirmed in our sense of the person. Henry James is exactly whom we expect him to be: warm and wittily generous with his siblings William and Alice, often cryptically ironic and circumlocutious in his responses to strangers, but always elegant, perfectly composed, often long-winded. Hart Crane, the suicide, reveals an uncanny joie de vivre and the publicly grave T.S. Eliot seems in his letters to Groucho Marx almost incredibly, light-heartedly amusing. D.H. Lawrence, always in character, is forever the moralist, never slipping into that life-of-the-party mode he was apparently loved for by his friends. Rilke to his 'young poet' is stoical and generously mentorly, while in correspondence with Magda von Hattingberg he is unreservedly narcissistic and manipulative. Neither persona quite matches the ethereal voice of *Sonnets to Orpheus.*

The letters of fictional characters, of course, cannot be read against the background of their deeds, misdeeds, or art. Their ostensive authors are ordinary people, and what we know about them is simply what they reveal about themselves and about each other through their letters and from any narrative context the author provides. In short, their authors have no biographies; they *are* their letters. Nevertheless, fictional correspondences have their advantages. The letters, for one thing, all have a point: to develop the tale. We are never in danger of wasting our time on an insignificant encounter or feeling. No landscape is described gratuitously, no colour introduced without deliberation. We read with faith in the novelist's invention and trust that all will finish satisfactorily, or at least with a sense of plausible completion. For fictional collections of letters *do* finish as surely as they begin, and they have middles, too. There is comfort in this, as there is not in the reading of genuine correspondences, which end as abruptly as they begin, dependent as they are on their author's real-life circumstances.

Fictional correspondences are, after all, fiction, which is to say, novels, or parts of novels. And if the novel, as some of us were taught in school, is a form invented to depict the situation of Man in Society, the epistolary novels of Natalia Ginzburg are no exception. While Ginzburg's novels do not exactly go about this task in a Balzacian manner, their subject is decidedly the *comédie humaine* and they do take seriously their traditional purpose. The society they depict is that of our time. In the novels, as in the plays and essays, Ginzburg explores relations among members of the bourgeois class. Their quarrels, failed attempts at marriage and parenting, their impotence and emptiness fill the pages of her work like so many pieces of dry straw.

Ginzburg's obsession with the fate of contemporary society and in particular with the institution of the family is particularly well served by her use of the epistolary novel, which is fragmentary by nature and therefore an ideal vessel for her concerns. The technique allows her to project herself impersonally into many different roles spread out over a wide spectrum of possibilities, from an aging, angst-ridden journalist to a young gay filmmaker. The letters, like dramatic monologues, are presented one at a time and always occupy centre stage while we read them. Each is separate from the others, yet all are strung together by the fiction of correspondence. The characters, themselves locked in their role as correspondents, have licence to ignore or respond to whichever parts of each other's letters they choose, thereby expressing the frail contingency of things, the arbitrariness of the reality they inhabit. The time lapse between letters is oddly jarring as well, as we realize that our privileged reading of the letters in rapid succession does not correspond to the experience of the writers themselves, who are sentenced to live their lives off the page, as it were, until the post arrives. We readers need not suffer any such delays, but the consequence of our not doing so is that we experience a sort of flatness in the world of these letters, a linear reality whose one-dimensionality defines everything.

When Giuseppe, in *La città e la casa*, for example, receives a letter from his son, Alberico, explaining that he wishes to give his adopted daughter the experience of having an attentive father unlike that which he, Alberico, had as a child, we read the hurtful words along with their humble response from Giuseppe, who pleads guilty without further ado. The effect is thereby diffused, relegating the potentially volatile exchange to the merely informational. Blows are dealt and received, it seems to the reader, almost simultaneously, and the plot moves forward. Reports to Giuseppe from his former lover, Lucrezia, about her new passion for 'I.F.' are immediately followed by Giuseppe's detached observations on her cruelty, which are, in turn, followed by an exchange between two minor characters, Albina and Egisto, whose reflections on Lucrezia and I.F. undercut Lucrezia's impassioned version of the affair. Letters begin and end, each delivering a staccato punch, each note sounding its isolated, hollow tone, responding to, without substantially connecting with, the previous note. The staccato rhythm aptly reflects the nervousness of the world in which the letters are written, a world without consoling structures or reliable institutions to smooth the painful edges of existence.

The corrupt worlds of Balzac, Zola, and Dickens, by contrast, exist in opposition to the explicit ideals of their critical authors, and even the most malignant of the societal cancers they reveal are shaped by metaphor, filtered and interpreted by authorial voice, given meaning by the intricate architecture of the books in which they appear. Even Richardson's *Clarissa*, to introduce perhaps the most famous of all epistolary novels, is essentially a didactic novel whose letters reinforce and undermine each other according to a predetermined theme or lesson, implicit in which is a stable set of societal codes, expectations, and assumptions. In *Clarissa* the characters sometimes violate those codes as they vie for power with each strategically composed missive they send. But the understanding is that there is something to violate, something to be lost in exchange for something gained.

In Ginzburg's epistolary novels the characters have no stratagems because they have nothing to hide. Neither past deed nor future intention shames or embarrasses them. They live in a post-Freudian, therapeutic universe where the goal common to bourgeois human beings is to live comfortably, without conflict and without stress. The way to accomplish this, as we know, is to turn our dark insides out, letting lightness shine where before there were shadows. Letters, it happens, are perfect occasions for externalizing inwardness, a handy confessional medium with none of the implications of sins committed or forgiven that real confessions effect. The letters of Ginzburg's novels matter-of-factly record their authors' fears, disappointments, and anxieties – rarely their joys. The eternal presentness of the epistolary novel further contributes to the weightlessness of the communications, contextualizing the past in a format which reinforces the here and now by definition.

The characters in both of Ginzburg's epistolary novels, *Caro Michele* and *La città e la casa*, could easily inhabit any of her other novels excluding *Tutti i nostri ieri*. With the sole exception of that book's modest hero, Cenzo Rena, the people in her stories, novels, and plays all speak in the familiar affectless tones of the postwar bourgeoisie. Giuseppe, the main character of *La città e la casa*, has undergone years of psychoanalysis and is frankly set on a course which will require little from him by way of depth or commitment. His goal, as a successful therapeutic, to borrow sociologist Philip Rieff's term for the contemporary social type,[1] is to distance himself from everything and everyone he claims to care about. Bored by his career as a journalist, tired of not having any money, and recently (in an unfortunate lapse from his therapeutic resolve to remain detached) disillusioned in love, he decides to move to America to achieve actual, as well as emotional, distance from his familiar Italian circumstances. The first letter of the novel, to his brother, Ferruccio, whom he plans to join permanently in America, reveals anxiety about his unsatisfactory fraternal relationship yet a wilful determination to go ahead with his plans to begin a new life. 'I am coming to America,' he writes to Ferruccio, 'like someone who has decided to throw himself into the sea and hopes he will emerge either dead or new and changed.'[2] ('Vengo in America come uno che ha deciso di buttarsi nell'acqua, e spera di uscirne fuori o morto, o nuovo e diverso') (*Opere II*, 1364).

Giuseppe has reached an emotional impasse and is doing something drastic to break the pattern which yields only boredom and emptiness in his life. We come to learn that, in fact, Giuseppe's social circle has reached a point of imminent disintegration and that his timing to escape before things fall apart is entirely accurate. In his initial letter Giuseppe assures his brother that, although he will miss some of his friends, he nevertheless wishes to make the break now. There is nothing, apparently, to keep him behind, not even his son: 'Di mio figlio non sentirò la mancanza perché non lo vedo mai' (*Opere II*, 1364) ('I won't miss my son because I never see him').

By the next letter, however, we learn to our astonishment that Giuseppe has fathered not only one son, but, according to Lucrezia, to whom he is writing, two. His refusal to acknowledge Lucrezia's child as his own seems to us less troubling than the fact that he has all but done the same to the son he knew at birth but abandoned when he divorced the boy's mother. He denies paternity of Lucrezia's boy, Graziano, simply because he does not like him. He would rather identify with Cecilia or Daniele, whose personalities he prefers, but understands that they couldn't possibly be his, since their births predate his affair with Lucrezia. Playful as his musings on such matters may be, they do reflect Giuseppe's inability to fathom the magnitude of paternal/filial connections. He admits to Lucrezia, with minimal emotion, that he was and is a poor father and reflects on this as he reflects on his other faults: as just another of his many imperfections, not as a definitive key to the failure of his character. A veteran of analysis, he is clearly used to dwelling on these failures with equanimity. In his rambling farewell letter to Lucrezia, he rehearses the sad story of Alberico's childhood with its early exposure to the unhappiness of his parents and, most damagingly, to their boredom. 'Io però pensavo che tutta quella noia che aveva respirato da piccolo, in mezzo a me e a mia moglie, doveva averlo intossicato e che in qualche modo un giorno sarebbe esplosa' (*Opere II*, 1370) ('I used to think that all that boredom which he breathed in as a child amidst my wife and me would have poisoned him and somehow eventually blown him up'). Giuseppe's way of acknowledging his indifference to his son and its damaging effects is to relegate the problem to a general condition of ennui, thus clearing himself and detaching the thought of his parental failure from any idea of individual responsibility. Impotence seems easier to admit than negligence, impotence carrying with it a range of psychological explanations and excuses for inadequate behaviour.

Giuseppe's first rambling confessional letter to Lucrezia is followed in the novel by a brief note from a mutual friend, Egisto, who was to deliver the letter to Lucrezia. Egisto's note, written in haste, serves in some ways as an inadvertent gloss on Giuseppe's, since Lucrezia will read them both together, delivered as they are by Albina, the only one of the friends to come to see her that weekend. In very few lines, Ginzburg, through Egisto, underlines certain impressions we have of Giuseppe, while undermining others. Egisto observes, for example, that 'Giuseppe 'è tanto depresso perché non ha più voglia di partire' (*Opere II*, 1378) ('is depressed because he doesn't want to leave any more'), while Giuseppe has just spent a good part of two letters going over the reasons why he is ready to make a new start elsewhere. The themes of loss of one's house and failed fatherhood are reiterated casually, as if Egisto, too, were already familiar with them by this time. Thematic repetition voiced in different contexts deepens the sense of a common experience among these friends, an experience rich in mutual reference, if not understanding.

Often linked with Giuseppe in *La città e la casa* is Lucrezia, his ex-lover and the central figure around whom the circle of friends frequently gather. She and her husband Piero have been proud participants in a so-called open marriage for some twenty years, entertaining friends on weekends at their ample Umbrian home Le Margherite. By the time the novel begins, something has gone awry in the happy circle. Not coincidentally, everyone is getting to be middle-aged. Lucrezia is past forty and Giuseppe is approaching fifty. They have not been lovers for years; while the affair got off to a passionate start, it cooled when Lucrezia wanted to leave Piero to marry and Giuseppe resisted. The relationship couldn't sustain itself under the hospitable umbrella of Piero's approval and was dissolved by Lucrezia in the end.

Although Giuseppe has remained a frequent guest at Le Margherite and admits to feeling as though they had just finished making love every time he sees Lucrezia, he is perhaps not as resigned to the arrangement as he seems. After all, he is leaving the whole lot of them for the unknown. The plasticity and open-endedness of modern relationships seem to have worn him out: he yearns for some authoritative figure in his life and has decided on his brother as the most likely candidate for this role. In his letter to Lucrezia of 5 November he writes:

> Anche adesso sento il desiderio della sua protezione autoritaria, leggermente sprezzante e imperiosa. Tu spesso mi rimproveravi di non proteggerti. Ma come facevo a proteggerti, con il desiderio che avevo io di essere protetto. (*Opere II*, 1394)

> Even now I feel the need for his authoritative, slightly contemptuous, and high-handed protection. You often reproached me for not protecting you. But how could I have protected you when I myself have such a need to be protected?

Giuseppe goes on to reflect on this as an infantile attitude, but seems satisfied with the admission: 'Ma forse né tu né io siamo mai diventati adulti, né Piero. Siamo una nidiata di bambini' (*Opere II*, 1394) ('Perhaps neither you nor I have ever become adults, nor Piero, either. We are a brood of children'). Again, expression of the observation passes for understanding. He closes the letter and the subject is dropped.

By the time Lucrezia replies nine days later, she has other matters on her mind and is full of newsy chatter and busyness. She allows herself a few personal words at the end, remarking that she is saying goodbye on this 'piece of paper' rather than seeing him in Rome. That Giuseppe has asked her *not* to come to Rome in an earlier letter, she ignores, choosing rather to represent the decision as hers. Better to be too busy than unwanted. That this is an unconscious manoeuvre we have no doubt, because Lucrezia is anything but conscious when it comes to the way she proceeds in relationships. She chastises Giuseppe – justifiably – about his failure to connect with his twenty-five-year-old Alberico, while regarding her own five children as so many little charges to parcel out here and there so that adult routines can resume. She is middle-class enough in both means and ways to see that they are fed and schooled and clothed. But they do not occupy her thoughts; she never writes in her letters about their activities, their interests, their personalities. They are identified by her according to their fathers: four are Piero's and one, she insists, is Giuseppe's. The final son, who dies two days after birth from – surprise – a malfunctioning heart, is Ignazio Fegiz's. Children exist for Lucrezia as legitimizing tags for her relationships; they have no weight of their own. Although she admits herself: 'Come sai, ho l'innamoramento facile' (*Opere II*, 1381) ('As you know, I easily fall in love'), she apparently only bears the children of her 'serious' flings. According to her logic, promiscuity which bears fruit is made wholesome.

Among Giuseppe's circle in Italy are a few auxiliary figures, most important of whom is his cousin, the busybody Roberta, who helps all and keeps everyone up-to-date on everyone else's affairs, by mail and in person. She is a down-to-earth, good soul with apparently little to do but be of service to her cousin, to Giuseppe's son, and to his friends. She does so willingly and with gusto. She never questions her own strong opinions or motives and just gets on with life and all of its daily challenges. An infinitely less complicated helper than Osvaldo, her counterpoint in *Caro Michele*, Roberta believes in causes and effects and in the intrinsic value of property. Her house, the apartment below Giuseppe's, is her prize possession, from which she will never part. And she advises others to subscribe to the same philosophy: 'Mai vendere il mattone, mai. Il mattone bisogna tenerselo stretto' (*Opere II*, 1365) ('Never sell bricks and mortar, never. You have to hang on to bricks and mortar for dear life').[3]

Giuseppe has, of course, not followed her sage advice and has instead sold his apartment for a song to his therapist, a gesture which could be seen as a substitute for genuine psychoanalytic transference. Property is transferred rather than feelings. Giuseppe never openly regrets this sale but does nevertheless continue to believe that his house in Rome will always be his only real home. For a brief moment it seems as though his mistake will be undone when, at the end of the book, Alberico decides to buy back the apartment for himself. But Alberico dies before paying for it, and so the circle of ownership is never completed. Giuseppe, therefore, does not retrieve the house; rather, I.F. and his woman insensitively initiate moves towards purchasing it as soon as they learn that it is free after Alberico's death. In fact, no one follows Roberta's advice. Houses, the most important one being Le Margherite, are passed on as relationships shift, and in general people find themselves in less and less satisfactory housing arrangements. The *domus*, that old bastion of family life and tradition going back at least to the ancient Romans, has no chance for survival among these contemporary Italians for whom bricks and mortar are as porous and insubstantial as the families they sometimes house.

Roberta's refrain about the indispensability of bricks and mortar is repeated throughout the novel, as are other phrases, which are passed from letter to letter, from voice to voice, used for different purposes, but essentially serving to bind this disparate group to each other and to their common past. They are the equivalent of the 'family sayings,' whose function Ginzburg so eloquently describes in *Lessico famigliare*, which are all the members need use to certify their place in the tight community. Each letter has its saying, a password to the familiar, precious world they once shared. So we think of Alberico's beautiful little white teeth, which are exposed at rare moments when he laughs; Giuseppe's storklike legs and nose, his cold hands; Lucrezia's pallor; I.F., also known as the 'The Fox,' and his habit of keeping one hand behind his back; Ippo, 'The Cat,' I.F.'s elegant, anorexic girlfriend and her beautiful hair; the contested sullenness of Graziano, the unacknowledged son of Giuseppe; Le Margherite, and its guest room with the checkered coverlet; the Women's Centre; Albina's 'difficult bed'; Serena's performances of *Mirra*. These talismanic references evoke a cozy world and elicit intimate responses. Though the letters take place in the present, their emotional life, it could be said, takes place in the past; the strongest feelings are those called up by common expressions. In this world it is written language that cues the recollection of intimacy. That the language is flat and the experience recalled one of relative emptiness doesn't change the fact that both language and past experience are shared and therefore have resonance and meaning for those who share in them.

The repetition of refrains and common references in the letters also serves to bind together the various threads of narrative in the novel. The main plot of *La città e la casa* has to do with Giuseppe and his move to America, his relations with his old crowd in Italy, most especially Lucrezia, and his new life in Princeton. Another main line of narrative follows Alberico through his various exotic adventures and misadventures. Giuseppe's story involves movement away from 'the city' and 'the house,' while Alberico's progresses from a state of loss of his house and nomadic citilessness to a settling in Rome. A third line of narrative involves Lucrezia, the dissolution of her marriage, and her consequent move from the house of houses, Le Margherite, to a series of unsatisfactory apartments in 'the city.' The letters report and reflect on these moves, admonishing, advising, or approving this or that decision all within the easy context of letters, whose a priori futility and impotence are what make their frequency and reliability possible. If correspondence is the surrogate for genuine relation (and, as Osvaldo reminds us, in *Caro Michele*, 'we all use surrogates'), at least for these people it makes possible the maintenance, and in some cases the evolution, of friendship.

By moving into an apartment (found for him by Roberta, the real estate advocate) in the same building as Egisto, Alberico begins to circulate among Giuseppe's old crowd, eventually ending up as Lucrezia's good friend. And, as in *Caro Michele*, the departed one takes pleasure in the fact that the ex-lover and the estranged family member have found each other back home – initially meeting, significantly, in Giuseppe's old building. We hear about Alberico mainly in letters from Roberta, Egisto, and Lucrezia, but eventually also from Alberico himself. Although he has chosen an offbeat life (his first film is revealingly entitled *Deviance*), he is in some ways the person with the most integrity in the book. Something of a bad boy when he was young, disappearing for days without notice, and homosexual, he has taken on the responsibility for a flaky woman and child, supporting them gladly, even adopting the child to give it legitimacy. Through others we learn about the filth and disorder of his apartment, the lack of hygiene and standards of safety with regard to baby care, the presence of great quantities of drugs in the house, and the generally desultory customs of its inhabitants. Alberico is a generous, sweet-spirited person, but, as Egisto remarks to Lucrezia, 'è un ragazzo perso' (*Opere II*, 1377) ('he is lost'). There are indications, however, that over the course of the book Alberico comes closer to achieving some sort of equilibrium. He suffers terrible losses – his friend Nadia is killed, her daughter is taken away by her Sicilian father – but he seems to come out on the other side of them sadder but wiser. The estranged tone of his early letters to his father ('Gentile padre') evolves to what seems to be filial affection ('Amato padre'). Ironically, the ocean between them has allowed father and son to achieve something like a genuine relationship – a correspondence, if you will – on paper. Alberico can admit, 'Fra le cose che dicevi non me ne ricordo molte, solo qualcuna. A dirti la sincera verità, io ti ricordo molto poco e molto confusamente' (*Opere II*, 1550). ('I don't remember many of the things you used to say, just a few. To tell you the honest truth I can only remember you very slightly and very vaguely'), and have it understood as a positive admission, one which allows a paper father, which he and Giuseppe construct together, to fill the vacuum where memory has failed. Paper father and paper son are attentive, courteous, and warm with each other. They have learned to console each other in times of need and to keep each other dutifully informed about their lives. Neither need notice squalor, drugs, deviance, narcissism, middle-age anxieties, or anything else; each is represented as he wants to be, an invented self on innocent paper.

Not surprisingly, *Caro Michele*, written in 1973, eleven years before *La città e la casa*, lacks the wit and clipped pace of the later novel. Partly, this is due to the fact that the characters are themselves rather joyless, unable as they are to transcend their circumstances. Where *La città e la casa* fairly gallops along to its conclusion, entertaining us as the characters entertain each other with their letters, *Caro Michele* runs its course more slowly, as the characters fail to engage each other but nevertheless compel us to read on. More important, this is a more sombre novel due to Ginzburg's formal decision to insert dialogue and passages written by an omniscient narrator in places where the letters need supplementing. The result is an interrupted rhythm and slowing down of the pace.

The letters in *Caro Michele* need supplementing because the decision to make the correspondence of the characters incomplete leaves too many questions unanswered. Neither the unheroic Michele, of the book's title, nor his friend Osvaldo is the sort of person who naturally writes letters, and we need to know more about them than they can tell us themselves. Nor can Michele's mother, Adriana, know what we know since it is her lot to be out of touch, a condition which defines her absolutely in the novel. By making it Adriana's fate not to know what we know, Ginzburg places us in a collusive relationship with those who keep her in the dark. Thus, as we read Adriana's angst-ridden complaints to Michele, we feel her ignorance all the more acutely. Irony is an old friend of Ginzburg's and she uses it masterfully in *Caro Michele,* augmenting its effect with extra-epistolary information which privileges the reader.

Of course, the letter is an intrinsically ironic form, seeming to be something that it is not. Fictional letters are ironic twice over, only *seeming* to seem what they are not. Where in *La città e la casa* the characters create surrogate relationships by corresponding with each other, in *Caro Michele* the characters do not succeed in establishing correspondences and therefore do not even connect through surrogates. In this sense their lives are even more impoverished than those of the later novel, failing as they do to succeed even socially on paper. The irony of Adriana's tireless letter writing is thus all the more painful in its futility: her direct, guileless missives are impossibly inept in their transparent efforts to effect a change in Michele; the more sincere they are, the more alienating they will be, and all the more inevitably destined to fail.

Neither Adriana nor Michele understands how to use the medium of letter writing to improve their relations. Neither enters into the spirit of creative role-playing in their letters and so the two never get past their differences. To be fair, Giuseppe and Alberico, in *La città e la casa,* are both professional writers – one for a newspaper, the other for the movies – and so are more plausibly practised in the manipulation of words than Adriana and Michele. Adriana, who is sophisticated enough to read Pascal and Proust with pleasure, hasn't the faintest idea of how to go about writing to her son in such a way that he will be moved to respond. But her ineptitude goes beyond having a writing problem: Adriana's character is not as malleable as Giuseppe's and so not susceptible to being reshaped with a pen. She is what she is, and her writing is an expression of her stoical, daily struggle to reckon with her mistakes. Where Giuseppe and his friends switch sexual partners and residences when the moment seems auspicious, Adriana stays put and tries to make sense of, if not improve, her circumstances. Her letters to

Michele, full of honesty and belated motherly advice, do not serve to bridge the estrangement between mother and son, and elicit, only rarely, return letters from Michele that can hardly be called replies. Questions like 'Se per caso è tuo il bambino di questa Martorello cosa farai tu che non sai fare niente?' (*Opere I*, 347) ('If by any chance this Martorello baby is yours what will you do, you who don't know how to do anything?') are not designed to invite warm answers. 'If you weren't so dense,' she writes elsewhere:

> Se tu non fossi così balordo, ti direi di lasciare il tuo scantinato e installarti di nuovo a via San Sebastianello ... Però essendo tu come sei mi rendo conto che è meglio che tu resti nel tuo scantinato. Se tu fossi là da tuo padre cresceresti il disordine e getteresti nella disperazione il cameriere. (*Opere II*, 346)

> If you were not so strange, I'd tell you to leave your studio apartment and move in again at via San Sebastianello ... But I realize that since you are the way you are it's better if you remain at your studio. If you were there with your father you would only add to the disorder and drive the manservant to despair.

Her letters, while written from a desire to retrieve something lost or, better, to find something she never had, are never without this acerbic tone and are therefore doomed to failure.

That Michele is not a letter writer accounts for the main tension in the book – a necessary device in a tale without much action. This imbalance in Adriana's life naturally does not occasion much wit on her part; her letters are hopelessly earnest, full of the kinds of concerns appropriate to a mother. When she is not haranguing him about his past failures, she is too worried about where and whether he does his laundry or if he has a warm coat in London to engage her son successfully in a paper conversation. But perhaps Michele's apparent indifference to his mother is so transcendent that the critical tone of her letters, as well as their content, is irrelevant. Letter after letter, over the course of five months, she pours out as much of her heart to him as she knows how – going over the past, reporting on the present, and chastising him for his misdeeds along the way – while his total of two short letters to her are nakedly practical, perfunctorily thanking her for the clothes and money she sent him in one, requesting more money in the other.

In the absence of genuine communications from Michele, Adriana nevertheless doggedly continues her one-sided 'correspondence' with her son, responding to him through what she learns of his circumstances from others. When she learns of his sudden departure for England, she writes: 'Non devi creder che io non abbia capito che la tua è stata una fuga. Idiota io non sono' (*Opere II*, 364) ('Don't think I don't understand that this trip of yours has been an escape. I'm not an idiot'). To Osvaldo's assurances that Michele looked in on his father before leaving, she has the following challenge: 'Ti sei affacciato, cosa vuol dire che ti sei affacciato, forse tu non ti sei reso conto che tuo padre sta così male' (*Opere II*, 363) ('What does it mean to "look in" on your father? Perhaps you did not realize that your father is so sick'). Similarly, she sees through Osvaldo's lie about the sculpture program Michele ostensibly had long been planning to attend in London. In vain she asks Michele to confide in her: 'Ti prego scrivimi subito e spiegami chiaro da cosa volevi fuggire o da chi. Osvaldo non è stato chiaro. O non voleva dirmelo o non lo sapeva' (*Opere II*, 364) ('I beg you, please write to me right away and explain what or whom you are running away from. Osvaldo wasn't clear. Or he didn't want to tell me. Or he didn't know'). But her pleas are to no avail; Michele for the most part remains silent. We infer from his general silence toward Adriana that he has neither interest in nor a filial sense of duty toward her.

In fact, it seems that Michele has no sense of duty to anyone; he is a 'free' agent, whose narcissistic evolution is complete. Universally regarded as charismatic and fun, he inspires in everyone the view that 'it is not in his nature' to be counted on, either in life or in the mail. He uses people for his purposes – some of which are not entirely dishonourable (he does marry the American physicist, apparently to help her conquer her drinking problem) – and drops them when they cease to serve or amuse. Ada, Osvaldo's shrewd ex-wife, has his number when she says to her ex-husband: 'Michele, sotto sotto, pensava che anche tu eri scemo. Non solo io. Succhiava il tuo sangue, però dentro di sé ti dava del cretino' (*Opere II*, 395) ('Michele deep down regarded not only me, but you too as a fool. He sucked your blood, but in his heart he considered you a fool').

While Michele is decidedly cold and unresponsive in his few communications with his mother, his letters to others in the novel do not exactly sparkle either, so that we wonder where his reputation for *simpatia* comes from. Although Mara, a young tramp and one-time lover of Michele's, tells Osvaldo in their dialogue early on in the novel that Michele is the only man she ever really had fun with, our impression of Michele is, on the contrary, rather dark. We have no evidence of him as much more than a rather desperate fugitive. What he seems to have enjoyed from Mara's occasional company is superficial relief from that darkness, as when he writes to his sister on 27 March:

> In questo momento, non mi dispiacerebbe avere qui Mara. Non la sopporterei a lungo, perché dopo avermi ascoltato mi rovescerebbe addosso i suoi guai e mi starebbe appiccicata come una caramella e non avrei più pace. Non la vorrei certo come moglie. Però in questo preciso momento non mi dispiacerebbe di averla qui. (*Opere II*, 457)

> At this moment I wouldn't mind having Mara around. I couldn't put up with her for long, though, because after having listened to me she would, in turn, load me up with all her own troubles; she would stick to me like caramel and wouldn't give me any peace. I definitely wouldn't want her as a wife, but at this moment I wouldn't mind having her here.

While Michele does have an affection for the zany Mara and urges his sister and others to look after her and the illegitimate son he may have given her, he wants nothing of direct responsibility for her. His marriage to the American physicist, we read later, lasted a total of eight days, after which Michele cut out to resume his old political activist ways. Presumably, the wife's problems got old in a hurry and conjugal life became too confining, too sticky.

We learn about Michele's failed marriage not from Michele, of course, but from a friend of his in England, an Italian named Ermanno Giustiniani, who writes to Michele's sister not only to give her the update on Michele's marriage, but in order to ask her to pay Michele's debts. The third avowed purpose of Giustiniani's letter is to let her know that Michele has not left an address, thus preparing the way for Michele's disappearance from the book. The formal, that is, novelistic, purpose of Ermanno's letter in the book is to render the ensuing letters addressed to Michele absolutely futile. Particularly poignant is the realization that Adriana's last letter to Michele, dated 9 April, will not even be read by him. It contains a vivid memory of her last time with her son, which was, if not satisfying, at least full of elements she lacks in her own life, namely energy and feeling. The memory of having followed Michele around the house screaming at him as he rifled through all the bureaux and turned all the drawers inside out while looking for a particular blanket is a happy one for her, full of a vitality she sorely misses in the present. In reviving the memory on paper, she tries to reach out to Michele in an imaginative and positive way for the first time, but the attempt comes too late.

Whereas we learn the crucial details of Michele's life, and eventually his death, from Ermanno Giustiniani, at home in Italy our chief contact with Michele is through Osvaldo, or rather through the dealings of others with Osvaldo. From the first, Osvaldo comes to us indirectly, in Adriana's original letter to her son, as the person who gave him his studio apartment and who might have connections with the phone company. Next, in Chapter Two, we are introduced to him formally by name, in one of Ginzburg's few authorial interruptions, complete with a concise physical portrait. Interestingly, the passage matches the one which opens the book, introducing Michele's mother, thus setting up a parallel between these two future friends: one the ex-lover, the other – for all practical purposes – the ex-mother of our absent hero. In a humorous dialogue between Osvaldo and the zany unwedded mother Mara (whose child may or may not be Michele's), we learn that Osvaldo manages his uncle's used bookstore, that he considers himself lazy, unpractical, and unproductive, and that marriage to the efficient and enterprising Ada was intolerably stressful. We suspect, as does Mara, that Osvaldo's failed marriage to Ada has something to do with his lack of avidity in other matters as well, but when Mara asks him whether or not he is gay he replies succinctly, 'No.' Mara, whose sexual barometer is highly functional, has picked up that Osvaldo's casually intimate way of revealing certain aspects of his personal life does not signal the often accompanying desire for other kinds of intimacies. He is not attracted to her, she notes, and he frankly confirms this notion when asked, much to her irritation. The dialogue ends on this comic note, the question of Osvaldo's ambiguous sexuality having thus been introduced with a light touch.

Although Osvaldo, Adriana's main source of information about her son, is deliberately vague when speaking of Michele, he is all Adriana has by way of connection to her son and she grows to depend on him more and more as the novel progresses. While Osvaldo cannot be said to have an ongoing relationship with Michele, the letters from all the characters to Michele reveal that he was at one time, at the very least, Michele's special friend, at most, his lover. One of the only communications Michele himself initiates in the book is to Osvaldo, and to this communication Osvaldo does respond very precisely. This happens only once in the novel, but significantly. Osvaldo's one letter to Michele is in response to a brief note received three months after Michele's departure from Italy, in which Michele informed him of his intention to marry an American physicist in England. Although the letter is fairly dry and direct in its description of his bride-to-be, Michele uses the occasion to close, almost lyrically, with a wish to make Osvaldo a present. He wants to give Osvaldo the cashmere scarf given to him by his recently deceased father, the father whom he didn't bother to visit when ill, and whose funeral he did not attend. Michele tells Osvaldo to go collect the scarf himself in Michele's abandoned apartment. Almost sentimental, the passage recalls their sunset walks together up and down the *lungotevere* as Michele anticipates the pleasure he will have imagining Osvaldo continuing those walks wearing this particular cashmere scarf. In Osvaldo's reply we immediately learn that the scarf, like the adoring father who gave it to him, has been carelessly abandoned, lost. But such connections are made by neither correspondent – certainly not by Michele, who, even as he embarks on a new union, gratifies his fancy with the idea of a tender gift to his old lover. He is as unaware that the scarf is gone as he is apparently indifferent to the death of the parent who gave it to him. But however careless and self-centred the spirit in which the offer is made – 'Sarei contento di sapere che hai al collo quella sciarpa, quando cammini per il lungotevere"' (*Opere II*, 431) ('It will please me to know that you have that scarf around your neck when you walk along the *lungotevere*') – it nevertheless *represents*, in the context of this sad book, a genuine gesture in the direction of the other, a gesture which is pregnant with past reference and remembered implication. Osvaldo, following Michele's lead, insofar as he is capable, is curtly congratulatory in his reply to the news of Michele's imminent marriage, and he responds in kind to Michele's sentimental indulgence, as well:

> La sciarpa di cachemire è introvabile. Io però mi sono comperato una sciarpa, credo non di cachemire, e senza strisce azzurre, una semplice sciarpetta bianca. La porto, e mi immagino che sia la tua. Mi rendo conto che è un surrogato. Ma d'altronde noi tutti viviamo di surrogati ...
>
> Per il resto, la mia vita è quella che tu conosci, diciamo sempre uguale. Vado al botteghino, ascolto la signora Peroni ... cammino per il lungotevere, sto con le mani in tasca appoggiato al ponte e guardo il sole tramontare. (*Opere II*, 432)

The cashmere scarf is not to be found. I have, however, bought another

> scarf, but I don't think it's cashmere, and it doesn't have blue stripes; it's just a simple little white scarf. I wear it and I imagine that it's yours. I realize it's a surrogate. But anyway, we all live by surrogates.
>
> As for the rest, my life is as you know it – shall we say, always the same. I go to the shop, I listen to Signora Peroni ... I walk along the *lungotevere*, and with my hands in my pockets, I lean against the bridge to watch the sun go down.

Thus Ginzburg, with characteristic economy, gives us pairs of materials from which to construe a relationship: a cashmere scarf and its fake surrogate; two walks by sunset, one with and one without Michele. The two letters, occurring as they do in the middle of the novel (chapters nineteen and twenty of forty-two), provide the fulcrum upon which the plot is balanced. They also form the emotional centre of the book, for they refer to a shared sense of past connection, however understated and oblique the reference – the *only* genuine connection between two people mutually agreed upon *in writing* in the novel. And it is on this tenuous, remembered connection that the other relationships in the book depend. The letters stop and the book ends logically when Michele dies, becoming the missing link without which the chain cannot continue.

We learn that Michele is stabbed to death in Bruges from his sister Viola, who breaks the news to Mara (and to us) in a letter. She tells Mara that she suspects a group of fascists did the deed, landing on the likely truth with a guess, for she is ignorant of Michele's political activities. We are not so ignorant, since we have read Michele's urgent earlier letter to his other sister, Angelica, asking her to take a machine gun from his apartment in Rome and throw it into the Tiber. Even though for a short period in England Michele has avowedly dropped politics (leaving that to his wife, who is a card-carrying party member) and plans to start reading Kant's *Critique of Pure Reason*, in the end he drops theory for *realpolitik* and pays the price. But we are never persuaded definitively that this is so; there is a lively possibility that Michele was murdered for other reasons, since the murderers have not been caught. In the final letter of *Caro Michele*, Osvaldo, whom Michele protected from direct knowledge of his political activities, says nothing of politics when he reports to Angelica on the state of affairs left behind by Michele in England. Rather, he has the following sharp observations to make about the companion Michele was with when he died:

> È un ragazzo. I ragazzi oggi non hanno memoria, e soprattutto non la coltivano, e tu sai che anche Michele non aveva memoria, o meglio non si piegava mai a respirarla e coltivarla. (*Opere II*, 495)

> He is a kid. Kids today don't have memories, mostly because they don't cultivate them; and you know that Michele himself didn't have a memory either, or, rather, that he never exerted himself to breathe it in or to develop it.

Osvaldo, who is clearly not like the 'kids today' he describes, concludes the letter (and the book), noting that he, Angelica, and her mother are among the only few left to cultivate their memories, not just because of their contemplative temperament but because they have nothing better going on: 'nella nostra vita presente non c'è nulla che valga i luoghi e gli attimi incontrati lungo il percorso' (*Opere II*, 495) ('in our present lives there is nothing that is worth the places and the moments that we've encountered along the way'). Thus he renders their inclination to remember pathetic rather than laudable and undercuts the implicit superiority to the contemporary norm suggested in his original observation. Osvaldo goes on, for the first time recalling directly his times with Michele, while at the same time reflecting on his recollection:

> Mentre io li vivevo o li guardavo, quegli attimi o quei luoghi, essi avevano uno straordinario splendore, ma perché io sapevo che mi sarei curvato a ricordarli. Mi ha sempre addolorato profondamente che Michele non volesse o non potesse conoscere questo splendore, e andasse avanti senza mai voltare la testa indietro. Credo però che lui senza saperlo contemplasse questo splendore dentro di me. E tante volte ho pensato che forse mentre moriva egli ha in un lampo conosciuto e percorso tutte le strade della memoria, e questo pensiero è per me consolante, perché ci si consola con nulla quando non abbiamo più nulla. (*Opere II*, 496)

> While I lived through those times and those places I noticed that they had an extraordinary splendour about them, and this is because I knew that I would keep these moments and remember them. It has always hurt me deeply that Michele neither wanted nor was capable of recognizing this splendour and that he always went forward without ever turning his head to look back. I think, however, that without understanding it he saw this splendour in me. And often I have thought that perhaps while he was dying he had, in a single bolt, understood and experienced all the paths of

> his memory, and this thought is for me a great consolation, because we console ourselves with nothing when we have nothing.

This passionate statement by Osvaldo at the end of the novel comes as a surprise not only because we are unaccustomed to hearing his voice, but because we have not experienced Osvaldo as the joyful, lusty partner of Michele. Within the time frame of the novel he is already an ex-lover and an ex-husband. His existence is defined by these negative identities, as he continues to circulate exclusively among the families and friends of his ex-partners. His kindness is exploited by others, but the exploitation at least gives him a reason for being, a kind of connection to those with whom he is no longer connected. Osvaldo is an unhappy therapeutic, a kind of contradiction in terms. He has transgressed cultural taboos, been marked by his transgression, but has not successfully made the leap into perfect narcissistic amorality. Therapeutically speaking, he has an Achilles' heel: he is loyal to a fault and, worse, sentimental. He has given up the goods of bourgeois marriage and parenthood and gotten nothing in return, neither a permanent companion in Michele nor comfortable membership in a circle of promiscuity. Instead, he whiles away the hours with Michele's mother, who places no demands on him and seems to find comfort, if not actual pleasure, in his company. They apparently do not speak to each other much, preferring, rather, that he read aloud from *Remembrance of Things Past*, a telling choice to be sure, in more ways than one.

When Michele dies, those he leaves behind to remember will no doubt continue their lives more or less as before; the novel must end because the formal device – everyone's connection to Michele – which moved it forward and which kept its various characters together has run its course. We imagine, however, that if we could follow these people who are associated with one another in life, not in letters, beyond the book's conclusion, we would observe them leading parallel bleak lives which never connect. However unworthy Michele was of a place in their collective memory, for each of the three he represented or occasioned something special. The vividness of Adriana's missives to Michele is matched nowhere in the extra-epistolary relationships the survivors have with one another. And Osvaldo misses the 'extraordinary splendour' of his times with Michele, however fleeting and inconsequential they ended up being. Angelica's connection to Michele is hardest to account for in terms other than those of ordinary sibling closeness, for while she is more naturally in touch with him than anyone else, it is hard to say how her life is diminished without him. She no longer need keep his secrets nor keep him posted on things back home; we don't know enough about her to imagine what else she'll miss. Sisters typically miss their dead brothers; perhaps that's all we need to know.

Though the memory of Michele binds the three together in a way, they have never achieved any other way of relating to each other naturally – not even mother and daughter. For these people do not correspond, and their everyday proximity to one another affords them only a limited array of imaginative possibilities with which to invent their relationships. With neither the facility for direct psychoanalytic discourse nor the resource of therapeutic self-invention on paper, they are left to deal with their own and each other's poor, unadorned selves. Without the paper medium to manipulate their respective identities, ironically, their capacity for friendship is impaired. The dynamics of mother/son, lover/lover, and sister/brother which served to inform their sense of themselves in relation to Michele are suddenly dissolved and there is no suggestion that substitutes are likely to be sought or found.

By contrast, the death of Alberico in *La città e la casa,* which also comes at the end of the book, does not substantially affect the lives of the other characters in the novel. His death is felt by the reader more than that of Michele in the other novel because we have, by the end, experienced Alberico's voice and felt his development as a person; the novel itself is not necessarily over *because* of it. Alberico's father, Giuseppe, is used to Alberico's absence, and though for a moment, just before Alberico's death, it seemed the two might somehow finally achieve something like a relationship, if only on paper, one does not feel that anything substantial will change in anyone's life, or in the letters they write about those lives, after Alberico is gone. Alberico's budding relationship with his father is the only ray of hope in a book populated by people bent on leading emotionally dead lives. But the hope is not felt genuinely by anyone except the reader, probably not even by Giuseppe, so that its disappearance has no deep impact on the community. Everyone is sad, to be sure, but we are reasonably sure that they will adjust. Egisto, from whom we get the gory details of Alberico's murder, finds it hard to continue to be in the apartment above the one that belonged to Alberico, but even as he writes the words he realizes that he will not move. Even Giuseppe will adjust, we are confident, and whether he remains in America or not, his life will contain more or less the same range of possibilities as before. His wife's death seems to have more reality for him, occurring as it does in his new environment, although we are never given the impression that theirs has been a good marriage. In his last letter of the novel, to Lucrezia, Giuseppe compares his relationship to Alberico with the one he has with his wife's son-in-law, Danny, and finds it wanting. 'Se Alberico non fosse stato mio figlio, avrei forse potuto star bene con lui' (*Opere II*, 1557) ('If Alberico hadn't been my son, perhaps I could have gotten along well with him'), he observes, still missing the point, the point being that family is different from friendship, that it requires discipline and unwavering standards of loyalty, support, and heavy regular doses of honest criticism. Most of all it requires love, and while both Alberico and Giuseppe have gradually managed to project something like love successfully in their letters, the paper surrogate does not finally have the impact of the real thing. Alberico passes away, Giuseppe mourns his loss, and life goes on – in Princeton with his son-replacement and, as ever, on paper with his Italian circle. The last letters between father and son will perhaps be filed away in the same place as earlier ones; perhaps they will come to mean something important, perhaps not.

The ironic lesson of these two novels when taken together is that in the absence of real connection, those who have recourse to letters, to language, can use their imaginations and find surrogate selves to fill in where reality has failed them. If Adriana, Osvaldo, and Angelica in *Caro Michele* seem more attractive to us than their counterparts in *La città e la casa* because of the integrity they exhibit in their epistolary dealings with Michele, they hardly serve as models of interesting and fulfilled human beings. For while they do not, in Yeats' words, 'lack all conviction,' neither are they filled 'with passionate intensity.' Lacking passionate intensity, they settle for numb relations with others in which there is seldom any real talk. Their failure is one about which Ginzburg has written often. 'Il silenzio,' she writes in *Le piccole virtù*, 'è un peccato' (*Opere I*, 859) ('Silence ... is a sin'), and it is the responsibility of individuals to recognize this and 'to resist ferociously its force in our time.' Ginzburg offers us these lessons with customary mischievousness in her novels, as with some bitter humour, but she leaves us in no doubt that she is dead serious about these 'little' matters which concern her throughout her work.

NOTES

1 Philip Rieff, *The Triumph of the Therapeutic: Uses of Faith after Freud* (New York: Harper and Row, 1966), 18. According to Rieff, contemporary men have gone 'beyond the old deception of good and evil, to specialize at last, wittingly, in techniques that are to be called in the present volume, "therapeutic," with nothing at stake beyond a manipulable sense of well-being. This is the unreligion of the age and its master science.'

2 All English translations are mine, unless otherwise stated.

3 The English translation in my text is from *The City and the House*, translated by Dick Davis (New York: Arcade, 1989), 8.

REFERENCES

Ginzburg, Natalia. *Caro Michele*. In vol. 1, *Opere*. Milano: Mondadori.

– *La città e la casa*. In vol. 2, *Opere*. Milano: Mondadori. Translated by Dick Davis under the title *The City and the House* (New York: Arcade, 1989).

– *Le piccole virtù*. In vol. 1, Milano: Mondadori.

Rieff, Philip. *The Triumph of the Therapeutic: Uses of Faith after Freud*. New York: Harper and Row, 1966.

Sagittarius: A Psychoanalytic Reading

GIULIANA SANGUINETTI KATZ

The short novel *Sagittarius* has often played the part of the unwanted child among Ginzburg's books. It was bitterly criticized by the author herself in the introduction she wrote to the 1964 Einaudi edition of *Cinque romanzi brevi* (*Five Short Novels*), where she republished the novel that had first appeared in 1957 in *Valentino*. In this introduction Ginzburg complained that *Sagittarius* had two main defects: its plot was too thick and tight and its story too contrived. Ginzburg remembered that she had to work and think too hard in order to compose the story, which therefore lacked the necessary spontaneity (*Opere I*, 1131). She concluded by stating: 'E' necessario scrivere e pensare col cuore e col corpo, e non già con la testa e col pensiero' ('It is necessary to write and think with heart and body and not with head and mind').[1] Even though the novel received some good reviews in the newspapers when it first appeared in 1957 and when it was republished in 1964, many of the critics were negative and often echoed Ginzburg's comments.[2]

It is my purpose in this article to show that both Ginzburg and her critics have been too harsh with *Sagittarius* and that the complex interweaving of characters, events, and imagery creates a surrealistic and poetic effect of deep psychological significance. Ginzburg explores in her novel basic relationships among relatives and friends: first and foremost between mothers and daughters and between sisters and girlfriends, then between fathers and daughters and between mothers-in-law and sons-in-law. These relationships, of course, are not clearly divided, but derive their richness from the fact that they are interchangeable: relationships between friends often mirror family dependencies, whereas family ties sometimes strive towards the more independent status of friendships among equals. Most of all, Ginzburg explores from many angles the complexities of female sexual development and the difficulties that women experience in finding their own identity, both as individuals and as members of society. And it is this psychological element of the story, up to now largely disregarded by critics, that I intend to analyse in this article.[3]

The story is narrated in the past tense by a young woman, a university student, who writes poetry and works as a secretary in a publishing firm (therefore duplicating some of Ginzburg's own activities). It centres on the figure of the narrator's mother, who vainly attempts to make herself at home in the world of the big city by opening an art gallery or a store and, most of all, by sharing her life with a congenial girlfriend and business partner. The fascinating character of the mother is a mixture of adolescent dreams and conventional middle-class ambitions: like the heroine of Fellini's movie *The White Sheik*, she moves from a narrow, provincial environment into the tempting life of the big city, dreams of wonderful adventures, and is duped by those who take advantage of her naïvety. But, whereas the protagonist's hopes in Fellini's movie are very simple and centre around the man of her dreams, in Ginzburg's novel, the mother's desires are more complicated and reflect various stages and needs in her life. The mother's adventures in the big city and her reactions to her new encounters not only provide us with a humorous criticism of middle-class society, but also give us a psychological insight into the problems and complexities of female sexuality.

The mother's wish to open a successful art gallery or a store in the city is an example of the many fantasies that she has had throughout her life and reflects different stages of her development. She wishes to assert her independence, give up her household routine, and move aggressively, like a man, into the new environment of the city; and she wishes to compete with her sisters and their profitable store; she wishes to gain the interest and admiration of the artistic and intellectual milieu of the city; and ultimately she wishes to be fed and taken care of by her business partner and by her gallery's future patrons, who would act as parental figures. That is, the mother regresses from her adolescent dreams of independence and success to her earliest stages of total dependence on parental figures.

As the symbolism of the art gallery develops, further and further layers of the mother's characters are revealed, until in the end she is left completely helpless and naked to confront death and despair. This emotional striptease proceeds rapidly, through a dizzying sequence of funny, grotesque, and melodramatic situations that accompany the mother's frantic search for identity and happiness. Ginzburg alternates melodrama with mystery, adventure with romance. She entertains us with her absurd tales, until in the end she slows down and suddenly confronts us with the tragedy of death and the sadness of irreparable loss.[4]

Ginzburg achieves a surrealistic effect by presenting to us a series of images and situations rich in symbolic meaning. The mechanisms of displacement and condensation (typical of the dream world) give the story its profound significance.[5] As happens in dreams, the deep-seated meaning of these images is concealed behind a more realistic one and is expressed indirectly, through the recurrence of certain key words and objects, which acquire a more and more condensed meaning. In the same way, the general meaning of the story is displaced, since the accent of the story falls on the grotesque elements of the novel rather than on the underlying feeling of anxiety and despair that is revealed only in the final scene. Ginzburg in her novel also adopts the dream mechanism of splitting the various sides of the same person into different characters, a technique which is typical of the psychological novel.[6] For instance, as we will see in the course of the article, the contrasting elements in the character of the mother are embodied in her two daughters and are also reflected in all the other female characters, by similarity or by contrast.

The protagonist, a mature, middle-class widow, has many grotesque characteristics that will be repeated in Elsa's mother, Matilde, in Ginzburg's next novel *Le voci della sera* (*Voices in the Evening*). However, she is also given a truly human dimension as she takes flight from loneliness and isolation into her dreams of glory and her pursuit of an impossible happiness. She is as domineering, controlling, and aggressive as Matilde in *Le voci della sera*. She charges into her sisters' china shop like a bull, to ask for money or to run the shop. She paces impatiently around the store, until she inevitably breaks one of the objects on sale, a figurine of a serenading Pierrot. Her bristling grey hair, her impulsive movements, and her mangy fur coat make her look like a wild animal.[7]

She is avaricious and uses her money to control her daughters and tell them what to do. She tells her adult daughters how to dress, how to comb their hair, what to eat, and she would also like, of course, to control their love lives. The reaction that the mother gets from her relatives to her intrusive and domineering behaviour is one of rejection:

daughters, sisters, and cousins try to avoid her and her insistent demands so as to preserve their independence. Her beautiful, married older daughter, who still lives with her, accepts her attentions in a passive way and withdraws behind a meaningless sequence of empty smiles and shrugs. Her ugly, intellectual younger daughter, the narrator of the story, fiercely defends her independent life as a student and worker and does not confide in her mother.

The mother's aggressive and domineering behaviour towards the rest of her family in reality covers a fundamental weakness and dependence. Her constant attempts at finding companionship and understanding show her desperate need for love and reassurance, which is a result of early losses and deprivations. Ginzburg underlines the mother's needs by showing her aimless wandering from coffee bar to coffee bar, in search of physical and spiritual nourishment. The protagonist hopes to find around her some congenial intellectual and artistic people who will befriend her and provide her with the appreciative environment she has always desired. While she eats one coffee granita with cream after another in the various coffee bars of the city, she eavesdrops eagerly on the conversations at the tables next to her in the hope of catching some interesting discussions to which she may be able to contribute. Needless to say, she only overhears fatuous dialogues and is continually disappointed. From this point of view, she is like a baby crying in vain for her mother's breast.

The protagonist's need for a mother figure is clear in her relationship with her sisters, a situation which is stressed at the very beginning of the novel. She is jealous and aggressive towards her two unmarried sisters, who live happily together in the city. They lead a quiet and contented life together, selling china and household ornaments to old-fashioned ladies like them. The protagonist would like to become part of their successful business store and be included in their serene life, but instead she feels excluded by them and consequently tries to seize by violence what she cannot obtain through love.

The mother buys a house in the city where her sisters live by compelling them to lend her a sum of money she has no intention of repaying. As soon as she arrives in the city, she immediately descends upon her timid sisters and takes over their business. She deals aggressively with the customers who come into the store, while the poor sisters withdraw into the back room, looking at each other with dismay. The mother is rivalrous with her sisters but, at the same time, nourishes the hope of being taken into their business. Their genteel way of life, looking back to the past, their quiet existence in the shadows, and especially their mutual understanding represent for the mother a happiness and a companionship for which she longs in vain. In fact, the perfect unity of the two sisters reminds one of the symbiotic unity of the mother and child during the first months of the child's life, and it is that type of unity which the mother tries to establish with her two daughters.

At this point it might be useful to look very briefly at the main points of psychoanalytic theories on female sexuality in order to understand the character of the mother in *Sagittarius*. In his two essays 'Some Psychical Consequences of the Anatomical Distinction between the Sexes' (1925) and 'Female Sexuality' (1931) and in his chapter on 'Femininity' in *New Introductory Lectures on Psychoanalysis*, Freud states that the little girl is conditioned in her psychological development by a lack of a clear sense of her sexuality, by an early clinging to her clitoris, and most of all by an unfavourable comparison of that organ with the boy's penis. This comparison leads in turn to penis envy, to castration anxiety, and to the turning of the little girl from her original prolonged attachment to mother to an Oedipal attachment to father. During her Oedipal period she gives up her previous masculinity complex and assumes a more passive and feminine position by replacing the wish for a penis with the wish for a baby by father.

In terms of family relationships, the little girl originally has a long attachment to her mother, during which she is first the passive recipient of her cares, and then feels intense active impulses towards her, wants her all for herself, and is jealous of her father and her siblings. At the end of the anal period, when the little girl discovers the difference between the sexes and believes herself to be a castrated being, she blames her mother for her mutilated condition and also often complains of not having been fed enough (loved) by her. At this point she takes her father as her love object, assumes a passive position towards him, and competes with the rest of his family for his attention. Only with the overcoming of the Oedipus complex, and the surrendering of the incestuous attachment to father, does the girl identify again with her mother and achieve feminine maturity.

Freud's theories on female sexuality were questioned from the beginning by his colleagues and followers and gave rise to several modifications of his opinions. Shahla Chehrazy, in a recent article on 'Female Psychology,' aptly summarizes the main differences between Freud's thought and current psychoanalytic views. In contrast with Freud's belief that the little girl has no vaginal awareness until puberty, present views stress the fact that the little girl has a preoedipal awareness of her vagina as early as the age of two and three, however vague that awareness may be, and has therefore an 'early sense of femaleness' (144). Whereas Freud sees penis envy as crucial to the little girl's development and more important than her subsequent awareness of her sexuality, current views hold that penis envy is 'a phase-specific developmental phenomenon' and that 'the little girl will soon come to value what she herself has, and relinquish the envy of what she does not have' (144). That is, the girl, who already has a sense of her femaleness, wants to possess a penis as well, as a result of the little boy's pride in his organ and because of the importance that family and society place on the masculine role. However, in subsequent reworkings of her penis envy, she comes to appreciate her own genitals and their capacity to bear children (145). Finally, whereas Freud believes that her entry into the oedipal phase is a reaction to the castration complex, modern theories hold that it is in fact an 'innately feminine process' and that the wish for baby 'is not *necessarily* a substitute for penis envy [as Freud suggested]' but is 'observed preoedipally as part of identification with mother' (150).[8]

In the light of this developmental theory, the little girl first identifies with mother and takes her as her exclusive love object during the oral and anal periods, competing with the other members of the family for her attention. During the oedipal period the girl turns away from mother to father and wants him as her exclusive love object. In subsequent years (especially in puberty and adolescence), the girl overcomes her Oedipus complex by identifying with mother and by turning her affectionate current towards father and her sexual current towards men outside the family circle. If earlier traumatic events create obstacles in this development, the little girl may regress from the positive Oedipus complex (taking father as exclusive love object) to a negative one (taking mother as exclusive love object) and may be unable to overcome penis envy and castration anxiety. Penis envy in this case does not represent the true desire to become a man, but stands for the impossible wish of acquiring the 'magic wand' that will heal the narcissistic wounds endured in previous years and bring strength, happiness, and fulfilment. It also represents the anger of the girl who wants to rebel against her mother, perceived as too authoritarian or not available, and who wants to stand up against her father, perceived as sadistic and destructive (Chehrazy, 150).

In the case of the mother in Ginzburg's novel, the aggressive, masculine stance that the protagonist takes towards her sisters might represent the particular oedipal development described above in which the little girl, instead of identifying with mother and having father as her love object (positive Oedipus complex), identifies with father and wants mother all for herself (negative Oedipus complex). The protagonist's behaviour towards her sisters might be due to her desire to move away from her original passive, dependent position from a domineering mother and to regain by force the good things present in the body of her mother (attack on the sisters' store). It might signify at the same time her anger at her mother for depriving her of love in earlier years and her wish to castrate father and to take over his strength (destruction of the statuette of the serenading Pierrot). It might also have a defensive purpose against a mother and father seen as domineering and destructive.

In *Sagittarius* the particular psychological development of the protagonist and the early traumatic events in her life become clear as the novel develops and the present becomes a mirror of the past. The protagonist's fantasies, fears, and desires are progressively illustrated to us by her past and present relationships with her family and by her friendship with a mysterious woman she meets by chance in the city. This strange woman, Antonietta Grossi, alias Scilla Fontana, seems to be the ideal companion for whom the mother has always been looking: a companion with whom to start a new life and make up for old disappointments. Scilla is an enterprising and domineering woman, a mirror image and an ideal self of the protagonist. Scilla, in fact, represents all the things the mother has ever wanted to be. She portrays herself as being an artist, a painter, and clothes designer: as a girl she studied ballet and lived a spoilt and easy life, and then, when her family lost all its money, she was compelled to support herself with all types of jobs:

> Aveva fatto parte di una compagnia di filodrammatici; era stata nel giornalismo; era stata segretaria d'un deputato, e siccome era un vedovo, lei doveva anche fargli da direttrice di casa: c'erano pranzi ufficiali dove stava seduta al fianco di ambasciatori e ministri. aveva conosciuto ogni specie di persone; la sua vita era tutta un romanzo; e forse, prima di morire, avrebbe scritto le sue memorie. (614)

> She had been a member of an amateur theatrical company; she had worked in journalism; she had been secretary to a politician and as he was a

> widower she had also run his household and acted as hostess at his dinners and official receptions where she sat next to ambassadors and ministers of state. She had rubbed shoulders with all sorts of different people; her whole life had been like the pages of a novel and maybe, before she died, she would write her memoirs. (87)[9]

Scilla appears to the mother as an example of the new woman, who is not only a capable housewife but also a sophisticated and modern person, ready to assert herself in a world dominated by men. According to the portrait that she paints of herself, she is a single mother, separated from a weak husband, looks after her daughter, the beautiful Barbara, and at the same time forges ahead in city life and claims her position in the world of business and of the arts. She appears to combine feminine and masculine qualities, that is, to be both a good mother and a successful, enterprising father figure. The name Fontana (Fountain) seems to point to Scilla's unlimited capacity for nourishing those around her. On the other hand, the name of her zodiac sign, Sagittarius (the Archer), which is also the name of the art gallery she is going to open with the mother, points to her aggressive and masculine characteristics, which will allow her to compete and be successful in public life. It is significant that Natalia Ginzburg uses Scilla's zodiac sign as the title of her novel, to convey the main message of her book.

Scilla presents herself as a masculine, aggressive woman, ready to make fun of the protagonist's fears of catching a cold or of walking in the rain. Scilla always wears sandals and does not need heavy shoes even in winter. She uses the same shoemaker as the mother does but, differently from her, she is able to stride boldly and recklessly in any weather (606–7). When the mother asks her for a book to read, Scilla gives her Dumas' *The Three Musketeers*, a novel designed to satisfy her adolescent craving for adventure in a man's world (619). Scilla is the protagonist's masculine ideal, who does not feel castrated and wounded by a series of narcissistic losses and can compete fearlessly with any man.

Scilla is also the caricature of the 'new' woman. I have already mentioned the many activities that she claims to have performed successfully in the working world and in the artistic milieu. The same attitude of bragging and bravado permeates all her life. For instance, as soon as she meets the mother and her family, she insists on painting a portrait of her daughter Barbara and of the narrator and calls it *Ragazze col maglione* (*Girls in Sweaters*). It is one of her typical desolate pictures, consisting of 'teste bislunghe e livide, una coi capelli a nuvola, l'altra con un pennacchio fiammeggiante; occhi a croce, bocca a sbarre' (622) ('livid, elongated heads, one topped by a frizz of hair, the other by a fiery plume, crosses for eyes and railings for mouths') (94). Yet Scilla thinks that she has captured 'la sostanza della vita moderna, ragazze ardite e spregiudicate, ragazze senza fronzoli né leziosaggini, fatte per battersi al fianco dell'uomo' (622) ('the very essence of modern life: these were today's young women, fearless, uninhibited, without frill or affectation, built to fight beside their menfolk') (94).

As I mentioned before, Scilla also presents herself as a maternal person who is ready to take care of and feed those who need her. She states that she is an expert in child rearing (one of her many jobs has been as worker in a kindergarten [614]) and declares that her house is open to all her friends, whom she entertains whenever they appear for dinner (609). She feeds the mother with all her adventurous tales about her family, her past life, her wealthy girlfriends and their love lives. The protagonist feels immediately won over by Scilla and identifies with her, to the point of despising her own middle-class way of life in favour of Scilla's more bohemian lifestyle.

In reality, Scilla will reveal herself as the bad mother, who feeds her child poisoned food: she gives the protagonist drugged wine in order to put her to sleep and rob her of her money. Her name is that of the mythical sea monster Scylla, who lived in a cave by the coast of Sicily and devoured all the fish and sailors that went near her, with her horrible six heads full of teeth. That name, in fact, points to her true nature as the cruel and orally sadistic mother.[10] Scilla is also the mother who deprives the child of the content of her bowels with too severe an upbringing. As Freud has explained, the attitude that the adult has towards money and possessions can be traced back to the anal period and to the pleasure she experienced as a child towards her most precious possession: her feces. In the light of these theories, the avaricious protagonist, who clings to her money, represents symbolically the constipated child, who is unwilling to surrender the content of her body to a parent perceived as hostile and depriving. Conversely, Scilla represents the parent who imposes a strict toilet training on her child and becomes a thief in her eyes.[11]

The optimistic world described by Scilla in her stories contrasts with the dreary pictures she paints, which represent 'delle teste livide e bislunghe, non si capiva se di uomo o di donna, con due crocette al posto degli occhi e al posto della bocca un'inferriata; e sullo sfondo case e case addossate contro un cielo a sbarre e comignoli storti, che mandavano fuori fumo livido' (613)[12] ('livid, elongated heads of indeterminate sex with little crosses for eyes and metal grills for mouths, set against backgrounds of rows and rows of houses with barred windows and crooked chimneys that emitted a livid smoke') (86). These figures are similar to de Chirico's mannequins, people who can neither speak nor see, who do not have a sexual identity, and whose extreme anxiety and anger are echoed by the prison-like landscape in which they are set. The only manifestation of their feelings is the livid smoke that comes out of the crooked chimneys in the background, a symbol of oral and anal aggression coming out of the only outlet in an otherwise closed world.[13]

The extreme deprivation portrayed in Scilla's paintings appears to reflect the psychological situation of the mother and her daughters. The two daughters cannot speak and barely function in the presence of a suffocating mother, and the mother herself constantly demands to be fed, entertained, and looked after, while at the same time she attacks all the members of her family with her oral and anal aggression. In fact, the trio of the mother and the two daughters, from the psychological point of view, seems to represent the different sides of a manic-depressive personality, which alternates between periods of melancholia (the repressed and passive condition of the two daughters, especially the older one) and periods of mania (the uncontrolled, instinctual outbursts of the mother).[14]

The part of the city where Scilla lives is as symbolic as her paintings and gives us an important insight into the psychology of the mother and her daughters. It is 'un quartiere di case nuove, su strade non lastricate, fra pozzanghere e lembi di prato imbrattati d'una neve grigia' (612) ('an area of newly-built houses and unpaved roads among puddles and patches of grass streaked with dirty snow') (85). The mother and her daughters, in the course of their first visit to Scilla, wander around in these utterly desolate surroundings until they find a road which is 'un fosso lungo una siepe, che terminava entro un cortiletto pieno di neve e di lastroni di ferro' (612) ('hardly more than a ditch bordered by hedges leading to a small courtyard heaped with snow and sheets of metal') (85). Finally, at the end of the road, they find Scilla's house, 'una casa alta e stretta come una torre, protesa nella nebbia sul ciglio della campagna' (612) ('a tall, narrow apartment block, reaching up like a tower into the fog and backing on to fields') (85).

As Ginzburg herself points out, the area in which Scilla lives has the same feeling of desolation that is reflected in her paintings.[15] The dirt and disrepair of the road and the junk heaps in the courtyard symbolize anal aggression and might refer to a trauma endured at an early age, during the anal period, by the protagonist and her daughters. Such a trauma might be caused, for instance, by a too-strict toilet training and upbringing that deprives the young child of her freedom of movements and of the control of her bodily contents. That this indeed is the case is confirmed both by the controlling and castrating behaviour of the mother towards her daughters, and by the robbery that the protagonist herself endures at the hands of a mother figure (symbolic deprivation of her feces).[16]

In her relationship with Scilla, the mother relives various stages of her life: her adolescent desire to grow up and find her own identity outside of the house and make a career for herself, and also her earlier desires to be cared for and protected by her parents. Scilla represents for the protagonist at the same time a bold and independent ideal self and a protective parental figure.[17] Just when the mother thinks that her wishes are going to be fulfilled, that her dream of running a successful business with Scilla and retiring afterwards with her on the Riviera will be realized, she is confronted with the devastating reality of being abandoned and robbed by her beloved friend.

Scilla's betrayal causes the protagonist to re-experience earlier traumatic deprivations suffered during the oral and anal periods. Old wounds are reopened. The mother suddenly regresses to helpless childhood, wanders around the city sobbing uncontrollably, and seems to lose all energy and desire to live. The extent of her early traumas is revealed in the final scene of the novel. Here we find the mother mourning the loss of her favourite daughter, Giulia, who has died in childbirth, and we see at the same time Giulia's newborn baby crying desperately in the arms of Teresa, a cousin of the mother.

At this point, the original trauma in the protagonist's life, the loss of maternal cares, is symbolically portrayed through Giulia's death in childbirth. The protagonist is left overwhelmed with sorrow and anger at the disappearance of the beloved one, who has 'betrayed' her by refusing life and withdrawing into death. Giulia's death, like Scilla's treachery, is only an echo of an earlier and much more traumatic loss: the loss experienced by the baby who feels abandoned by mother. Giulia's baby, who cries in cousin Teresa's arms, mirrors the anguish and sorrow of the mother and explains her complete helplessness in this situation. Behind the mother's frantic search for happiness lies the inextinguishable sorrow and mourning for this early loss of parental love.

The protagonist's problems in relating to family and friends reflect her inability to overcome the enormous ambivalence created by these early traumas. We have already indicated that the narrator and her sister may be seen as portraying the various parts of the protagonist's character and the different ways of dealing with the same internal and external conflicting situations. The older daughter, Giulia, represents the ultimate stages of the depressive personality. She accepts passively anything her mother imposes on her and gets married only for the sake of finding another 'mother' figure, a person ready to take care of her from an emotional and physical point of view. She is a permanent invalid, who makes no effort to communicate with the people around her and who expresses her rejection of the world in the most primitive ways. The blood that she spits from her mouth as well as her enigmatic, empty smile represent the way the infant refuses the world around her, by spitting the milk of the bad mother or by refusing to take it altogether (Fenichel, 62–6). Giulia's death in childbirth is described by Ginzburg as the ultimate refusal of life and is equivalent to a suicide:

> Sul letto ricomposto, Giulia giaceva nell'abito di quando s'era sposata, e aveva le gracili braccia venate d'azzurro incrociate al seno. Con le labbra spianate in un vago sorriso gentile e malinconico, Giulia sembrava dire addio a questa vita che non era stata capace di amare ... Adesso mia madre capiva il senso di quel sorriso. Era il sorriso di chi vuol essere lasciato in disparte, per ritornare a poco a poco nell'ombra. (666)

> Laid out on her bed, dressed in her bridal gown with her thin, blue-veined arms crossed over her breast and her lips parted slightly in a vague, sweet, melancholic smile, Giulia looked as though she was bidding farewell to this life, a life that she had never managed to love ... My mother understood that smile now. It was the smile of someone who wants nothing more than to be left alone to retreat softly into the shadows. (134)

The younger daughter, the narrator of the story, who most overtly mirrors some of Ginzburg's own activities as a writer and as an editor in a publishing house, represents an active way of dealing with depression. She is clearly more independent and more in control of the situation than any of the other characters. She strives for economic and emotional independence from her family. She is able to channel her creativity in a constructive way through her writing career and her university studies. Most of all, she has a clear perception and understanding of what is going on and is the only person the mother respects: on many occasions she acts, in fact, as a mother to her own mother.

And yet the narrator too is repeatedly portrayed as a shy, introverted person. She feels ugly and unwanted and relies desperately on the woman with whom she shares her apartment to provide her with maternal love and protection. When her companion leaves to get married, the narrator feels a sense of loss and isolation, which echoes, in a muffled way, the piercing sorrow felt by the mother at the end of the novel. The little apartment in which the narrator lives, which belongs to her companion, is portrayed almost like a protecting womb. The apartment and the little square in front of it are a safe enclosure and an extension of the maternal figure with which the narrator longs to share all her life.

The protagonist's attitude towards men is coloured by the same ambivalence that is so obvious in her relationships with women. She alternately longs for a father figure to take care of her and solve her problems, and resents any man who may separate her from her daughters (she symbolically competes with father for the possession of mother). The protagonist feels 'abandoned' by her husband, who has left her a widow and compelled her to bring up her daughters all alone (589). She tries to regain a protective milieu by marrying off her daughter Giulia to some well-to-do, middle-class young man, thereby validating her own success as a woman and as a mother. Yet when Giulia finally marries the gentle and kind doctor Chaim Wesser, the mother shows overt hostility towards him. She thinks of him as dirty and repulsive and cannot understand how his patients can stand being touched by him (582).

It is an interesting and telling point that the money the mother invests in her business venture could have been given to her son-in-law Chaim to help him pay for a medical office in the city and establish his practice. The mother thus chooses to further her own career at the expense of her son-in-law's. Chaim is compelled to run all over town on his bicycle to visit his clients, cannot afford a new overcoat, and has to wear the same old jacket he was given as a war refugee (583).

The mother keeps the son-in-law in a state of miserable subjection and constantly humiliates him, taking away any money he earns and making him feel guilty for any little pleasure he may have (she even grudges him the cigarettes he smokes). In this situation she is clearly the castrating woman, who wants to deprive the man of the family of his potency so as to acquire it herself. In fact, she competes with her son-in-law for the exclusive possession of her older daughter's affection, just like a little girl who competes with father for the exclusive possession of mother.

The protagonist's aggression towards men covers up old wounds and fears. We have already seen her dependence on her husband and her desire to find a substitute father figure. The mother's fear of a critical and severe father figure is revealed in the episode when, after discovering Scilla's robbery, she goes to a police inspector to report the theft. The inspector has little patience with the poor woman, who is beside herself with grief, and accuses her of having acted 'col giudizio d'un bambino di quattro anni' (660) ('with the circumspection of a four-year-old') (128). Afterwards, the mother does not want to have anything to do with the police: 'Nutriva ormai una piena sfiducia, e anche un sordo odio, verso i commissariati di questura: e in questura non voleva tornarci mai più a nessun costo' (661–2) ('Her attitude towards the police was one of total mistrust now, even of unreasoning hatred, and nothing on earth would ever induce her to set foot in a police station again') (130).

Sexual fears and dependencies are apparent in the mother and in the female characters who surround her. The mother's fear of male sexuality is clear in her reaction to Scilla's intention to employ a manservant rather than a maid. The mother is alarmed and warns her friend that a man would eat too much and that he might suddenly get some dangerous ideas in his head: Scilla and Barbara might not feel safe alone with him at night (626).

These feelings are made clear even further in the behaviour of her two daughters. Giulia, the tall, attractive one, with long hair and long legs, avoids sex and discourages all her suitors. When she finally meets someone she likes, she develops tuberculosis and spits blood, driving away her beau. The condition of Giulia in love, not dissimilar to that of the famous heroine of *La dame aux camélias,* shows us that love can be a dangerous and destructive passion. Giulia's sexuality is symbolically represented by tuberculosis, the disease that killed so many people in the nineteenth century. The loss of blood in the menstrual cycle is here displaced to the upper part of the body and seen as the result of an internal sickness.[18] But in contrast to the passionate Marguerite Gautier, after the appearance of her disease Giulia will never love again. She will marry Dr Wesser only out of need for a protector and will bitterly resent being made pregnant by him. In the end, she will die in childbirth, rejecting life and maternity.

The second daughter, the narrator, is portrayed as small and unattractive, with a mass of wavy, frizzy hair sticking out. She conceals her femininity inside bulky, dark clothes, much to her mother's disappointment. She is painfully shy and aware of her physical shortcomings and turns to intellectual life for those satisfactions that she cannot find in her love life. Both the mother and her younger daughter have intellectual aspirations and value the world of the artists (though the mother appears like a caricature of her daughter). Both have masculine characteristics, in their physical appearance and in their desire to find a place in a world dominated by men.

The two daughters embody different reactions to the dangers of feminine sexuality. Giulia, the beautiful one, who accepts the dictates of family and society and appears to represent the typical middle-class girl, avoids sexuality by carrying her passivity to extreme lengths and almost regresses to the helpless state of a baby. Her illness and her death in childbirth represent adolescent fears about menstruation and pregnancy, which obviously constitute an obstacle to the acceptance of female sexuality.[19] The more rebellious younger sister, the narrator, who opts for independence and an intellectual career, defends herself from the dangers of sexuality by identifying with father and assuming a more masculine and aggressive role.

The two daughters are in fact complementary, the two sides of the same coin, separating in an exaggerated way the passive and active characteristics present in a normal personality. They represent the typical oscillations between a positive and a negative Oedipus complex that can be found in adolescents struggling for a sexual identity. Ginzburg, however, emphasizes the anxiety of this situation because she does not indicate any way to solve the problem, which, in the case of the protagonist and her daughters, is the outcome of childhood traumas. Scilla's pictures of creatures of uncertain sex, locked in their inner world and incapable of communicating, sum up the complex issues explored throughout the novel.

The masculine and feminine attitudes embodied in the protagonist's two daughters are repeated in different ways in the couple of Scilla and her daughter Barbara. The latter is completely the opposite of her mother. While Scilla is very active and claims to be an intellectual and an artist, Barbara is a beautiful, voluptuous, and empty-headed girl, the equivalent of the American 'dumb blonde,' all instinct and no brains.

Barbara, with her joy of life and combination of good-natured naïvety and flirtatiousness, also represents the carefree and healthy sexuality of the person who is close to nature, as opposed to the neurotic sexuality and perversions of civilized man. She has many of the ideal traits of the actress, interpreted by Anita Eckberg in Fellini's *La dolce vita,* and her flaming red hair is a beacon and a reminder to the other women of the pleasures of sex. The pale and wan Giulia is completely captivated by the fiery Barbara: only in her company does she acquire some vitality and is able to laugh.

However, even Barbara, who would seem destined to have an easy and enjoyable life next to an adoring man, dies tragically at the hand of her paranoid husband Pinuccio. Although he appears to be an ideal suitor – a wealthy, handsome, and educated Sicilian aristocrat – unfortunately the young man suffers from paranoid jealousy and condemns Barbara's open sexuality because he thinks she is always ready to betray him. Once they are married, he ill-treats her and finally, in a fit of rage, shoots her in the lungs and kills her. The protagonist's and Scilla's plan of conquering the male-dominated environment by means of a store, bearing the warlike name of Sagittarius, literally backfires. Instead of the two women shooting their arrows into the crowd, like proud Dianas, we have Pinuccio shooting his gun at Barbara.

Barbara's violent death is soon followed by Giulia's death in childbirth. The two beautiful young women who get married both end tragically. Barbara, who actively embraces life and love with enthusiasm, is shot in the chest by her brutal husband (the shooting might here be symbolic of the sexual act).[20] Giulia, in spite of her passive attitude and her withdrawal from life and love, is rendered pregnant by her husband and dies as a result of it. Both situations represent a sadomasochistic view of sexuality, destined to cause woman's death. The tragic end of the two women stresses the fact that the masculine stance of Scilla and of the protagonist conceals a fundamental fear of male sexuality, perceived as brutal and destructive.

Scilla's behaviour towards men is particularly interesting because of the ambiguities and secretiveness that surround her character. In fact, Scilla's life is viewed by the protagonist with the same avid curiosity with which children watch the world of adults and try to understand adult sexuality. Though Scilla presents herself as an independent, modern woman, the opposite of her seductive daughter, she is in fact quite similar to Barbara in many ways and dreams of a happy marriage as a way of ensuring her daughter's happiness. She encourages Barbara to put up with her fiancé's scenes of jealousy, in spite of the young man's unstable personality. She even leaves Barbara alone for a long time with the young man so as to catch him in a compromising situation with her and compel him to marry her. She refuses to accept the reality of Barbara's unhappiness with her husband and keeps thinking of her as a bride enjoying her honeymoon.

Scilla's apparent daring and success in many careers is belied by other features of her personality. She is in reality only a humble dressmaker, who strains her eyes to embroider blouses for her rich clients. She makes up for that dreary side of her existence by talking of her wealthy 'friends' and of their luxurious lives and love affairs. She recounts to the mother the imaginary adventures of her 'friend' Valeria with the same enthusiasm with which young people watch soap operas on television, thereby fulfilling vicariously their oedipal fantasies.

Though she claims to be completely independent from her husband, she has an ambiguous relationship with him. Scilla's husband is a gambler and a drunkard, a weak and narcissistic man, who does not seem to be very concerned with his daughter in spite of her affection for him. Scilla speaks of him as an unreliable person, who cannot give her the support she needs and who is only a friend, and yet she runs away with him after stealing the mother's money, thereby revealing her strong link to him.

In conclusion, the only couple who seem to have a 'healthy' relationship are the narrator's girlfriend and her fiancé. The girlfriend is physically unattractive but has a nice personality and cares deeply for the narrator. She is a practical woman, who does not abandon herself to daydreaming and appears to know what she wants and to have no doubts about her future. She is economically independent thanks to her teaching position and is getting married to find a companion rather than a saviour or protector (as in the case of Giulia and Barbara). The fiancé is a nice-looking man, an engineering student, who is introduced to us briefly at the beginning of the novel. The two of them seem to be the only ones capable of attaining happiness, and their fleeting appearance is like a ray of sunshine in an otherwise overcast and stormy sky.

The various psychological themes so far examined are rendered effectively by Ginzburg's writing technique. The author links the various scenes of the novel through a repetition of key images, situations, and symbols in a way that is typical of dreams and that has been generally adopted by filmmakers. We have already seen how the various characters of the novel are reflected in the buildings they inhabit and in the landscapes and art work that surround them. We have also seen how the various characters mirror each other or represent the various sides of the same personality and sometimes undergo a similar fate (in the case of the two couples of the protagonist and Giulia and of Scilla and Barbara, the daughters come to a tragic end and the mothers remain hopelessly bereaved).[21]

There are, moreover, various visual symbols that are repeated throughout the novel and become increasingly meaningful as the story unfolds, just as certain images acquire particular value within the context of a dream.[22] For instance, the symbol of the fountain, with its clear associations of nourishing food and drink, of beginning of life and of early childhood, is present not only in the name of one of the main characters, Scilla Fontana, but in two landscapes that have a particular meaning attached to them. In the first case, the narrator eats with her girlfriend the supper which the latter has prepared. From the safety of their little apartment the two girls watch 'la piccola piazza dove gli uomini entravano ed uscivano dall'osteria, si fermavano in circolo sotto i lampioni, scalciavano e scalpitavano per il freddo, e facevano deviare per scherzo lo zampillo della fontanina sull'angolo' (623) ('the little square below, where people were going in and out of the *osteria* or standing in groups around the street lamps, stamping their feet with the cold while others played with water jetting from the little fountain on the corner') (95).

It is clear from this description that the actions of the people in the square, going in the *osteria* and playing with the fountain, reflect the feelings of sadness and longing of the narrator, who regrets the pleasures of childhood and knows that the happy time spent with her maternal companion is almost over. Now the narrator will not be able to 'play' happily while mother is preparing dinner for her: she will have to behave like a mature adult and look after herself:

> Mi pareva che quella piccola piazza, e quel nostro cucinino e la nostra stanza, coi libri e il tavolo dove la sera io studiavo, fosse un porto sicuro a cui tornavo per trovare quiete e conforto. Fra qualche mese, la mia amica si sarebbe sposata; e io sarei rimasta sola in quella stanza, sempre sola la sera a segnare con la matita rossa, in margine alle dispense, le cose che dovevo ricordare. (623–4)

> For me, the square and our tiny kitchen and the room with its books and the table I used for studying were a haven of refuge, to which I could

> always return for peace and comfort. In a few months' time, my friend would be married and I should be left alone in that room, spending every evening alone jotting down notes with a red pencil in the margins of the texts of my university lectures about all the things I had to remember. (95)

The other appearance of the fountain is in the house of Scilla's rich client, Valeria Lubrani. It is 'una villetta signorile, con un giardino ricoperto di ghiaia e una vasca con lo zampillo' (662) ('a pleasant house with a neatly gravelled garden and a pool with a fountain') (130). The mistress of the house is a distinguished lady dressed in black, with a fox fur draped over one shoulder, who works deftly at a piece of crochet, seated in a leather armchair in a study lined with bookshelves. In this case, Valeria represents an ideal of feminine domesticity within the frame of an orderly life and against the background of Valeria's husband's intellectual activities (he is the director of an archive and Valeria knits in the library).

Once more, the landscape of the garden with the pool and the fountain reflect the character of the mistress of the house and represent for the protagonist a certain model of femininity. The mother tries for a while to imitate Valeria and starts crocheting a cot-cover for Giulia's baby. She dreams of striking a friendship with Valeria and spending the time with her, crocheting in her library, but recognizes that this fantasy is unrealistic and that she is too old to behave like an adolescent.

Other recurrent symbols are certain physical characteristics on which the author insists: hair, feet (and shoes), legs, hands, mouths, which come to represent also psychological traits of the various characters.[23] I have already mentioned how the wiry hair of the mother (578), the frizzy, shapeless hair of the narrator (595), and Scilla's shock of straw-coloured hair (606) represent their lack of feminine attraction and their masculine characteristics, in contrast with Giulia's beautiful long hair (585) and Barbara's flaming ponytail (608).

Masculine characteristics are also represented in the way the mother and Scilla stride along: the first with her imperious stiletto heels (578) and the second with her sandals and galoshes (606–7), which allow her to wade even in the mud. The fact that the mother has to lie in bed in Dronero, with a broken leg, just at the time when Giulia falls in love for the first time with a suitable young man, might indicate the destructive (and castrating) effect of sexuality and be a prelude to Giulia's illness and the disastrous effects of Giulia's and Barbara's marriages (586). Yet shoes and legs can represent femininity as well: the mother insists with the narrator that she should dress better and have her shoes made at the mother's shoemaker so as to appear more feminine and more attractive to men (581–2).

Hands are particularly significant in the various contexts of the novel. At the very beginning of the novel we are told that the mother, when moving house from Dronero to the city, takes among her few belongings 'una mano di marmo posata su un cuscinetto' (577) ('a marble hand resting on a cushion') (53). This gruesome ornament (a typical nineteenth-century knick-knack) is possibly an allusion to the protagonist's penis envy and feelings of mutilation and deprivation, since hands and feet are often eroticized and given phallic significance.

The large, protective hands of the narrator's girlfriend well represent her capable, maternal attitude towards other people (624), whereas Valeria's 'larga mano ossuta, dalle nocche sporgenti' (663) ('broad bony hand, with big knuckles') (131) which crochets non stop, embodies masculine strength combined with feminine skills. Dr Wesser's hands, full of cuticles and with broken and bitten nails, reveal his constant inner turmoil and anxiety, which he turns on himself as well as his castrated position (582).

Mouths and teeth are naturally important, since they reveal directly the emotions of the various characters. I have already mentioned Giulia's permanent empty smile, which is symbolic of her passive rejection of life and love. Dr Wesser's broken teeth are a reminder of the persecution he endured in Poland at the hands of anti-Semites, but they also represent the present persecution he suffers silently at the hands of his mother-in-law (621).

The narrator has crooked teeth, which the mother wanted to straighten with braces when she was a little girl but was prevented from doing so by a decision of the father. In this case the situation of the mother who worries about her daughter's crooked teeth, in contrast with the eccentric father, gives us an insight into the daughter's character (595–6). The narrator's silent rebellion, her desire to write and to move out of the house, and her identification with a masculine model might be represented by her crooked teeth, which her father has insisted should not be straightened and which now keep boyfriends away from her. Since teeth can have a symbolic meaning at both the oral and phallic levels, the narrator's crooked teeth might symbolize in a condensed way the bond between the narrator and her parents: in particular her fear of her authoritarian and possessive mother (a cause for her silence) and her oedipal attachment to her father and identification with him in her search for intellectual achievement and recognition in a man's world.

Animal symbolism plays an important part in the story and stresses both the grotesque and surrealistic elements present in the novel. The mother, with her wiry grey hair, her mangy fur coat, and her jerky movements, is like a wild animal. When poor Giulia is in hospital in Viareggio, her mother paces up and down the hospital corridor 'come un orso in gabbia' (590) ('like a bear in a cage') (65). In an earlier part of the novel the image of the bear appears as an absurd object consisting of a bear supporting a table lamp, which the mother intends to take from her sisters' china shop and exhibit in her projected art gallery with a view to selling it (581). Clearly, the bear with the lamp is a reflection on the mother herself, who, with her clumsy movements and awkward personality, has invaded her sisters' delicate china shop and created havoc in their lives.

The mother's personality is also associated with the image of other wild animals: tigers, buffalo, bison, and elephants. We are told at the beginning of the novel that the mother, in her move to the new house in the city, has taken with her a tiger skin among the few objects from the old house. Later on, after her friend Scilla has refused to spend the afternoon with her, alleging tiredness, and has pushed her out of the apartment, the mother goes to a movie about African safaris:

> Davano un film di cacce africane, a colori; e lei rimase a guardare, nella sala semivuota, mandrie e mandrie di bufali su sconfinati orizzonti color rosso fuoco; non c'era intreccio, non succedeva niente, si vedevano solo bufali, bisonti e elefanti. (650)

> They were showing a film in colour about African safaris, and she sat in the half-empty auditorium watching endless herds of buffalo seen against a boundless, fiery-red horizon; there was no plot, nothing actually happened and one saw nothing except buffalo, bison and elephants. (119)

The wild animals in these cases clearly represent the anger the mother feels inside her at previous deprivations and present frustrations in her instinctual life.

Animal symbolism is used to make fun of the characters in the novel. A symbolic meaning might be given to the scene in which Valeria laughs frankly at hearing the mother's adventures and then swallows her laughter, 'come una gru che inghiotte un pesciolino' (663) ('like a crane swallowing a fish') (131). This is a comic commentary not only on Valeria's jutting chin but also on the mother's unrealistic expectations and childish behaviour. In fact, the mother herself has been like a crane, greedily swallowing all the lies that Scilla has fed her (Valeria's laughter also mirrors Scilla's insolent laughter when she first meets the mother in the hairdresser's store and makes fun of her constant complaints).

Animal imagery is also used to describe Giulia's failed suitors and to stress their inadequacies in the eyes of the mother. The rich and aristocratic Tuscan industrialist whom the mother sees at a coffee bar and whom she imagines as her future son-in-law, suddenly 'agitava d'un tratto fiaccamente le mani in direzione d'una ragazza lontana e faceva un verso nella gola che pareva un chioccolare d'uccello' (585) ('waggled a feeble finger in the vague direction of a girl in the distance and made a noise in his throat like the trilling of a bird') (61). This causes the mother to consider him a 'ciula' (Piedmontese expression meaning 'stupid').

Giulia's first fiancé, who is compelled by his parents to abandon the poor girl without a word when her tuberculosis is discovered, says goodbye to Teresa, the mother's cousin, while crying like a lamb (590). Clearly the young man is seen as a feeble and childlike person, who follows his parents' orders and does not have the courage to fight for his love. The image of the little lamb serves to emphasize the young man's ineffectual and weak personality.

The dog and the cat, which are connected with Giulia and with Scilla's household, also have a particular meaning. Poor Giulia who, after developing tuberculosis, has withdrawn into herself, finds comfort in the company of a little white poodle which she takes for brief walks around the house or cuddles in her lap (583–4). There is something very poetic and Chekhovian in the elegant figure of the young lady, sick with tuberculosis and knowing that her life will be brief, walking with her little dog. Giulia's puppy is her link to life and to childhood.

On the contrary, Menelao, Barbara's Siamese cat, with his name and with his unhappy destiny, represents the castrated condition of some of the characters in the novel. The cat bears the name of Helen's betrayed husband, who had to fight a long and bloody war to get back his faithless wife and regain power and honour. But unlike the Greek hero, who wins in the end, the poor cat loses an eye in a fight with another cat and is 'put to sleep' by his mistress, who cannot tolerate the sight of such an ugly animal (642).

I would like to conclude this list of animal symbolism on a literary note. Ginzburg, with the biting irony of an insider, describes the 'intellectual' world of the city as being made up of a few old people, who fall asleep during the lectures held at a literary club:

> Poi un'altra volta un giovinottino aggraziato ed esile, bellino e quasi senza naso, aveva sfarfallato per la stanza in punta di piedi, leggendo qualche pagina di un romanzo che parlava d'una balena. Mia madre s'era annoiata con quella balena; e nelle seggioline intorno a lei c'erano quei vecchietti appisolati; tuttavia s'era trattenuta fino all'ultimo, immobile in prima fila, fissando il giovinottino coi suoi occhi neri lampeggianti. Visto un po' da presso, il giovinottino aveva una faccetta stanca di quarantenne, un roseo frutto avvizzito dal freddo. (603)

> On another occasion a slender, pretty young man with a tiny button nose had flitted about the room on the tips of his toes, reading extracts from a novel about a whale; the whale had been very boring and all the little old people around her had dozed off, but my mother endured to the end, sitting motionless in the front row and fixing the youth with her bright black eyes. Seen close up, the youth had the face of a worn forty-year-old, like a rosy fruit pinched by the frost. (77)

The whale, with its enormous proportions and its mythical and literary importance, is set in deliberate contrast to the ridiculously effeminate reader of the novel, who performs ineffectually in front of a sleeping audience. This might be a possible comment on the failed ambitions of some of Ginzburg's contemporary writers, who behaved like helpless children in front of a gigantic mother.

Food, as we have seen above, has great importance in the novel in representing the oral dependency of most of the characters. The mother goes from coffee bar to coffee bar in the city, eating coffee ices with cream, in search of an ideal milieu (603). She has a sweet tooth and is forever buying pastries for herself and her daughters (604). The empty store she hopes to buy with her friend Scilla in order to set up her art gallery is strategically located near a pastry shop (648). She constantly feeds her daughters with eggs and other foods in the hope of keeping them dependent on her and of asserting her maternal importance (580, 597).

On the other hand, she bitterly resents having to feed people other than herself and her daughters. She is very much aware of having to pay Scilla's bills when they go to coffee bars together (629). She leaves Dronero so as not to feed the father of her maid Carmela and see him constantly in her kitchen (598–600). She resents the burden of having to feed her son-in-law, whom she considers a good-for-nothing (604), and the one time she invites Chaim's brother Jozek for dinner, she counts the slices of meat he eats (610).

During the 'last supper' she has at Scilla's house, the mother is served an overdone steak and a bottle of wine containing a sleeping powder (655). One of the mother's sources of indignation, when the swindle is revealed, is that Scilla did not even pay for the steak at the butcher (661).

The mother's weakness for sweets is shared by the beautiful Barbara, who, on her first appearance, immediately consumes at the coffee bar a large quantity of fresh strawberries with whipped cream, for which the mother has to pay (608). Barbara cannot resist the chocolates with liqueur that her fiancé Pinuccio brings her, even if the sweets cause her do develop acne on her pretty face (617–18). Barbara eats even the tangerines, which were to be used as part of the portrait that her mother wanted to paint of her and the narrator (621–2).

We have already seen that Barbara represents the joy of life and the pleasures of sexuality. It is significant that poor Barbara, who likes food so much, does not like the spicy Sicilian sausages and the excessively sweet cakes that her fiancé receives from his family as a special treat (616). It is almost as if her distaste of Sicilian food is a warning to her of the dangers that await her if she marries jealous Pinuccio.

Scilla, on the other hand, seems to have problems with food, suffering from frequent indigestions and keeping to a diet limited to vegetables. When she first meets the mother, she orders a bitter drink in contrast with the mother's coffee ices with cream and feels nauseated by the mother's rich food (607, 654). When she does not feel well, she eats only vegetables and stewed fruit purée (627), and on the day she swindles the mother, she is pale, shivers, and complains about indigestion (654). After robbing the mother and running away with her money, she leaves in the house a ball of cooked chicory and a celery stalk in a glass (658). As we have already seen, she is a symbol of the bad mother, who does not feed her children or who gives them 'poisoned' food.

It is interesting to note that the narrator, like Scilla, lives on a meagre diet. In order to assert her independence, she refuses to go to live with her mother, who would feed her too well, and does not even want to follow her mother's advice of having a more nourishing diet. Yet she longs to be fed by a mother figure and is comforted by her girlfriend, who is about to get married, with the promise that the girlfriend will invite her into her new home and feed her with some wonderful milkshakes (624).

Colour symbolism also plays an important part in the novel. We have already mentioned the symbolism of Barbara's flaming red hair to represent her exuberant sexuality. Her link to the mother's personality is established by the flaming red silk dressing gown that the protagonist wears in the morning before applying purple powder and greasy lipstick to her face in an effort to assert her femininity (580).

In contrast with this bright colour, we have the grey skirt and dark blue sweater of the unassuming and depressed narrator (582) and the foggy sky and muddy ground against which the story unfolds. Bright colours, in this case, represent instinctual life ready to burst out in spite of the repressive environment (the grey sky and dreary setting of the novel).

In conclusion, this novel not only explores the difficulties that women experience in searching for their identity but also gives us an insight into the meaning of creativity and writing for Natalia Ginzburg. The act of storytelling on the part of the narrator, who is both an editor in a publishing house and a poet, is mirrored by the colourful dreams of the mother and by the exciting stories that Scilla tells the protagonist. The dreams and fantasies of the two older women and their hopes for a bright future are a denial of and an escape from the dreary world that surrounds them.

The narrator offers a further dimension to the story by telling us these dreams in a detached and critical way and showing us how the pleasure principle, embodied in the mother's hopes, has to give way to the reality principle, embodied in the tragic ending. The narrator defends herself from the pain and rage implicit in the story by presenting the facts in a humorous way, telling them at breakneck speed, and mixing the elements of a detective story with those of a melodrama and of a soap opera. Only in the last scene does she slow down and let us feel the tragic sorrow of loss of love and of premature death.[24]

Writing, then, truly acquires a cathartic function, since it gives the narrator an insight into her life, into her repressed instincts, and into the mechanisms with which she defends herself from those instincts. It also provides her with a safe way of releasing her pent-up emotions as well as a means of sublimating her sexuality, through the creative act of writing.

NOTES

1 The translation of this Italian passage is mine.

2 Among the positive critcisms of the novel, see Pina Sergi's review of

Valentino in *Il Ponte* 13 (1957): 1882–4; Ferdinando Virdia, 'Tre romanzi brevi di Natalia Ginzburg,' *Fiera Letteraria* (4 August 1957); Mario Bonfantini, 'Il "muto" segreto di molte esistenze,' *Corriere della Sera* (14 February 1965). More recently, Alan Bullock shows appreciation for Ginzburg's psychological insight into the character of the mother (98).

Among the negative critics of *Sagittarius* we find Seroni, who complains that the author has lost her ability to portray inner reality (84–5); Manacorda, who, in his *Storia della letteratura italiana contemporanea, 1940–1965* (321) and in *Vent'anni di pazienza* (376–7), writes about the novel's lack of depth and its shadowy and unsubstantial characters; and De Tommaso, who points out the lack of a unifying source of inspiration (828). Also on the negative side we find Marchionne Picchione, who comments on the lack of realism in the psychology of the characters and in the dramatic events of the story (52–6), and Clementelli, who criticizes the plot as too artificial and complicated (74–5).

3 For my psychoanalytic interpretation of the novel I shall rely on the Freudian theories discussed by Chehrazy and Chasseguet-Smirgel.

4 Marchionne Picchione, commenting on the last scene of the novel, speaks of 'un brusco, inaspettato ritorno della Ginzburg al tono narrativo dei suoi momenti migliori' ('a brusque, unexpected return of Ginzburg to the narrative tone of her best moments') (55).

5 For the mechanisms of condensation and displacement in dreams, see Sigmund Freud's chapters on 'The Work of Condensation' and on 'The Work of Displacement' in *The Interpretation of Dreams, Standard Edition*, vol. 4, 279–304, 305–9.

6 Freud mentions the mechanism of splitting in dreams in *The Interpretation of Dreams, Standard Edition*, vol. 4, 90–1. Later on, in 'Creative Writers and Day-Dreaming,' when comparing the work of artists with the fantasies and daydreaming of adults, Freud writes: 'The psychological novel in general no doubt owes its special nature to the inclination of the modern writer to split up his ego, by self-observation, into many part-egos, and, in consequence, to personify the conflicting currents of his own mental life in several heroes' (*Standard Edition*, vol. 9, 150).

7 Marchionne Picchione comments on the 'masculine aggression' of the protagonist and finds that there is too great a contrast between the mother's frenetic activity and the passive attitude of Giulia and her aunts, who tend to disappear in the shadows (55). According to my interpretation, what appears excessive from a realistic perspective is very significant from a psychological point of view.

8 For Freud's theories on female sexuality, see 'Some Psychical Consequences of the Anatomical Distinction between the Sexes,' *Standard Edi-*

tion, vol. 19, 241–58; 'Female Sexuality,' *Standard Edition*, vol. 21, 221–43; 'Femininity,' *New Introductory Lectures on Psycho-Analysis*, *Standard Edition*, vol. 22, 112–35.

9 For the quotations in Italian from the novel I am using the first volume of the 1986 edition of Ginzburg's *Opere* published by Mondadori. For the English version of *Sagittarius* I am using Avril Bardoni's translation of the novel. I would like to caution the reader, however, that Bardoni's translation of *Sagittarius* (the only one available, to my knowledge) sometimes omits or mistranslates the original Italian text. The passages quoted in this article are correctly translated.

10 For a description of Scylla, the sea monster, see Homer *Odyssey* 11.85–100. The oral stage of the development of the child has been studied in detail by Karl Abraham. This stage corresponds to the first year of the infant's life, when the child's interest and pleasure are concentrated first in the action of sucking from the mother's breast and then in the action of biting when the first teeth appear.

Abraham distinguishes sucking, which he sees as a purely positive action, from biting, which is aggressive and can be destructive when used in anger and not just to satisfy one's basic needs.

Jacques Schnier, in his article 'Dragon Lady,' examines the psychological origin of many devouring female monsters, including Medusa and Scylla. Schnier concludes that the figures are fantasies of a child who is angry because he or she is denied the breast and projects his or her aggression onto the mother.

For examples of oral aggression see my study of Nievo's life and works, *The Uses of Myth in Ippolito Nievo*, 25, 89–91, 207.

11 Freud repeatedly points out that the proud and possessive attitude of the child towards his feces, the product of his body, is subsequently transferred to objects in general and to money in particular. See Sigmund Freud, 'Character and Anal Erotism,' *Standard Edition*, vol. 9, 167–75, and 'On Transformations of Instinct as Exemplified in Anal Erotism,' *Standard Edition*, vol. 17, 125–33.

12 Scilla's denial of reality can also be seen in the way she transforms the dreary winter landscape around her apartment into an idyllic spring setting where she can go and paint the beauty of nature (86).

13 Since the house can symbolize the human body, as evidenced by its frequent personification in everyday language, the chimney could represent various orifices of the human body belching out or evacuating its refuse.

14 For an explanation of the nature of depression, see Freud, 'Mourning and Melancholia,' *Standard Edition*, vol. 16, 237–58.

15 Marchionne Picchione aptly comments on the fact that the sinister and

squalid landscape near Scilla's house forebodes the outcome of her relationship with the mother (52).

16 During the anal development in the second year of age, the child is toilet trained and taught to be clean and neat. When this period of the child's life is affected by traumatic events, the personality develops certain traits that denote fixation on the anal stage. Such traits include obstinacy, rebellion, the desire to control and be controlled, and excessive concern about money, cleanliness, and order. See note 11 for Freud's articles on the subject.

For examples of anal erotism and aggression, see Giuliana Sanguinetti Katz, *The Uses of Myth in Ippolito Nievo*, 30–7, 39–42, 47, 57–8, 91, 207–9.

17 For the issues concerning the development of girls during puberty and adolescence and the difficulties of separating from the parents and identifying with them, see Helene Deutsch, *The Psychology of Women*, vol. 1, 91–148.

18 For an example of the displacement of the female genitals to the upper part of the body, see the symbol of the Medusa's head as discussed by Freud in his article 'Medusa's Head,' (*Standard Edition*, vol. 18, 273–4).

Speaking of the flower symbolism in Dumas' novel *La dame aux camélias*, Freud in the *Interpretation of Dreams* connects the camellias with Marguerite's sexuality and points out that she usually 'wore a white camellia, except during her periods, when she wore a red one' (*Standard Edition*, vol. 4, 319). Freud does not comment on Marguerite's tuberculosis, but there is no question that Armand is completely fascinated by Marguerite when he first comes to her house, remains alone with her in her room, and sees her coughing blood. We are also told that if Marguerite gave up her dissolute life and remained chaste, her disease would disappear. In short, tuberculosis is clearly linked with Marguerite's promiscuous sex life, first, and passionate love for Armand afterwards.

19 For a discussion of female fantasies and fears about menstruation and pregnancy, see Helene Deutsch, *Psychology of Women*, vol. 1, 15, 78–80, 87, 149–84, 321; vol. 2., 126–201.

20 Freud, in *The Interpretation of Dreams*, points out that there is no doubt 'that all weapons and tools are used as symbols for the male organ: e.g. ploughs, hammers, rifles, revolvers daggers, sabres, etc.' (*Standard Edition*, vol. 5, 356).

21 Marchionne Picchione had already commented on the similarities between Scilla and the protagonist (53–4).

22 For the importance of visual representation in dreams, see Freud, 'On Dreams,' *Standard Edition*, vol. 5, 659–60.

23 For the phallic significance that certain parts of the body can acquire, see

Freud, 'Fetishism,' *Standard Edition*, vol. 21, 147–57. Freud explains that the individual who suffers from castration anxiety reassures himself by imagining that women are provided with a penis and gives phallic significance to some part of the body or to some object in contact with the body. Fashionable garments for women provide us with many examples of fetishism: for instance, padded shoulders, thick boots, leather jackets, and stiletto heels.

24 The defence mechanisms used by the narrator are paralleled by the attitude of Ginzburg herself, who transforms autobiographical material into fiction. It has already been remarked that the narrator – a university student, a poet, and a magazine editor – seems to represent various facets of the author herself (Bullock, *Natalia Ginzburg*, 98). The narrator seems to have inherited some of the characteristics of the adolescent Ginzburg: her painful shyness, her feelings of being excluded by the outside world, her need of being fed and taken care of by her mother, her fear of men, her obstinate search for identity and for her own artistic voice, and her unconventional way of dressing, much criticized by her mother.

REFERENCES

Abraham, Karl. 'The First Pregenital Stage of the Libido.' In Karl Abraham, *On Character and Libido development*, edited by Bertram D. Lewin, 35–66. New York: Basic Books, 1966.

Bonfantini, Mario. 'Il "muto" segreto di molte esistenze.' *Corriere della Sera* (14 February 1965).

Bullock, Alan. *Natalia Ginzburg*. New York/Oxford: Berg, 1991. Chasseguet-Smirgel, Janine. 'Feminine Guilt and the Oedipus Complex.' In *Female Sexuality*, edited by J. Chasseguet-Smirgel, 94–134. London: Maresfield Library, 1970.

– 'The Femininity of the Analyst in Professional Practice.' In *Sexuality and Mind*, 29–44. London: Maresfield Library, 1986.

– 'Freud and Female Sexuality: The Consideration of Some Blind Spots in the Exploration of the "Dark Continent"' (1976). In *Sexuality and Mind*, 9–28. London: Maresfield Library, 1986.

Chehrazy, Shahla. 'Female Psychology: A Review.' *Journal of the American Psychoanalytic Association* 34, no. 1 (1986): 141–62.

Clementelli, Elena. *Invito alla lettura di Natalia Ginzburg*. Milano: Mursia, 1972.

De Tommaso, Piero. 'Natalia Ginzburg.' *Letteratura Italiana*, vol 3: *I Contemporanei*, 817–33. Milano: Marzorati, 1975.

Deutsch, Helene. *The Psychology of Women. A Psychoanalytic Interpretation*. 2 vols. New York: Grune & Stratton, 1944–45.

Fenichel, Otto. *The Psycho-Analytic Theory of Neurosis*. New York: Norton, 1945.

Freud, Sigmund. *The Interpretation of Dreams. Standard Edition of the Complete Psychological Works of Sigmund Freud*. Vols 4, 5. London: Hogarth Press and the Institute of Psycho-Analysis, 1953.

– 'On Dreams.' *Standard Edition*. Vol. 5. London: Hogarth Press and the Institute of Psycho-Analysis, 1953.

– 'Medusa's Head.' *Standard Edition*. Vol. 18. London: Hogarth Press and the Institute of Psycho-Analysis, 1955.

– 'On Transformation of Instincts as Exemplified in Anal Erotism.' *Standard Edition*. Vol. 17. London: Hogarth Press and the Institute of Psycho-Analysis, 1955.

– 'Character and Anal Erotism.' *Standard Edition*. Vol. 9. London: Hogarth Press and the Institute of Pyscho-Analysis, 1959.

– 'Creative Writers and Day-Dreaming.' *Standard Edition*. Vol. 9. London: Hogarth Press and The Institute of Psycho-Analysis, 1959.

– 'Female Sexuality.' *Standard Edition*. Vol. 21. London: Hogarth Press and the Institute of Psycho-Analysis, 1961.

– 'On Fetishism.' *Standard Edition*. Vol. 21. London: Hogarth Press and the Institute of Psycho-Analysis, 1961.

– 'Some Psychical Consequences of the Anatomical Distinction between the Sexes.' *Standard Edition*. Vol. 19. London: Hogarth Press and the Institute of Psycho-Analysis, 1961.

– 'Mourning and Melancholia.' *Standard Edition*. Vol. 16. London: Hogarth Press and the Institute of Psycho-Analysis, 1963.

– 'Femininity.' *New Introductory Lectures on Psycho-Analysis. Standard Edition*. Vol. 22. Hogarth Press and the Institute of Psycho-Analysis, 1964.

Ginzburg, Natalia. *Family Sayings*. Translated by D.M. Low. Manchester: Carcanet Press, 1984.

– *The Little Virtues*. Translated by Dick Davis. Manchester: Carcanet Press, 1985.

– *Opere*. 2 vols. Milano: Mondadori, 1986–7.

– *Two Novellas: Valentino and Sagittarius*. Translated by Avril Bardoni. New York: Seaver Books Henry Holt and Co., 1988.

Manacorda, Giuliano. *Storia della letteratura contemporanea, 1940–1965*. Roma: Editori Riuniti, 1967.

– *Vent'anni di pazienza*. Firenze: La Nuova Italia, 1972.

Marchionne Picchione, Luciana. *Natalia Ginzburg*. Firenze: La Nuova Italia, 1978.

Sanguinetti Katz, Giuliana. *The Uses of Myth in Ippolito Nievo*. Ravenna: Longo, 1981.

Schnier, Jacques. 'Dragon Lady.' *American Imago* 4 (1947): 78–98.

Sergi, Pina. Review of *Valentino*, by Natalia Ginzburg. *Il Ponte* 13 (1957): 1882–4.

Seroni, Adriano. *Esperimenti critici sul Novecento letterario*. Milano: Mursia, 1967.

Virdia, Ferdinando. 'Tre romanzi brevi di Natalia Ginzburg.' *Fiera Letteraria* (4 August 1957).

Natalia Ginzburg and the Craft of Writing

EUGENIA PAULICELLI

The aspect of things that are most important for us are hidden because of their simplicity and familiarity. (One is unable to notice something because it is always before one's eyes.) The real foundations of enquiry do not strike a man at all.

Wittgenstein, *On Certainty*

Introduction

I would like to start my discussion of 'Il mio mestiere' ('My Craft,' 1949) by Natalia Ginzburg with two quotations which reveal both her complex, ambivalent, and twofold relationship with language, and the way she inhabits reality.[1]

The first quotation is at the very beginning of *È stato così* (*It Was Like This*, 1946–7):

> Gli ho detto: – Dimmi la verità, – e ha detto: – Quale verità, – e disegnava in fretta qualcosa nel suo taccuino e m'ha mostrato cos'era, era un treno lungo lungo con una grossa nuvola di fumo nero e lui che si sporgeva dal finestrino e salutava col fazzoletto.
> Gli ho sparato negli occhi.

> I told him: 'Tell me the truth,' and he said: 'What truth?' and he hurriedly drew something in his notebook and showed me what it was, it was a long, long train with a big cloud of black smoke and showed him leaning out of the window saying good-bye with his handkerchief. I shot him in the eyes.

The second is taken from an interview:

> Scrivendo *La strada che va in città* volevo che ogni frase fosse come una scudisciata o uno schiaffo. Invece quando scrissi *È stato così* mi sentivo molto infelice e non avevo né la voglia né la forza di schiaffeggiare o di scudisciare. Si penserà che avessi voglia di sparare, dato che questo racconto comincia con un colpo di pistola: ma no. Ero del tutto senza forze, infelice.[2]

> While I was writing *The Road to the City* I wanted each sentence to be like a whip or a slap in the face. When I wrote *It Was Like This*, however, I was feeling so unhappy that I did not have either the desire or the strength to whip or slap anybody in the face. You might think that I felt like shooting someone since this novella starts with a gunshot: but this is not true at all. At the time I was unhappy and devoid of all strength.

These two quotations illustrate a number of contradictory issues that recur in Ginzburg's writings. Moreover, from these two quotations we can gauge the problematic rapport that the writer establishes with words and different uses of language, which is evident, for example, when she writes a story, or when she comments on one, or again when she attempts to explain her use of language in a given context. All these aspects are present and developed in her 1949 essay 'Il mio mestiere,' republished in *Le piccole virtù* (*Small Virtues*), the text which will constitute the main point of reference in my analysis.

It seems necessary to underline in my introductory remarks the coexistence in Ginzburg of two distinct movements in her use of language. This coexistence reveals in turn a sort of ambivalence or a duality in her mode of approaching reality. This duality becomes apparent in both her fictional and critical writing. On the one hand, we can notice the way she proceeds almost brutally towards her readers, in her project to eliminate any kind of equivocal term. Her prose is in fact characterized by the use of very short sentences and language that is sharp, precise, sometimes as final as a gunshot that goes straight to the heart of things. On the other hand, her writing contains a distinct awareness of something minimal and almost invisible, like the fleas she talks about in 'Il mio mestiere.' Simplicity and familiarity are specifically for Ginzburg the realms in which both truth and mystery hide. Hence her complex notion of language, which is never completely optimistic. For Ginzburg words are means by which we can either reveal or hide important parts of our human condition. That is why even in some of her apparently 'clearest' writings imperceptible shadows surround her crystalline words. For us readers then, the question remains open and unsolved: what is this invisible worm that undermines the compact body of language, of words – those words that in Natalia Ginzburg's narrative project try to recollect the shattered fragments of experience and transform them into the stories she tells?

These different facets of Natalia Ginzburg function side by side in her writing and contribute to the puzzlement rather than the reassurance of the reader, who lives among the masks of the apparent 'clarity' and 'linearity' of her style, a style that is very atypical in the history of Italian literature. The effect she often produces in the reader is one that follows the conflagration of a gunshot after which some words survive. In this battle with language there are words that hold an imperceptible splinter, or residue, that undermine the project toward clarity.

'Il mio mestiere' is an explicit discussion of Ginzburg's poetics, but it is also an attempt to define something that escapes the very rules of definition: creativity. For its intimate link to *mestiere*, creativity is not for Ginzburg either a metaphysical entity or a romantic stereotype. Rather, her notion of creativity nourishes and lives thanks to the meticulous work she does with her hands, her body, and her mind: writing, or, better, her *mestiere di scrivere*. In the text, the reader can perceive the pain implied in the creative process at every moment in which Ginzburg as a writer responds to her mysterious and internal need to write, to give aesthetic form to different events in life. At the very beginning of the text Ginzburg says:

> Il mio mestiere è quello di scrivere e io lo so bene e da molto tempo. Spero di non essere fraintesa: sul valore di quel che posso scrivere non so nulla. So che scrivere è il mio mestiere. Quando mi metto a scrivere, mi sento straordinariamente a mio agio e mi muovo in un elemento che mi par di conoscere straordinariamente bene: adopero degli strumenti che mi sono noti e familiari e li sento ben *fermi nelle mie mani*. (73; my emphasis)

> My *mestiere* is that of writing and I have known it well and for a long time. I hope not to be misunderstood: I do not know anything about the value of what I can write. I know that writing is my *mestiere*. When I start writing, I feel extremely at ease and I live in an element that I seem to know extremely well: I use the tools that I am familiar with and I feel them very *firmly in my hands*.

Before beginning a discussion of this text, let me say that the word *mestiere* linked to the question of creativity represents a starting point and a return. More precisely, Ginzburg's notion of *mestiere* becomes a nerve centre from which two fundamental questions can be linked and problematized. Let me say first that we will not understand the strong ethical implications of *il mestiere di scrivere* and *di vivere* for Natalia Ginzburg if we fail to consider her experience in the light of the cultural debate which took place in and around the Turin-based publishing house Einaudi where she worked. Ginzburg believed, especially during her formative years there, that it was the intellectuals' task and duty to build a new concept of culture and consequently a different cultural politics, after the tragedy of Fascism. This important background, which I will discuss in the second section of my paper, helps me to take a step forward in the analysis of the relationship between certain ethical political issues that Ginzburg brings to our attention in her writings and other questions which bear on contemporary feminist cultural politics. This will be a topic of the third section of my discussion, a problematic consequence and development of the issues which will have emerged from the previous section. Before starting my discussion, though, I think it is necessary to clarify that it is not my intention here to associate Natalia Ginzburg with feminism. Ginzburg's polemics with some Italian feminist groups are well known. What is important for me, in this context, is to investigate how certain issues which arise in Ginzburg's writing can actually contribute to the creation of new spaces for women in our society. More precisely, I would like to address the question of creativity not only as an individual right but also as a fundamental appropriation of a political space for women in the family, in society, and within themselves. I believe that Natalia Ginzburg has a lot to say on these topics, especially insofar as she sees women's creativity as it is manifested from the minimal and the personal to the ethical-political. In so doing, I will see to what extent the implications coming out of my discussion of Ginzburg can serve a project which articulates a new dimension for the subject in general and for women in particular.

With these premises in mind, let me now turn to the discussion of *mestiere.*

The Craft of Writing and Its Ethical-Political Implications

The etymological roots of the word *mestiere* in different Romance languages include several different meanings. First, the Latin *mestiere* is associated with manual work, the result of practical experience in the workshop or laboratory; it implies a deep knowledge and mastery of technical skills. Second, the Latin *mestiere* is opposed to art and profession. Moreover, *mestiere* is also related to *mysteriu/misterioso* (mysterious), from which *ministeriu* also derives. This combination appears in religious Latin texts of the Middle Ages. Third, in the Gallo-Romance language, the meaning of *mestiere* extends to 'need' or 'to be necessary.'[3]

In Ginzburg's writing, one can trace all of these connotations of the word *mestiere*. These meanings of manual work, mystery, task, function, necessity, supply the interpretive frame which allows us to read Natalia Ginzburg's 'Il mio mestiere' in an ethical-political perspective. In this context, I consider writing to have an intimate link to the idea of *making* or *forging*. It is this gesture that for Ginzburg embraces the political as well as, in broader terms, her relationship with history.

'Il mio mestiere' reiterates themes that are always present in Ginzburg's fictional work. She is aware that a writer has the ethical responsibility to show that words are, on certain occasions of one's life, very poor and insufficient in explaining oneself and events. Hence, an important interaction is constructed between microhistory and History. Ginzburg's work demonstrates vividly an ever-present and intricate rapport between the individual and the collective body of history. Narration is situated in this space. As an example of this we can see how in a novel like *Lessico famigliare* (*Family Sayings*, 1963) personal history beautifully intermingles with important events from Italian history, such as the rise of Fascism, Leone Ginzburg's assassination, and the postwar years. All these events are filtered through a narrative voice that is sometimes almost invisible, hidden in a corner of a room, from which she observes those present and records their dialogues and thoughts in her notebook of memory. At the same time, however, in other parts of the novel readers perceive a much stronger presence of the narrative voice, who declares very clearly her ideas and intents. As examples of this dual narrative technique, let me point to two episodes in *Lessico*. One is Leone Ginzburg's death, which is narrated by or filtered through another character – Cesare Pavese, who at the time in which Ginzburg wrote *Lessico* was already dead. Of his suicide, in fact, we will be informed towards the end of the novel. In Leone's death, which was one of Ginzburg's most crucial experiences, the author of the autobiography disappears as in a filigree fading where her emotions lie concealed and out of reach (155). The second episode comes later, when the narrative voice talks about the difficulties the antifascist intellectuals had in finding an authentic language to express the change in reality that accompanied the fall of Fascism, the end of World

War II, and the project to construct a new society. I will discuss this part later in the essay, but what I wish to bring attention to here is that on this occasion the narrative voice regains her strong presence (164–7). All these problematics are already present in the foreword to the readers, in which Natalia Ginzburg clearly states that all the narrated events and characters are real, but at the same time underlines that *Lessico* is not a *chronicle*, but rather a *novel*. Consequently, all the text is constructed on the borderline between reality and the memory of the writer who *lovingly* evokes the places and the personal lexicon of the characters whose language is situated between orality and writing. As she says at the end of the foreword : 'La memoria è labile e ... i libri tratti dalla realtà non sono spesso che esili barlumi e schegge di quanto abbiamo visto e udito' (vi) ('Memory is fleeting ... the books based on reality are often only thin glimmers and splinters of what we have seen and heard').

Writing, in Ginzburg's sense of *mestiere*, had, for those intellectuals who gravitated around the Einaudi publishing house, such as Pavese, Italo Calvino, and Ginzburg herself, essentially the meaning of construction, which responded to the ethical sense of duty they all felt. Their aim was to build a new literature and concept of the individual for a new society after the 'dark years' of Fascism. Translated into Gramscian terms, into the figure of the 'intellettuale organico' (organic intellectual), their notion of culture bore not on intellectualism, nor on a cultural activity completely separated from the rest of society; this, rather, was to be a culture in which intellectual activity itself constituted a political act. It is not by chance, then, that Pavese defines the writer as 'un operaio della fantasia' (a worker of fantasy),[4] and this in 1946, a difficult year full of projects, new aspirations, and yet disappointments. These are years beautifully described in Paolo Spriano's book *Le passioni di un decennio: 1946–56* (*The Passions of a Decade: 1946–56*), the first two chapters of which are dedicated to Calvino and Pavese.

Similarly, Natalia Ginzburg conceives the act and the body of writing as a laboratory where a meticulous craftsperson forges in his or her hands the words which build a narrative. Hence the experience of pain and joy described in 'Il mio mestiere,' which becomes almost a religious vocation. As we said in the beginning, Natalia Ginzburg's words seem to aim straight at the heart, at the neuralgic point of the event. Here her apparent clarity is a result of her calling things by their proper names and avoiding reassuring metaphors that can lessen the writer's anxiety to understand and to grasp historical and subjective reality.

These elements are always present in a number of Ginzburg's journalistic and literary texts, and they establish recurrent themes throughout her work. For the new edition of her *Cinque romanzi brevi* (*Five Short Novels*, 1964), Natalia Ginzburg wrote a new preface in which she goes through the stages of her *mestiere di scrivere*, trying, she says, 'di rintracciare le ragioni che in questi anni mi hanno governato nel mio scrivere' ('to track down the principles that in these years ruled my writing'). This is an intent that also underlies 'Il mio mestiere' of 1949. In the present context, I would like to underline her recurrent preoccupation with and discourse on *clarity*. It seems to me that clarity constitutes a project that subtends her *mestiere di scrivere* as well as her search for explanations, for the inner and ethical motivations of the act of writing. Hence her relationship both with language and with the different experiments she uses in her narrative technique, which is full of problematic passages that provide clues to her definition of *mestiere*. It is for this reason that Natalia Ginzburg's style is not composed of canonical metaphors. Moreover, her way of dealing with language and words transforms her 'clarity' in a complex tangle of different avenues and interpretations. She calls the reader to think and *rethink* continuously the meanings of the words used. That is why Ginzburg starts with words that are closer to us, using the objects and atmosphere of the everyday. She seems to suggest that it is exactly in the 'boring and monotonous' everyday, in the *familiar*, that mystery and shadow fall, surrounding our life like a dream or a film. It is also in the everyday that 'History' celebrates its cunning mysteries and passages, as she has shown in *Lessico*.

It is interesting to note that in one of her journalistic articles, called 'Chiarezza' ('Clarity,' 1944)[5] for *L'Italia libera* (*Free Italy*), the newspaper of the Action Party to which she was affiliated, she established certain elements that as we said previously will recur throughout her work. Let me show some of the passages from this article and compare them with other passages in *Lessico*. The main concern of Natalia Ginzburg in 'Chiarezza' is to distinguish the relationship that intellectuals were forced to establish with language during the years of Fascist dictatorship from the *new* relationship to be established after the Liberation. In other words, intellectuals had to bring back to light the 'clarity' and 'truth' that were prohibited during Fascism. The article starts and ends with a metaphor, an absent or rare figure in Ginzburg's fiction: 'Gli uomini cadevano inciampando fatalmente nella *propria* rivoltella carica' (emphasis mine) ('Men fatally tripped over their loaded guns'), and later, 'Esso – [il fascismo] – dovette fatalmente perire, precipitando nella fossa che s'era scavata con le sue proprie mani, "inciampando nella sua rivoltella carica"' ('Fascism was fatally to perish, falling into the ditch that it had dug for itself with its own hands, "tripping over its loaded gun"'). 'Chiarezza' ends with a declaration of a strong ethical-political intent:

> Ma io credo che il primo atto da compiere sia questo, ritrovare noi stessi: ricondurci alle forme più elementari e spontanee della parola, nei rapporti umani, nei pensieri e nei sentimenti.

> But I think that the first thing to do is to find ourselves again: going back to the most primary and spontaneous forms of words, in human relationships, in one's thoughts and feelings.

Let us now look at the following passage from *Lessico*, published in 1963, which shows how she goes back to analyse the same themes after many years:

> Era il dopoguerra, un tempo in cui tutti pensavano d'essere dei poeti, e tutti pensavano d'essere dei politici; tutti s'immaginavano che si potesse e si dovesse anzi far poesia di tutto, dopo tanti anni in cui era sembrato che il mondo fosse ammutolito e pietrificato e la realtà era stata guardata come di là di un vetro, in una vitrea, cristallina e muta immobilità. Romanzieri e poeti avevano, negli anni del fascismo, digiunato, non essendovi intorno molte parole che fosse consentito usare ... Si determinò una confusione di linguaggio fra poesia e politica, le quali erano apparse mescolate insieme. Ma poi avvenne che la realtà si rivelò complessa e segreta, indecifrabile e oscura non meno che il mondo dei sogni; e si rivelò ancora situata di là dal vetro, e l'illusione di avere spezzato quel vetro si rivelò effimera ... Così il dopoguerra fu triste, pieno di sconforto dopo le allegre vendemmie dei primi tempi ... Certo, per molti anni, nessuno fece più il proprio mestiere, ma tutti credettero di poterne e doverne fare mille altri insieme ... era necessario tornare a *scegliere* le parole, *a scrutarle per sentire se erano false o vere, se avevano o no vere radici in noi, o se avevano soltanto le effimere radici della comune illusione.* (165–7; my emphasis)

> It was the postwar period, a time in which everybody thought they were poets, and everybody thought they were politicians; everybody imagined that one could and should make poetry out of everything, after many

> years in which it had seemed that the world was reduced to silence and petrified, and reality was looked at from behind a glass, in glasslike, crystalline, and dumb immobility. During the years of fascism, novelists and poets had fasted since there were not many words around that they were allowed to use ... A confusion of language between poetry and politics occurred since these two appeared to be mixed together. But then reality revealed itself with its complexities and secrets, undecipherable and obscure, not less than the world of dreams; reality once again revealed itself beyond the glass and the illusion of having broken that glass turned out to be ephemeral ... So the postwar years were sad, full of discomfort after the happy crops of the first times ... Certainly, for many years, no one did his own job, but everybody believed that they could and should do thousands of them at the same time ... it was necessary to go back and *choose* the words, *to scrutinize them in order to feel if they were false or true, if they had true roots inside of us, or if they only had the ephemeral roots of the common illusion.*

This 'common illusion' was shared by many anti-fascists after the Liberation. In these passages there is a sharp critique and analysis not only of the historical-political situation after the war, but also of her role as an intellectual in that precise social and political environment. Those new projects evoked at the end of the article 'Chiarezza' remained in Ginzburg's eyes just dreams, and twenty years later in *Lessico* she realizes the failure of those noble purposes shared by an entire generation. The reasons for that failure are still under scrutiny, but what I would like to focus on in the quotation from *Lessico* is the impossibility for the two languages of politics and poetry to correspond. They respond in Ginzburg's eyes to two different needs and yet are both fundamental for the evolution of human beings. Furthermore, the political, in this context, is very problematic because it is also linked to particular party lines. Indeed, the difficulties of intellectuals such as Pavese, Calvino, and Ginzburg to fit in with these rules are well known.[6]

The two passages I have quoted are also important because they show a very precise and emblematic example of the way memory works and is constructed. The different events which happened during Fascism are seen and discussed by Ginzburg in a new and revised manner each time she goes back to analyse them. This vividly demonstrates what the neuroscientist Oliver Sacks affirms about the essential quality of memory, that it 'is not to *reproduce* but *to rebuild*.'[7] It is exactly this act of rebuilding that implies the formation of a fundamental creative space which enables Natalia Ginzburg to revisit and reshape her multifaceted identity as a writer in the course of time and history. In so doing, she touches upon some aspects of her identity as a person and as a woman, trying to find a language which can express from time to time her complex approach to both reality and creativity.

The Craft of Living: Natalia Ginzburg and the Feminine

The act of writing and ultimately the text produced are for Ginzburg a continuous outgrowth of roots searching for new spaces in which to dwell. Ginzburg distinguishes between her critical essays and journalistic articles on the one hand, and her fictional writing on the other. She has a different attitude towards these two kinds of writing and language, together with two diverse functions of the same. Writing is for her a means of approaching the elusiveness of events in life, an act of recollecting them, reshaping them in order to reach again the ultimate lost object, language:

> Quando scrivo invece non penso mai che c'è forse un modo più giusto di cui si servono gli altri scrittori. Indendiamoci, io posso scrivere soltanto delle storie. Se mi provo a scrivere un saggio di critica o un articolo per un giornale *a comando,* va abbastanza male. Quello che allora scrivo lo devo cercare faticosamente come *fuori di me* ... E ho sempre l'impressione di truffare il prossimo con delle parole prese *a prestito o rubacchiate qua e là. E soffro e mi sento in esilio.* Invece quando scrivo delle storie sono come uno che è *in patria,* sulle strade che conosce dall'infanzia e fra le mura e gli alberi che sono suoi ... Questo è il mio mestiere, e io lo farò fino alla morte. (74; my emphasis)

> When I write, however, I never think that there is another better way that other writers employ. Let me make myself clear: I can only write stories. If I try to write a critical essay or an article for a newspaper that I have been *commissioned* to write, it does not go very well. Because what I write in this case I have to find with difficulty as if it were outside of me ... And I always have the impression of cheating somebody *with words that I borrow or steal here and there. And I suffer and I feel as if I am in exile.* When I write stories, on the other hand, I feel I am like someone in his *homeland,* on the roads he has known well since childhood and among the walls and trees that are his own ... This is my craft, and I will do it till I die.

In this passage we can notice her deep awareness of the inevitable differences in language, rhetoric, and attitude required for those texts that are born 'a comando.' These texts are unlike those that are born out of an intimate need which belongs to a completely different universe and to a distinct order of discourse. Natalia Ginzburg clearly faces two questions here: first, her personal relationship with her creativity, which is profoundly ethical; and second, the complexity of different rhetorical codes of language which focus on the multifaceted rapport between the denotative and connotative elements of words. We also see in the above passage how the two languages of criticism and poetry are for Ginzburg incompatible insofar as they respond to two different needs and functions. As we also have previously seen, a similar concern emerged from *Lessico* as regards the languages of politics and poetry.

'Il mio mestiere' is also a text which describes the trajectory of Ginzburgs Ginzburg's evolution as a writer, a trajectory that is full of difficult passages and painful and contradictory phases which were all necessary for a definition of a more lucid awareness of reality through writing. There are different temporal sequences that mark the unfolding of her evolution, which becomes itself a narrative and self-narrative gesture. 'Il mio mestiere' starts in fact with the present indicative and then switches into the past and the imperfect, the tense of memory and nostalgia. All through this evolution we perceive several selves that express different parts of her identity. On several occasions she directly addresses the readers: 'E badate, non è che uno possa sperare di consolarsi della sua tristezza scrivendo' (87) ('And remember, don't think that you can hope to console yourself about your sadness writing'). And a little earlier:

> Ho scoperto allora che ci si stanca quando si scrive una cosa sul serio. È un cattivo segno se non ci si stanca. Uno non può sperare di scrivere qualcosa di serio così alla leggera, come con una mano sola, svolazzando via fresco fresco. Non si può cavarsela così con poco. Uno, quando scrive una cosa che sia seria, ci casca dentro, ci affoga dentro proprio fino agli occhi. (78–9)

> I discovered then that one gets tired when one writes something seriously. If you do not get tired it is a bad sign. One cannot hope to write something serious so lightly, as if with only one hand, fluttering here and there ... You cannot manage it with just a little effort. When one writes something serious, one falls inside, drowning up to one's eyes.

The image of hands is present in this passage and underlines a strong corporeal element in the act of writing as *mestiere*. In so doing, this act involves some of the etymological suggestions I have mentioned at the beginning of the essay. Moreover, this corporeal element is not perceived and conceived by Ginzburg as strong, heavy, encumbering, but is instead understated, first announced in the body of the text and then almost dispersed in the shadow of imperceptible gestures of the everyday, minimal details and her 'stubborn search for fleas,' which are mentioned in 'Il mio mestiere.' I consider them a symbol of the minimal, the almost invisible details of reality that Ginzburg believes are important to observe and to be taken into account in her act of narration.

An archaeology of memory, the secret mechanism of Ginzburg's work on language, is here in action. Hence her ongoing and painful search – as any deep analysis must be – of possible spaces that would violate the easy rhetoric of common places, of stereotypes, and the conventional meaning of words and ideas. Ginzburg seems to be always committed to exploring those places like family, friends, and lovers' relationships, thereby reinventing and reshaping them in her writing. But within these spaces there is also a constant search to build up roots, especially for the female characters when they are victims of society, life, or themselves, or they are simply not inscribed in the laws of the family. Ginzburg's controversial and polemical relationship with feminism – or with particular aspects of it – and with certain qualities that traditionally define the feminine universe is well known. These questions are addressed in different ways in 'Il mio mestiere':

> L'ironia e la malvagità mi parevano armi molto importanti nelle mie mani; mi pareva che mi servissero a scrivere come un uomo, perché allora desideravo terribilmente di scrivere come un uomo, avevo orrore che si capisse che ero una donna dalle cose che scrivevo. Facevo quasi sempre personaggi uomini, perché fossero il più possibile lontani e distaccati da me. (82)

> Irony and meanness seemed very important weapons in my hands; it seemed to me that they were useful for me to write like a man, because then I really wanted to write like a man. I was horrified at the idea that someone could detect from what I wrote that I was a woman. I always created male characters so that they could be as far and detached from me as possible.

In this context it is interesting to bring attention to another example in which Natalia Ginzburg likes to use a male mask perhaps also to study herself. The essay I would like to mention is 'Ritratto di scrittore' (Portrait of a Writer) written in 1970 and published in the collected essays *Mai devi domandarmi* (*Never Ask Me*). 'Ritratto di scrittore' is Ginzburg's disguised self-portrait, in which she talks of the different stages and changes of style and concerns in the evolution of a male writer's career. An important issue for Ginzburg in this essay is the relationship the writer establishes with 'il vero' and 'la fantasia':

> È diventato così lento e paziente, anche perché il vero traccia davanti a lui arabeschi che gli sono difficili da decifrare. Decifrarli però gli sembra essenziale. Il suo pensiero a volte vi rimane impigliato. (253–4)

> He has become so slow and patient because the truth traces before him arabesques that are difficult for him to decipher. Deciphering them, though, seems to him essential. His thought sometimes remains entangled in this.

We can notice that almost twenty years after 'Il mio mestiere' she is still deeply engaged in describing her *mestiere*, but this time once again using a completely different narrative technique. We can also perceive a sort of movement toward a reality that is very difficult to grasp and decipher.

Ginzburg's fear of being identified as a 'woman,' as overtly stated in 'Il mio mestiere,' must also be read as her resistance to certain commonplaces that identify women as being 'sentimental' or having shown in history a certain 'defect of reason.' We all know that these are not exactly commonplaces but more precisely represent those narrow and limited spaces in which women have been confined and imagined. Moreover, the 'natural' space for women, the family, had often turned out to be more an attractive 'cage' than a place where they could express themselves. Consequently, the language we speak is a language that included women not as subjects, but as objects to be thought, imagined, or destined to certain places or categories in the symbolic order. These are some of the reasons why Ginzburg always tries in her writing to escape the obvious trap of a common rhetoric about pain, loss, and death. She often reaches a shocking effect in her prose and takes the reader by surprise with the 'cruelty' of her words.

But what changes when a woman enters into the relationship with writing that is itself composed of numerous masks and multivoiced selves? Here a woman is a subject that inevitably faces and struggles at the same time with a language that is marked by her absence or by her being defined in oppositional terms as 'something else,' ultimately as the negative pole, which becomes the negation of her-self. In this absence of the woman as subject, a *being* (man) is not delineated as opposed to a *non-being* (woman). I think that the terms of this relationship in history(ies) that is/are apparently oppositional are much more ambiguous, complicated, multifaceted, and rich in elusive nuances. We are all still looking for answers. Being a woman has existed as *being for others*, but has not existed *for her-self, to-her-self*. Her voice in the history of institutionalized disciplines did not have a *space*. Women have constructed another order to escape a logic that reproduces her identity as something that is 'thought' and not as an autonomous thinking of events and herself [*che pensa e si pensa*].

It is then no surprise if Natalia Ginzburg was often afraid of being identified as a 'woman,' especially in the early stages of her career. Moreover, this preoccupation persists, even though it is expressed differently from time to time. It might be interesting to recall that in December 1992, the Italian journal *Tuttestorie* republished Ginzburg's 'Discorso sulle donne' ('Discourse on Women') and Alba De Cèspedes' response: 'Lettera a Natalia Ginzburg' ('Letter to Natalia Ginzburg'). Both pieces were written in 1948 and originally appeared in the journal *Mercurio*, which was founded in 1944 by Alba De Cèspedes.[8] In her 'Discorso,' Ginzburg addresses the question of 'sexual difference.' Let me specify though that Ginzburg does not explicitly use the term 'sexual difference.' I am borrowing the term from Luce Irigaray and from the Italian feminist philosophers' group known as Diotima. The main reason why I am using the concept of 'sexual difference' is because the issues Ginzburg addresses here can be analysed in the light of the most recent research and discussion within contemporary feminist groups. We must bear in mind though that Ginzburg wrote this article in 1948. She states clearly that all women are different from men, and the main reason is because women have the tendency to fall into a well, namely the well of melancholy and depression. The problem for Ginzburg is that women are so ashamed of admitting this tendency that they pretend to have no troubles and to be completely free. She addresses this issue again with words that are as cutting as a samurai sword, not excluding herself from this cruelty. She says, in fact, that what she wrote in a previous article on women right after the fall of

Fascism and her Einaudi years, was completely wrong and false, simply because:

> In vent'anni di fascismo uno aveva perduto il senso dei valori più elementari, e bisognava ricominciare da capo, ricominciare a chiamare le cose con il loro nome, e *scrivere pur di scrivere per vedere se eravamo ancora delle persone vive*. Quel mio articolo parlava delle donne in genere, e diceva delle cose che si sanno, diceva che le donne non sono poi tanto peggio degli uomini e possono fare anche loro qualcosa di buono se ci si mettono, se la società le aiuta, e così via. Ma era stupido perché non mi curavo di vedere come le donne erano davvero: le donne di cui parlavo allora erano donne inventate, niente affatto simili a me o alle donne che m'è successo d'incontrare nella mia vita; cosí come ne parlavo pareva facilissimo tirarle fuori dalla schiavitù e farne degli esseri liberi. E invece avevo tralasciato di dire una cosa molto importante: che le donne hanno la cattiva abitudine di cascare ogni tanto in un pozzo, di lasciarsi prendere da una tremenda malinconia e affogarci dentro, e annaspare per tornare a galla: questo è il vero guaio delle donne. (58; my emphasis)

> In twenty years of Fascism one had lost the meaning of the most elementary values, and it was necessary to start calling things again by their proper names and to write, for writing's sake, to see if we really were still alive. That article of mine talked about women in general and it said things we all know. It said that women are not worse than men after all and that they can do something good if they try, if society helps them and so forth. But this was stupid because I did not bother to see how women really were: the women of whom I was talking at that time were invented, not at all similar to me or to those women that I happened to meet in my life; so in the way I was talking it seemed to be very easy to free them from slavery and make them free human beings. I had omitted to say something very important: that women have the bad habit once in a while of falling into a well, of being taken over by a tremendous melancholy and drowning in it, and struggling to come to the surface: this is the real trouble with women.

De Cèspedes' brilliant answer is that it is exactly the awareness of that well of pain and melancholy that helps women to establish an intimate and unique relationship with their inner and often hidden world. According to her, it is this deep contact with the hidden world that is within them that men miss and fail to see, simply because they are too self-centred and more interested in their public figure. Hence, the well for De Cèspedes is 'la nostra forza' (our strength), by which she also means 'la nostra differenza' (our difference) because it constitutes a necessary and inevitable phase in life which is the starting point for women's impulse and need towards liberation. The two positions are both problematic and they certainly deserve much more space and attention than I can give them in the present essay. But let me point out that Ginzburg's and De Cèspedes' discussion represents a wonderful example of dialogue built on the *different* positions assumed by the two women, which is a very important enabling condition for a nonauthoritarian dialogue and/or criticism. Furthermore, it is also an example of a sincere attempt at communication and perhaps also undermines a one-sided definition of feminism. This perhaps helps us to understand some of the reasons for Ginzburg's resistance to identifying her discourse in straightforward feminist terms, even though she here helps the cause of feminism. Moreover, a problematic notion of *alterity* is present in her approach to women, reality, and language. It is no surprise then that the language of politics is for her too tight a dress to wear.

It would be useful at this point to expand our analysis by drawing attention to Ginzburg's controversial and polemical relationship with certain language used by feminist groups in Italy. In a 1973 newspaper article entitled 'È davvero una servitù? Essere donna,' a returning to the general question of women she had raised thirty years earlier, she offers a further articulation on the subject. First, borrowing from the Marxist analysis of class struggle, Ginzburg thinks that it is completely wrong to speak of women as a class. Her reason for this position is quite simple. In a given society, there are women who are privileged and women who are not:

> Non amo il femminismo come atteggiamento dello spirito. Le parole 'Proletari di tutto il mondo unitevi' le trovo chiarissime. Le parole 'Donne di tutto il mondo unitevi' mi suonano false ... Nel femminismo, la condizione femminile è concepita come una classe sociale. Essendo state le donne umiliate e adoperate per secoli, è nata in loro una coscienza di classe. Il femminismo vede le donne oggi come un esercito, in marcia per la propria liberazione. Le donne non sono però una classe sociale. La coscienza di classe non basta a creare una classe sociale inesistente. Una classe sociale è una comunità di persone che hanno le medesime necessità, le medesime privazioni, i medesimi problemi e disegni. Ora fra la vita delle donne che

sono in stato di servitù, e la vita delle donne che appartengono alle società privilegiate, non esiste la più pallida rassomiglianza.

> I do not like feminism as an attitude of the soul. I find that words like 'Workers of the world unite' are very clear. Words like 'Women of the world unite' sound false to me ... In feminism, women's condition is conceived as a social class. As women have been humiliated and used over the centuries, a class awareness is born in them. Feminism sees women today as an army marching for their liberation. Women are not, though, a social class. Class awareness is not sufficient in order to create a nonexistent social class. A social class is a community of people who have the same needs, the same deprivations, the same problems and projects. In this light, I do not see even a pale likeness between those women who belonged to privileged societies and those who are in a state of slavery.

This article is an important text that not only problematizes Ginzburg's ideas about women and feminism, but also adds important questions to the present debate on women. She is uncomfortable with slogans that she considers harmful. She sees it as the starting point from which a certain feminist ideology has constructed its political analysis and strategy. Ginzburg says in fact that:

> Il sentimento essenziale espresso dal femminismo è l'antagonismo fra uomo e donna. Tale antagonismo, il femminismo lo giustifica con le umiliazioni subite dalle donne. Le umiliazioni danno origine a un desiderio di rivalsa e di rivendicazione. Il femminismo nasce dunque da un *complesso d'inferiorità,* antico di secoli. Ma sui complessi d'inferiorità non si può costruire una visione del mondo. Il pensiero è chiaro quando li ha conosciuti e ne cammina lontano. Sui complessi di inferiorità non si può costruire nulla di solido. È come voler costruire una casa con del materiale deteriorato e scadente. (183; my emphasis)

> The essential feeling expressed in feminism is the antagonism between man and woman. Feminism justifies this antagonism by reference to the humiliations experienced by women. The humiliations give origin to a desire for revenge and vindication. Feminism, then, is born of an age-old *inferiority complex.* But we cannot build a vision of the world on inferiority complexes. Thought is clear when it has come to terms with this inferiority and so can walk very far from it. We cannot build anything solid on

inferiority complexes. It is like building a house using second-rate and cheap material.

In this passage Ginzburg strongly states her critique of the politics of the feminist movement in the seventies: namely that in its early stages it was based on the opposition between men and women, at many different levels, to the point of denying the experience of maternity, love, and all the domestic tasks which were seen as constricting. For many women this also meant denying a more intimate relationship with their particular feminine world and body. The same principle of *denying*, so typically identified with women's history, was paradoxically reproduced in this feminist ethics and politics.

One of the limits of contemporary feminist thinking and practice is that it has not come to terms with the question of creativity at different levels of everyday life. That is why I think that certain questions raised by Ginzburg have not yet been unequivocally resolved or answered either by different schools of contemporary feminist thinking or by political institutions. As we can see in 'Il mio mestiere,' creativity played a fundamental and vital role in Ginzburg's life; writing was a vocation, and a subtle lifesaver:

> Quando scrivo qualcosa, di solito penso che è molto importante e che io sono un *grandissimo scrittore*. Credo succeda a tutti. Ma c'è un *angolo* della mia anima dove so molto bene e sempre quello che sono, cioè un piccolo, piccolo *scrittore*. Giuro che lo so. Ma non me ne importa molto. Soltanto, non voglio pensare dei nomi: ho visto che se mi chiedo: 'un piccolo scrittore come chi?' mi rattrista pensare dei nomi di altri piccoli scrittori. Preferisco credere che nessuno è mai stato come me, per quanto piccolo, per quanto pulce o zanzara di scrittore io sia. (87; my emphasis)

> When I write something, I usually think that it is very important and that I am a *great writer*. I believe that this happens to everyone. But there is a *corner* of my soul where I know very well and always what I am, that is, a little, little *writer*. I swear I know. But I do not care much about it. The only thing is that I do not want to think of names: I realized that if I ask myself: 'a little writer like whom?' it makes me sad to think of names of other small writers. I prefer to believe that nobody has ever been like me, even so small, even such a flea or mosquito-like writer as I am.

The problem of gender returns here ambiguously and is apparently solved with the term 'scrittore.' Being a woman or a man does not seem to matter here on the level of a text, whether it is a short story or a novel. Nevertheless, it is interesting to note that these observations follow a period (her experience of maternity) in which she had stopped writing. As Ginzburg explains in 'Il mio mestiere,' during the years of her family's political exile in a small town of the Abruzzo region she feels nostalgia in two different directions: for her native city Turin and for her own *mestiere*. From her nostalgia, the need and desire to take up her writing once again, is born her search for a new space and dimension. The events in her life – war, exile, love, maternity, widowhood – as I have previously shown, are always intermingled with an individual story and a collective history:

> Ricominciavo a scrivere come uno che non ha scritto mai, perché era già tanto tempo che non scrivevo, e le parole erano come lavate e fresche, tutto era di nuovo come intatto e pieno di sapore e di odore. Scrivevo nel pomeriggio, quando i miei bambini erano a spasso con una ragazza del paese ... mi venivano fuori certe parole che dicevano e che io non sapevo prima, certe imprecazioni e certi modi di dire: e queste nuove parole lievitavano e fermentavano e davan vita anche a tutte le altre vecchie parole. Adesso non desideravo più tanto di scrivere come un uomo, perché avevo avuto i bambini, e mi pareva di sapere tante cose riguardo al sugo di pomodoro ... in un modo *misterioso e remoto* anche questo serviva al mio mestiere. (84–5)

> I started to write again like someone who had never written, because I had already not been writing for a long time and words were fresh and clean, everything was again untouched and full of flavour and savour. I used to write in the afternoon when my children were taking a walk with a girl from the village. Some new words, ways of expression and curses that they used there that I didn't know came out of me: and these new words rose up and fermented and gave life to the other old words as well. At that time I did not want to write like a man anymore, because I had had children and it seemed to me that I knew so many things about tomato sauce ... in a mysterious and distant way, this too was useful to my *mestiere*.

The experience of maternity allows Ginzburg to distinguish her own relationship with life and with writing from that of a man. More precisely, being a mother implies a new awareness of her past and of the different ways of revisiting history. Ginzburg is touching upon specific elements of femininity, which for her is a highly problematic and controversial question. As I have already discussed, femininity and masculinity are worlds that traditionally have been defined in oppositional terms. In addition, the boundaries within which women had to fit acted more as a prison than as a definition of identity. On the other hand, in more recent times, the principles defining 'masculinity' have collapsed, thanks to the efforts of the feminist and gay movements. But most of the problems deriving from all of this still remain, in the majority of cases, either unsolved or not even posed.

The important question for Natalia Ginzburg when she says 'Non amo il femminismo. Condivido però tutto quello che *chiedono* i movimenti femminili. Condivido tutte o quasi tutte *le loro richieste pratiche*' ('È davvero una servitù? Essere donna') ('I do not love feminism. I share, however, everything that feminist movements demand. I share all or almost all their practical demands') is the *language* of feminism and the political practice derived from it. Ginzburg thinks that the feminist movement's specific language is false, confusing, and unclear. It is a language that helps neither women nor men to free themselves from the heavy stereotypes that construct their identities. Moreover, it fails to distinguish individual lives from one another or to help us understand ourselves as human beings – what we really are and what we really want to do. Instead, it responds (sometimes unconsciously) to fashionable ideas that give us easy or ready-made answers to our questions and doubts.

Ginzburg's conception of her *mestiere* seems to contain the connections between mystery and necessity that are also, as we have previously seen, part of the etymological evolution of the word. Hence two different tendencies manifest themselves: first, her withdrawal from both the time and space that belongs to the everyday and that can have the power of crushing us if we are led to reproduce uncritically a series of pre-established rules, and second, her continuous effort to forge a creative space 'misterioso e remoto' ('mysterious and removed') within the everyday life. Ginzburg says that she knows many things about 'il sugo di pomodoro' (tomato sauce), and this experience gives a new flavour and taste to her writing. Consequently, this 'sugo di pomodoro' can represent and become a creative space which also narrates our stories. Memory is also made of flavours.

Clara Sereni, one of the most interesting contemporary Italian writers, has subtly and beautifully shown in her novel *Casalinghitudine* (1988) how food and recipes, which form the structure of her book, contribute to the recollection of individual and collective history. Real recipes appear in each chapter of her novel, introducing a new phase in the lives of the narrator and the other characters who surround her. The book starts with recipes for a small child and ends with a long quotation from a study by her father, Emilio Sereni, on poverty in southern Italy.[9]

Is Ginzburg's project one which takes root within and through the creative space – that precise space which cannot be contained in the production and re-production of time, a space that traditionally was denied to or simply not destined for women? The same question of women's space has recently been addressed by the Italian philosopher Adriana Cavarero, a member of the Verona-based Diotima group, in her book *Nonostante Platone* (*Despite Plato*). In *The Odyssey* Penelope, according to the reinterpretation proposed by Cavarero,[10] constructs in her ritual gesture of weaving, which has traditionally been seen as the time of waiting, an autonomous space. Confined to the room to which she was doomed as a woman and where she weaves with her handmaidens, Penelope fulfils her role of 'spouse' inside the royal palace occupied by the Proci, Odysseus' enemies. Penelope creates her own time and space within the places that tradition assigns her. In her room by night, Penelope unweaves the 'text' that she had woven during the day. She does this in order to postpone her forced marriage with Odysseus' enemy while she waits for his return. Penelope's gesture, in its infinite and rhythmic rituality, creates a world separate from the rest of the people who surround her. The act of writing clearly parallels Penelope's weaving and unweaving, with all its symbolic weight. Writing produces a texture whose making is contingent on both adding to and subtracting from the obligation to reproduce old rules. This kind of logic implies the basis of a narrative that proceeds through the interplay established between forgetting and remembering, two of the mechanisms that constitute memory's selective quality. In this way both memory and writing share the same selective quality.

What seems to me problematic, although fascinating, in Cavarero's essay is that Penelope's and her handmaidens' acts of weaving and unweaving remain strictly inscribed within their own space. Their symbolic acts are in a way revived by the philosopher, who translates them into modern terms to mean the construction by women of an autonomous space in order to elaborate their thought and discourse and in so doing create a new symbolic order and language. Although this is a very attractive idea, I am sceptical about it for several reasons. I think that the ambiguous relationship created between the establishment of roots within and around oneself in a given space and the resulting displacement requires a continuous questioning of the closed space itself. As a consequence, a problem arises: How can this space be built in such a way that it actually interacts with a construction of a political and decision-making space within the production of cultural models of a given society? A necessary step has to be that this space created by women is able to corrode not only those other already predetermined and pre-established spaces where conventional power resides, but also those spaces 'traditionally' destined to women, like the family. In other words, the creative space of resistance that Penelope forms and which women can create must function, I think, not only as an internal dwelling, but also as an *interactive* dwelling.

The strongest point in Natalia Ginzburg's 'È davvero una servitù? Essere donna' is when she affirms that it is completely wrong to consider women as a class for the reason that in our society there are women who are privileged and women who are not. And one of the most fundamental tasks of feminism is not only to spread the word among as many women as possible but also to change some of the rules on which a given society is based. This means, for example, creating the *practical* conditions which will allow women who are less privileged to have enough time and resources to forge their own space and identity. These aspects, it seems to me, are missing from Cavarero's writings.

One of the most complex and least resolved questions that contemporary feminism needs to address is that of breaking with an oppositional logic that is present in the description of events as well as in norms which build relationships and 'genders.' In this sense the shadowy parts of Ginzburg's texts require a sharp critical analysis by the readers not only towards language, as any literary text requires, but also towards unresolved and thorny questions such as the subtle relationships between the *mestiere di scrivere* and the search for a creative space for the woman as subject. This gesture is always located on a borderline between the heaviness of a tradition and a language that no longer speak to present concerns and of a present that needs to be reformulated within writing. It is for this reason that I have talked above of dwelling, of language taking root within the white space of blank pages and of memory.

In 'Il mio mestiere' Ginzburg examines the act of writing and mentions the dangers of being frivolous and false that confront every writer:

> Siamo continuamente minacciati da gravi pericoli proprio nell'atto di stendere la nostra pagina. C'è il pericolo di mettersi a un tratto a civettare e a cantare ... E c'è il pericolo di truffare con parole che non esistono davvero in noi, che abbiamo *pescato a caso fuori di noi* e che mettiamo insieme con destrezza perché siamo diventati piuttosto furbi. (89–90; my emphasis)

> We are continuously threatened by serious dangers in the very act of laying out our page. The danger is to begin all of a sudden to flatter and sing ... And there is also the danger to cheat with words that do not really exist in us, those words that we *picked at random outside ourselves* and that we put together with dexterity since in the meantime we have become rather cunning.

Ginzburg is aware that cheating with language is fundamentally a game that underlies the act of writing. But 'cheating with words that do not really exist inside us' changes its meaning to a cheating with language that is part of the rules of rhetoric. As Ginzburg's work shows, looking for words that are authentic or that 'truly exist in us' is a risky challenge and requires deep analysis to get rid of commonplaces and prejudices. I think that Natalia Ginzburg helps us to see the fragility of definitions of social and historical phenomena that we tend to take for granted. Her ambivalent relationship with reality is exemplified in her outward search, shooting sometimes at the readers or hiding the remnants of words so that they surface in the texture of memory:

> È un mestiere che si nutre anche di cose orribili, mangia il meglio e il peggio della nostra vita, i nostri sentimenti cattivi come i sentimenti buoni fluiscono nel suo sangue. Si nutre e cresce in noi. (90)

> This is a *mestiere* that nourishes itself on terrible things, it eats the best and the worst of our life; our bad feelings as well as the good ones flow into its blood. It nourishes and grows within us.

This is a metaphor of the maternal womb, which is both protective and devouring. It hints at the fragile borderlines which divide the inner from the outer, but which, however, are not in opposition. Rather, they coexist in a discrete conflagration which suspends the interpretation of those who listen, read, and write and also, perhaps, detains the reader, who is waiting for a revelation about human experience. That revelation however, remains in shadow, in process. Even in 'Il mio mestiere,' a text that aims to explain what this craft of writing is for a woman, Ginzburg leaves the explanatory elements to whisper in the readers' ears. 'Clarity' becomes a shadowy place where the strange presences of what we cannot see but only perceive as traces *really* appear in the meticulous task that Ginzburg has called 'her stubborn search for fleas.' And perhaps these persistent and invisible fleas insinuate the benefit of doubt in her strenuous attempt to capture the reasons of her writing, to explain them rationally and to ask herself if writing after all was a duty or a pleasure. Perhaps men do not ask themselves questions like these, but she likes to think the contrary in her thinly disguised self-portrait 'Ritratto di scrittore':

> [Lui] Pensa che non ha fatto mai altro che ammucchiare errori su errori. Che stupido è stato. Si è anche posto una grande quantità di domande stupide. Si è chiesto se scrivere era per lui un dovere o un piacere. Stupido. Non era né l'uno né l'altro. Nei momenti migliori, era ed è per lui come *abitare la terra*. (255; my emphasis)

> [He] thinks that he has never done anything other than to accumulate mistake after mistake. How stupid he has been. He has also asked himself a number of stupid questions. He asked himself if writing was for him a duty or a pleasure. Idiot. It was neither one nor the other. In the best moments, writing for him meant and means living the land.

There is only one answer for Natalia Ginzburg: writing gives her the sense of *living the land*; or, better, writing coincides with her being in the world. There are no possible metaphors or adjectives that can describe writing simply because, for Ginzburg, writing is. Writing is the space where she creates and re-creates life, memory, and history.

NOTES

1 I have chosen not to translate *mestiere* with the English *job* or *work* because this would have been misleading. As here *mestiere* refers to writing, I thought that the best translation would be *craft*. On the other hand, in the context of this essay, I have used the various implications of the etymology of the word *mestiere* as an interpretive frame. For this reason, I have

elected not to translate it and keep the original word in the text. All quotations in this article, unless otherwise indicated, are my own.

2 Ginzburg, quoted in Peggy Boyers, 'On Natalia Ginzburg,' *Salmagundi* 96 (Fall 1992): 57.

3 For a detailed linguistic analysis of this argument, see Steven N. Dworkin, 'Mester and Menester – An Early Gallicism and a Cognate Provençalism as rivals in Older Hispano-Romance,' *Romance Philology* 25 (1971–2). I wish to thank Hermann Haller for having drawn my attention to this article.

4 See Cesare Pavese, 'Di una nuova letteratura' article originally published in the Communist Party journal *Rinascita*, 26 January 1946 and later republished in the collection *Saggi letterari* (Turin: Einaudi, 1951).

5 I wish to thank David Ward for having brought this article to my attention.

6 See Paolo Spriano, *Le passioni di un decennio* (Milan: Garzanti, 1986).

7 See Oliver Sacks, 'Memoria e identità' in Lina Bolzoni and Pietro Corsi, eds, *La cultura della memoria* (Bologna: Il Mulino, 1992), 379.

8 See 'Racconti letture trame di donne,' *Tuttestorie* 6/7 (December 1992).

9 The title quoted in Clara Sereni's *Casalinghitudine* is E. Sereni, 'Note di storia dell'alimentazione nel Mezzogiorno: I Napoletani da "mangiafoglia" a "mangiamaccheroni,"' in *Terra nuova e buoi rossi* (Turin: Einaudi, 1981).

10 See Adriana Cavarero, *Nonostante Platone* (Rome: Editori Riuniti, 1990).

REFERENCES

Boyers, Peggy. 'On Natalia Ginzburg,' *Salmagundi* 96 (Fall 1992).

Cavarero, Adriana. *Nonostante Platone*. Rome: Editori Riuniti, 1990.

De Cèspedes, Alba. 'Lettera a Natalia Ginzburg.' *Tuttestorie* 6/7 (December 1992): 61–3.

Dworkin, Steven N. 'Mester and Menester – an Early Gallicism and a Cognate Provencalism as Rivals in Older Hispano-Romance.' *Romance Philology* 25 (1971–2).

Ginzburg, Natalia. 'Chiarezza.' *L'Italia libera* 3, no. 7 (9 January 1945).

– *È stato così*. Turin: Einaudi, 1947.

– *Piccole virtù*. Turin: Einaudi, 1962.

– *Lessico famigliare*. Turin: Einaudi, 1963.

– *Cinque romanzi brevi*. Turin: Einaudi, 1964.

– *Mai devi domandarmi*. Milan: Mondadori, 1970.

– 'È davvero una servitù? Essere donna.' *La Stampa* (15 April 1973).

– *Vita immaginaria*. Milan: Mondadori, 1974.
– 'Discorso sulle donne.' *Tuttestorie* 6/7 (December 1992): 58–61.
Lilli, Laura. 'Noi donne nel pozzo della malinconia.' *Repubblica* (28 November 1992).
Pavese, Cesare. 'Di una nuova letteratura.' In *Saggi letterari*. Turin: Einaudi, 1951.
Sacks, Oliver. 'Memoria e identità.' In Lina Bolzoni and Corsi Pietro, eds, *La cultura della memoria*. Bologna: Il Mulino, 1992.
Sereni, Clara. *Casalinghitudine*. Turin: Einaudi, 1983.
Spriano, Paolo. *Le passioni di un decennio*. Milan: Garzanti, 1986.
Wittgenstein, Ludwig. *On Certainty*. New York: J. & J. Harper, 1969.

The Eloquence of Understatement: Natalia Ginzburg's Public Image and Literary Style

JEN WIENSTEIN

In her essay 'Moravia,' which appears in the 1974 collection of essays and articles *Vita immaginaria,* Natalia Ginzburg discusses her famous friend Alberto Moravia and bitterly complains about the untruthful nature of his public image. According to Ginzburg, Moravia's public image, which portrays him as cool, detached, and condescending, distorts and denies his true self:

> Lo conosco da molti anni ... Però è molto famoso, e allora uno che non lo conosce di persona, oppure uno che sta a lungo senza vederlo, ha davanti la sua immagine pubblica. Questa immagine pubblica spesso mi infastidisce e non mi piace ... In particolare, per quanto riguarda Moravia, mi sembra che la sua immagine pubblica risulti esattamente il contrario di quella che è la sua persona reale. La sua immagine pubblica appare altezzosa, autoritaria, sprezzante e compiaciuta di sé. Nell'avvicinarlo, uno si trova davanti di colpo la sua grande innocenza, la sua profonda e candida serietà.
>
> I've known him for many years ... but he is very famous, and so someone who doesn't know him personally, or someone who sees him infrequently, is faced with his public image. This public image often annoys me and I don't like it ... Particularly in Moravia's case, it seems to me that his public image is the exact opposite of the real person. His public image is arrogant, authoritarian, scornful, and self-righteous. When you get close to him, you unexpectedly discover his great innocence, his profoundly honest seriousness.[1]

Curiously, however, Ginzburg's own numerous autobiographical essays, and magazine and newspaper articles and interviews convey a public image of her which is just as puzzling and controversial as that of her famous friend. The self-effacing, overly modest Ginzburg openly belittles, berates, and underestimates herself. She downplays her literary triumphs;[2] she ruthlessly focuses on her personal weaknesses, hesitations, and insecurities. She is the object of constant and severe self-scrutiny.

The first hint of this curious display of humility, so precious to Ginzburg, is detected in the essay 'He and I,'[3] an amusing portrayal of the author and her second husband, Gabriele Baldini. He, of course, is all-knowing and all-powerful, while she, on the other hand, is totally incompetent. According to 'He and I,' Natalia Ginzburg has no sense of direction: she is easily confused; she's shy, uncertain, lazy; she doesn't understand a thing about music; she doesn't know any one language really well; she doesn't manage her time efficiently; she can't sing, dance, type, or drive a car. She is inept and insecure. Her imperfections are endless!

In *Le piccole virtù* and *Mai devi domandarmi,* our author repeatedly pleads ignorance when it comes to art, music, and film;[4] in *Mai devi domandarmi* and *Vita immaginaria,* she warns us no less than four times in three different essays that she knows absolutely nothing about politics.[5] And as if this weren't enough, in her hurry to belittle herself, she shamelessly adds further inadequacies to the already exaggerated list of her 'infinite' shortcomings:

> Oltre alla politica, vi sono infinite altre cose che io non so e non capisco per nulla, come l'economia, o la chimica, o le scienze naturali, o le scienze esatte. (*Vita immaginaria,* 169)

> Besides politics, there are an infinite number of things that I don't know and I don't understand at all, like economics and chemistry and the natural sciences and the exact sciences.

Now, if we as obedient readers were to take her at her word, we would have to conclude (as her mother and teacher had done many years before) that our 'somewhat slow' author is, after all, nothing but 'a nuisance,' 'an ignorant donkey' (*Mai devi domandarmi,* 161, 191, 75). Her essay 'Pigrizia' ('Laziness') dwells on her 'great ignorance,' her 'great sloth,' her absolute 'lack of ideas'; it is overwhelmingly self-condemning.[6]

> Avrei voluto che qualcuno mi desse un posto senza conoscermi e per mie

competenze. Il male era che io competenze non ne avevo ... L'ostacolo principale ai miei propositi di lavoro, consisteva nel fatto che non sapevo far niente ... Nella mia vita, salvo allevare i miei propri bambini, fare le faccende domestiche con estrema lentezza e inettitudine e scrivere dei romanzi, non avevo mai fatto niente. (*Mai devi domandarmi*, 37)

I would have liked someone to give me a job not because he or she knew me but for my qualifications. The problem was I didn't have any qualifications ... The main obstacle in my getting a job was the fact that I didn't know how to do anything ... Besides bringing up my children and doing housework slowly and inefficiently and writing novels, I had never done anything in my life.

When it comes to her 'novels' (last on the list of her 'few' accomplishments), Ginzburg softens slightly and is somewhat forgiving. But not for long. She starts off by thinking that her writing is very important and that she is a great writer, but her initial optimism fades quickly, as does her self-esteem. She readily accepts a defeatist attitude and defines herself as a 'little, little writer,' an insignificant writer, a 'flea' or a 'mosquito' on the literary scene:

Quando scrivo qualcosa, di solito penso che è molto importante e che io sono un grandissimo scrittore. Credo succeda a tutti. Ma c'è un angolo della mia anima dove so molto bene e sempre quello che sono, cioè un piccolo, piccolo scrittore. Giuro che lo so. Ma non me ne importa molto. Soltanto, non voglio pensare dei nomi: ho visto che se mi chiedo: 'un piccolo scrittore come chi?' mi rattrista pensare dei nomi di altri piccoli scrittori. Preferisco credere che nessuna è mai stato come me, per quanto piccolo, per quanto pulce o zanzara di scrittore io sia. (*Le piccole virtù*, 89)

When I write something I usually think that it is very important and that I am a fine writer. I think this happens to everyone. But there is one corner of my mind in which I know very well what I am, which is a small, a very small writer. I swear I know it. But that doesn't matter much to me. Only I don't want to think about names: I can see that if I ask myself 'a small writer like who?,' it would sadden me to think of the names of other small writers. I prefer to think that no one has ever been like me, however small, however much a mosquito or a flea of a writer I may be. (*The Little Virtues*, 67–8)

An unimportant, insignificant writer therefore – but unique, special!

The hesitant, insecure, and apologetic tone in Natalia Ginzburg's voice is not unfamiliar; it is, in fact, reminiscent of other literary voices heard in different places and at different times – and almost exclusively women's voices.[7] Our author's self-deprecating attitude is in no way exceptional but rather traditional in women's literature; she fits in. Her need to apologize, to belittle, to downplay, on one hand, and her urgency to make herself heard, on the other, are two sides of a typically feminine literary approach – a recurring theme in women's literature.

The examples of female writers faithful to the tradition of self-deprecation are numerous. Famous members of this sisterhood include Sylvia Plath, Betty MacDonald, Margaret Cavendish, Duchess of Newcastle, Erma Bombeck, Ivy Compton-Burnett, Emily Dickinson, and Annie Vivanti.

As P.M. Spacks illustrates, the American writer Sylvia Plath, in her autobiography *The Bell Jar* (1966), lists one by one (as does Ginzburg in 'He and I') all her defects: 'I was a terrible dancer. I couldn't carry a tune ... I couldn't speak German or read Hebrew or write Chinese.'[8] And Betty MacDonald, in her 1940s bestselling autobiography *The Egg and I*, describes herself as a failure in her role as the wife of a Washington egg farmer. Like Ginzburg in 'He and I,' MacDonald is forever incompetent while her husband is always efficient. We recognize Natalia Ginzburg in Spacks's comments on MacDonald: 'Her husband does everything right, she does everything wrong.'[9] Similarly, Margaret Cavendish, Duchess of Newcastle, when comparing her literary talents with those of her husband, belittles herself. When he writes, he 'creates himself' with his pen; she merely 'scribbles.'[10] The American journalist Erma Bombeck also fits neatly into this category of self-deprecating female authors. According to Spacks, the successful Bombeck portrays herself as 'fat, unattractive, no longer an object of sexual interest, incompetent at all activity, butt of her children and her friends for her stupidity and her middle age.'[11]

The literary critic Clotilde Soave Bowe includes Ivy Compton-Burnett and Emily Dickinson among those who deny their artistic and personal talents; she groups these three together and explains that Ginzburg, 'a self-confessed and self-condemned minore,' like Ivy Compton-Burnett and Emily Dickinson, 'would have us believe that the little she had to say was said in the slightest possible way.'[12]

And Luigi M. Personé compares Ginzburg's at times coy attitude to that of Annie Vivanti, who flaunts her ignorance in order to capture the attention of and entertain Giosuè Carducci. Personé explains: 'Ginzburg reminds me of Vivanti, who, when asked by Carducci what most interested her in the *Divine Comedy*, answered: "Doré's illustrations."'[13]

Sylvia Plath, the Duchess of Newcastle, Betty MacDonald, Erma Bombeck, Ivy Compton-Burnett, Emily Dickinson, Annie Vivanti – the similarities are numerous and the examples do not end here. These authors, chosen from different eras and literatures, share the same outlook; they follow a common agenda. These women writers suffer from feelings of inadequacy; they feel like second-class citizens in a male-dominated society, in the world of the 'others.' Ginzburg, Plath, Cavendish, MacDonald, and Bombeck compare themselves with their husbands; Vivanti measures herself against her mentor; and they don't reach the mark. They deem themselves inferior, insignificant, and irrelevant in their daily dealings with their husbands, families, and the outside world. And finally, this typically female feeling of inadequacy is inevitably present in their writings. The works of Natalia Ginzburg, who willingly joins the ranks of the inadequate, are no exception.

However, when it comes to Ginzburg, other problems enter into play; other questions arise. At first, defining Ginzburg's public image as characteristic of a female literary tradition seems questionable, almost suspicious. It is Ginzburg herself who tries to mislead us by minimizing and by focusing away from the relationship between her positions as woman and as writer. Although she admits in her essay 'The Female Condition'[14] that everything she thinks and does is influenced by the fact that she is a woman, she tries to minimize the importance of her feminine temperament. She longs for a space which does not admit differences between male and female writers; she aims at a higher level; she yearns for a Utopia, 'un momento migliore,' in which one's thoughts are neither male nor female. Her ultimate desire, her 'fine ultimo,' is to transcend the personal, to rise above the female condition.

In the Preface to her 1964 collection of five short novels *Cinque romanzi brevi*[15] she describes her early feelings of 'horror' and 'terror' when confronting her feminine side. She abhors, but is tempted by, her autobiographical tendencies; she fears and rejects the definition of herself as a sentimental, 'sticky,' or 'sickeningly sweet' female writer; she wants to 'write like a man.'

In her early writings, in the short story *Un'assenza* (1933), written in the third person, she chooses a male protagonist, and later, in the short story *Casa al mare* (1937), the first of her stories written in the first person, she makes use of a male narrator. In the Preface of *Cinque romanzi brevi* she explains how in *Casa al mare* she actually 'pretended to be a man.' Gradually, however, she takes on a female first-person narrator in *La strada che va in città* (1945), *È stato così* (1947), *Tutti i nostri ieri* (1952), *Valentino*, and *Sagittario* (1957), and finally, after initially rejecting her autobiographical tendencies, she comes to accept them. Memory seeps into her writing; she overcomes her feelings of horror and terror; she gives in completely to the temptation of autobiography and writes her autobiographical novel *Lessico famigliare* (1963). Her collected writings *Mai devi domandarmi* (1970) and *Vita immaginaria* (1974) continue in this vein.

Natalia Ginzburg's tendency to belittle, to reduce, to minimize is not strictly confined to her autobiographical works and to her public image; it is, in fact, prevalent throughout her narrative and theatrical works. The author's need to downplay, her tendency to focus on the flaw, translates into and ultimately defines her literary style. In the Preface to *Cinque romanzi brevi*, she explains: 'You must write with your heart and your body and not with your head.' She refuses the intellectual and the cerebral; she shuns the literary, the scholarly, the academic; she rejects all sophistication. Her literary style is neither flowery nor frilly. Her language is clear, concise, colloquial. She is never wordy or pretentious. Her sentences are brief, to the point. Her style is undeniably plain, simple, and eloquent in its understatement[16]

The relationship between our author's self-deprecating public image and her literary style is best revealed in Ginzburg the portrait artist. The author's keen attention to detail, her sensitive awareness of glances and gestures, and her tendency to minimize beget a whole range of fictional characters. Portraits abound in Ginzburg's narrative. They are often proof of her sense of humour; they always bear witness to her love of the concrete, the real, the down-to-earth. Ginzburg's portraits are not flattering. Her discerning eye zeros in on and exposes the embarrassing flaw, the sore spot, the peculiarity, the idiosyncrasy in physical appearance or behaviour. She focuses away from the grandiose and seeks out the trivial; a minor detail becomes major. Even the most heroic of figures seems human in his or her vulnerability.

Several unforgettable portraits in *Valentino* are proof of Ginzburg's expertise. The sad yet humorous short novel recounts the failed marriage of Valentino and Maddalena, and the aborted engagement of Valentino's sister Caterina (the narrator) to Kit, Valentino's lover. The following is a detailed portrait of Valentino's mother as she appears at her son's wedding; notice the particular of the 'old fox with one eye missing':

Mia madre si fece fare un cappello, dopo tanti anni: un cappello alto e complicato, con un nodo di nastro e una veletta. E tirò fuori la sua vecchia volpe con un occhio in meno: se puntava la coda contro il muso non si vedeva che mancava l'occhio: mia madre aveva già speso tanto nel cappello, che non voleva più sborsare neanche una lira per quel matrimonio[17]

For the first time in many years, my mother had a hat made for her: a tall, complicated creation with a bow and a little veiling. And she unearthed her old fox fur that had one eye missing; by arranging the tail carefully over the head she could hide this defect, and the hat had been so expensive that my mother was determined not to spend any more on this wedding.[18]

And just as funny and compassionate is the eloquent description of Valentino's wife-to-be Maddalena when she first meets her future in-laws:

Allora quando lui arrivò con la nuova fidanzata eravamo così sbalorditi che nessuno aveva fiato di parlare. Perchè questa nuova fidanzata era qualcosa che non avevamo potuto immaginare. Portava una lunga pelliccia di martora e delle scarpe piatte con la suola di gomma ed era piccola e grassa. Aveva degli occhiali cerchiati di tartaruga e dietro gli occhiali ci fissava con degli occhi severi e rotondi. Aveva un naso un po' sudato e dei baffi. In testa aveva un cappello nero tutto schiacciato da una parte: dove non c'era il cappello si vedevano dei capelli neri striati di grigio, ondulati al ferro e spettinati. Doveva avere almeno dieci anni più di Valentino. (*Valentino*, 160)

She was quite unlike anything we had ever imagined. She was wearing a longish sable coat and flat rubber-soled shoes and was short and fat. From behind tortoise-shell glasses she regarded us with hard, round eyes. Her nose was shiny and she had a moustache. On her head she wore a black hat squashed down on one side and the hair not covered by the hat was black streaked with grey, crimped and untidy. She was at least ten years older than Valentino. (*Valentino*, 10)

And here is Clara, Valentino's jealous and cranky older sister:

Mia sorella abitava all'ultimo piano d'una casa in periferia. Tutto il giorno batteva a macchina degli indirizzi per una ditta che le dava un tanto ogni

> busta. Aveva sempre male ai denti e stava con una sciarpa intorno alla bocca. (*Valentino*, 161-2)

> My sister lived in a top-floor flat on the outskirts of town. All day long she typed addresses for a firm that paid her so much for each addressed envelope. She had constant toothache [sic] and kept a scarf wrapped round her face. (*Valentino*, 12)

And finally Valentino himself upon return from his honeymoon:

> Eravamo felici di vederlo: eravamo così felici che quasi ci pareva che non fosse più niente importante la moglie che aveva preso. Era di nuovo seduto in cucina con la sua testa riccia e i denti bianchi e la profonda fossetta nel mento e le grosse mani. Carezzava il gatto e diceva che voleva portarselo con sé: c'erano dei topi nella cantina della villa e così avrebbe imparato a mangiare i topi che adesso invece aveva paura. (*Valentino*, 168)

> We were so happy to see him that it no longer seemed important whom he had married. There he was, sitting in the kitchen once more with his curly head and white teeth and deeply-cleft chin and big hands. He stroked the cat and said that he would like to take it away with him: there were mice in the cellar of the house and the cat would learn to kill and eat them instead of being afraid of them as he was at present. (*Valentino*, 19)

We are amused at the beginning of *Valentino* by Ginzburg's portrayal of the protagonist's mother, with her complicated hat and her one-eyed fox; we smile when we first read the description of the 'short and fat' Maddalena, who has a shiny nose and a moustache; we may even laugh at the grumpy Clara, who always has a toothache. But Ginzburg's attention to detail makes the final abandonment and frustration of these lonely women all the more pathetic. The contrast between the minor details and the major life events is heart-rending in its eloquence. At the end of the novel, the desperately humiliating sorrow of the now aged and worn-out Maddalena is reflected in the suffering of the younger (yet similarly defeated) Caterina; the mirror image of sorrow which results is therefore twice as moving for the reader.

And Ginzburg's real-life characters do in no way receive preferential treatment. Prominent figures in the political and cultural life of Italy, such as Filippo Turati, Adriano Olivetti, Felice Balbo, Leone Ginzburg, and Cesare Pavese, are all cut down to size in Ginzburg's 1963 autobiographical novel *Lessico famigliare* (*Family Sayings*). They seem to shrink in stature under our author's diminishing gaze, as do Alessandro Manzoni, Cesare Beccaria, Giulia Beccaria, Teresa De Blasco, and Claude Fauriel in the 1983 novel *La famiglia Manzoni*. The following is a portrait of Adriano Olivetti in *Lessico famigliare*. Notice how Ginzburg draws attention to the 'awkward,' the 'goofy,' the 'unkempt' in his less-than-'soldierly' appearance:

> Fra questi amici ce n'era uno, che si chiamava Adriano Olivetti; e io ricordo la prima volta che entrò in casa nostra, vestito da soldato, perché faceva, a quel tempo, il servizio militare; anche Gino faceva il servizio militare, ed erano, lui e Adriano, nella stessa camerata. Adriano aveva allora la barba, una barba incolta e ricciuta, di un colore fulvo; aveva lunghi capelli biondo-fulvi, che s'arricciolavano sulla nuca, ed era grasso e pallido. La divisa militare gli cadeva male sulle spalle, che erano grasse e tonde; e non ho mai visto una persona, in panni grigio-verdi e con pistola alla cintola, più goffa e meno marziale di lui.[19]

> Among these friends was one called Adriano Olivetti. I remember the first time he came to the house in uniform, since he was doing his military service. So was Gino just then, and he and Adriano were in the same dormitory. Adriano at the time had a reddish beard which was unkempt and curly, and he had long, fair reddish hair which curled down his neck. He was pale and fat. His uniform fitted badly on his fat round shoulders and I have never seen anyone in grey-green uniform with a pistol at his belt who looked more goofy and less soldierly than he did.[20]

And it seems particularly fitting and funny that the 'very dry' Franco Rasetti, who is described as obsessed with bugs and minerals, should have a 'sharp nose,' 'a pointed chin,' a greenish lizard-like complexion, and a bristling porcupine-like moustache;[21] and notice how he plays with the crumbs on the tablecloth as he talks:

> Il nipote di Galeotti si chiamava Franco Rasetti. Studiava fisica: aveva però anche lui la mania di raccogliere insetti e minerali; e questa mania l'aveva attaccata a Gino. Tornavano dalle gite con zolle di muschio nel fazzoletto, scarabei morti e cristalli dentro al sacco da montagna. Franco Rasetti, a tavola, parlava incessantemente, ma sempre di fisica, o di geologia, o di coleotteri: e parlando tirava su col dito tutte le briciole sulla tovaglia.

> Aveva il naso puntuto e il mento aguzzo, un colorito sempre un po' verdognolo da lucertola, e baffetti spinosi. (*Lessico famigliare*, 54)

> Galeotti's nephew was called Franco Rasetti. He was a physics student and he too was mad on collecting insects and minerals. Gino caught this mania too. They returned from expeditions with clumps of moss in their handkerchiefs, dead beetles and crystals in their rucksacks. Franco talked incessantly at meals, and always about physics, geology, and beetles, and as he talked he gathered all the crumbs on the table-cloth with his finger. He had a sharp nose and a pointed chin and a rather lizard-like greenish complexion[22] and a bristling moustache. (*Family Sayings*, 45–6)

And the count Felice Balbo, who is later to become Ginzburg's best friend, is 'a little man' with 'a red nose':

> Fu così che io sentii parlare di Balbo per la prima volta. Era un conte, mi disse sul corso Umberto, piccolo, col naso rosso. Balbo doveva diventare tanti anni dopo, il mio migliore amico: ma io allora certo, non lo sapevo: e lo guardai senza nessun interesse, quel piccolo conte, che imprestava a Lisetta i libri di Croce. (*Lessico famigliare*, 134–5)

> That was how I first heard of Balbo. [Lisetta] told me that he was a count. She pointed him out to me one day on the Corso Re Umberto – a little man with a red nose. Balbo was to become my best friend years later. But of course I did not know that then and I did not look with any interest at the little count who lent Lisetta Croce's books. (*Family Sayings*, 110)

And Filippo Turati, alias Paolo Ferrari, the founder of Italian socialism, who takes refuge in the Levi household before fleeing Italy, is a big old bear of a man with little white hands:

> Ferrari [Turati] era vecchio, grande come un orso, e con la barba grigia, tagliata in tondo. Aveva il collo della camicia molto largo, e la cravatta legata come una corda. Aveva mani piccole e bianche; e sfogliava una raccolta delle poesie di Carducci, rilegata in rosso. (*Lessico famigliare*, 82)

> Ferrari was old, as huge as a bear, with a grey goatee beard. He had a very big collar size and a tie like a piece of string. He had small white hands, and he was leafing through a volume of Carducci's poems, bound in red. (*Family Sayings*, 68)

And finally there are no exceptions to the rule in Ginzburg's gallery of portraits. No one is spared – not even the anti-Fascist Leone Ginzburg, Natalia's first husband, who in 1943 dies tragically at the hands of the Germans in the Regina Coeli prison in Rome. Leone, described by the author's mother as a 'very cultivated, intelligent man, who does very fine translations from Russian,' is in the end reduced to being the 'ugly' Jew:

> 'Cos'ha da fare Mario con quel Ginzburg?' disse a mia madre ...
> 'È uno,' disse mia madre, 'coltissimo, intelligentissimo, che traduce dal russo e fa delle bellissime traduzioni.'
> 'Però,' disse mio padre, 'è molto brutto. Si sa, gli ebrei son tutti brutti.'
> 'E tu?' disse mia madre, 'tu non sei ebreo?'
> 'Difatti anch'io son brutto,' disse mio padre. (*Lessico famigliare*, 96)

> 'What has Mario got to do with Ginzburg?' he asked my mother ...
> 'He is a very cultivated, intelligent man, who does very fine translations from Russian.'
> 'But he is very ugly,' said my father. 'We know Jews are all ugly.'
> 'And what about you?' said my mother. 'Aren't you a Jew?'
> 'Well, yes, I am ugly too,' said my father. (*Family Sayings*, 79)

We may snicker at Professor Levi's definition of all Jews as ugly, but when we read later on of Leone's tragic death, we are overpowered by emotion. The contrast between the trivial, light-hearted description of Ginzburg's physical appearance and the profound tragedy of his death is devastating in its eloquence.

And so, all fall victim to Ginzburg's understated style; their greatness is taken for granted; their idiosyncrasies make them human, vulnerable; as a result, the pathos in *Family Sayings* is overwhelming.

The 1983 novel *The Manzoni Family* bears further witness to our author's style. The literary critic Giulio Nascimbeni is curious about Ginzburg's 'metodo riduttivo,' her use of understatement in this particular novel. In a newspaper interview with her, he asks why she chooses to underestimate, to minimize the great moments in Alessandro Manzoni's life. The interview appears with a heading that reads 'My Manzoni is knocked off his pedestal.'

> A pagina 29 del suo libro c'è un momento decisivo per la storia del

> Manzoni: la conversione avvenuta nella chiesa di San Rocco a Parigi il 2 aprile 1810. Il Manzoni aveva perso la moglie Enrichetta tra la folla, aveva provato un senso di vertigine, si era rifugiato in chiesa 'pregando con vera preghiera.' Eppure lei sembra propendere per la tesi di una crisi di nervi ... Anche altri grandi momenti come la composizione del '5 maggio' come l'inizio e la stesura dei *Promessi sposi*, passano nel suo libro inavvertiti. Che cosa l'ha indotta a questa scelta di metodo?
>
> On page 29 of your book there is a very important moment in Manzoni's life: his conversion which took place in San Rocco Church in Paris on April 2, 1810. Manzoni had lost his wife Enrichetta in the crowd, had felt dizzy, and had gone into the church and had 'prayed fervently.' And according to your theory, this was all due simply to an anxiety attack ... And other great moments (such as the composition of 'The Fifth of May,' and the beginning and the writing of *The Betrothed*) also pass unnoticed in your book. What led you to this choice of method?[23]

Ginzburg's straightforward answer to Nascimbeni's question explains her motivation; her purpose is clear:

> L'ho fatto intenzionalmente. Volevo raccontare la famiglia Manzoni, non lui. Dei *Promessi sposi* si parla molto ma mai nel cerchio della vita famigliare. Volevo vedere questo evento del grande romanzo proiettato sugli altri più che vissuto da lui ... Volevo che da questo libro [Manzoni] venisse fuori senza cipria, più vero. In genere lo si è sempre visto su un piedistallo: ho cercato di farlo scendere.
>
> I did it intentionally. I wanted to write about the Manzoni family, not about Manzoni. Much is said about *The Betrothed*, but never in the context of Manzoni's family life. I wanted to see the event of this great novel projected onto others rather than lived by him ... I wanted a Manzoni free of face powder, I wanted a truer Manzoni. Usually Manzoni is perched up on a pedestal. I tried to knock him off his pedestal.

And according to Ginzburg, Manzoni unmasked, off his pedestal, examined from up close, is never natural or genuine; he is a 'bad father' and, above all, 'a tremendous egoist.'

Another telling example of Ginzburg's style of portraiture is the depiction of Cesare Beccaria, author of *Of Crimes and Punishments* and Manzoni's maternal grandfather. The image of Cesare Beccaria as the 'enormously fat' grandfather who fetches a 'cioccolatino,' a little chocolate, hidden away in his drawer, is comical, almost embarassing in its effect; the character's great girth and his great literary fame are given equal weight by a somewhat amused Ginzburg:

> Prima di partire per Merate, Giulia lo portò a salutare il nonno, Cesare Beccaria; egli era diventato, con gli anni, enormemente grasso; Alessandro, che lo vedeva per la prima volta e non l'avrebbe riveduto mai, lo ricordò più tardi mentre si alzava dalla poltrona pesantemente per prendergli da un cassetto un cioccolatino. Non sembrava troppo contento di quella visita. Alessandro aveva allora sette anni.[24]

> Before setting off for Merate, she [Manzoni's mother] took him to see his grandfather, Cesare Beccaria, who with the years had become enormously fat; Alessandro, who was seeing him for the first time and would never see him again, later recalled him rising heavily from an armchair to get him a chocolate from a drawer. He did not seem too pleased at their visit. Alessandro was then seven.[25]

The first paragraph of *The Manzoni Family* is particularly eloquent and most indicative of Ginzburg's understated style. The passage which presents Manzoni's mother, Giulia Beccaria, and his grandparents, Cesare Beccaria and Teresa De Blasco, deftly weaves significant and insignificant details.[26] Equal emphasis is given to the great and the small:

> Giulia Beccaria aveva i capelli rossi e gli occhi verdi. Nacque a Milano nel 1762. Suo padre era Cesare Beccaria e sua madre Teresa De Blasco. Suo padre era di famiglia nobile, sua madre era figlia d'un colonnello. Il matrimonio era stato aspramente contrastato. I due avevano difficoltà di denaro, ma sempre vissero in maniera dispendiosa. Cesare Beccaria scrisse in età giovanissima un libro che gli diede gloria, *Dei delitti e delle pene*. Teresa era nera di capelli e gracile. Divenne amante d'un ricco, certo Calderara. (*La famiglia Manzoni*, 7)

> Giulia Beccaria had red hair and green eyes. She was born in Milan in 1702. Her father was Cesare Beccaria and her mother Teresa De Blasco: he belonged to the nobility, she was the daughter of a colonel. The marriage had met with bitter opposition. The couple had financial difficulties, but they always lived extravagantly. When he was very young, Cesare Beccaria wrote a book which brought him a certain fame, *Of Crimes and Punish-*

> *ments*. Teresa was a delicate woman with black hair. She became the mistress of a rich man called Calderara. (*The Manzoni Family*, 11)

In the same breath, Ginzburg describes Giulia Beccaria's red hair and green eyes, Teresa De Blasco's black hair and thinness, and Cesare Beccaria's great literary fame as author of *Of Crimes and Punishments*. She places historical data and petty gossip side by side, the public and the private on the same level; she gives equal attention to major events and minor details.

The secret of Natalia Ginzburg's art rests in her attention to detail, to the trivial and the minute – to that which may, at first glance, seem petty, negligible – and in her passionate love of the concrete. The literary critic Donald Heiney rightfully draws our attention to the deeply 'tragic' and complicated sense of life hidden beneath what appears to be a simple narrative style:

> The narrating consciousness takes refuge in a world of trivia, but the trivia are in some way elevated to the archetypal. Furniture, family quarrels, broken engagements, bicycles, the way of washing windows: the tiny details, massed together and linking one by one, begin finally to form vague metaphysical shapes. The dominant shape that emerges, subsuming and strengthening the others, is a recognition of the tragic sense of life, a pessimism relieved by good humour ... Things are simple on the surface and complicated underneath, and all the difficulty of art lies in this illusion.[27]

And, similarly, Italo Calvino states that the secret of Ginzburg's style lies in her use of 'a very limited number of tools to express that which is extremely complex.' Calvino compares poetry in general (and Natalia Ginzburg's art in particular) to 'the sea passing through a funnel.'

> Il segreto della semplicità di Natalia è qui: questa voce che dice 'io' ha sempre di fronte personaggi che stima superiori per le sue forze, e i mezzi linguistici e concettuali che essa usa per rappresentarli sono sempre un po' al di sotto delle esigenze. Ed è da questa sproporzione che nasce la tensione poetica. La poesia è sempre stata questa; far passare il mare in un imbuto; fissarsi uno strettissimo numero di mezzi espressivi e cercare di esprimere con quello qualcosa di estremamente complesso.

> This is the secret of Natalia's simplicity: the first-person narrator is always

> confronted with people whom she deems superior to her, and the tools which she possesses and which she uses to describe these people are always slightly below the mark, always inadequate. Poetic energy is born of this inequality, of this imbalance. Poetry has always been just that: having the sea pass through a funnel – allowing oneself a very limited number of tools and trying, with those meagre tools, to express something which is extremely complex.[28]

And so, Natalia Ginzburg's art is a struggle between great and small, significant and insignificant, useful and useless, in which the small, the insignificant, the useless win out. Our author's public image presents her as a less than perfect human being and a 'small, small writer.' Her writing produces no larger-than-life characters; no one and nothing is oversized in her eyes; the dimensions remain small. Her work promotes the 'little virtues' and neglects the great. In an essay entitled 'Collective Life' she chooses the useless over the useful:

> E' totalmente impossibile all'uomo stabilire cosa gli sia utile e cosa gli sia inutile ... Utile viene oggi decretata la scienza, la tecnica, la sociologia, la psicanalisi, la liberazione dai tabù del sesso ... Il resto è disprezzato come inutile. Nel resto però c'è un mondo di cose ... Fra esse c'è il giudizio morale individuale, la responsabilità individuale, il comportamento morale individuale. Tutto quello che costituisce la vita dell'individuo. (*Mai devi domandarmi*, 141–2)

> It is totally impossible for men to establish what is useful or useless to them ... Today what is considered useful is science, technology, sociology, psychoanalysis, freedom from sexual taboos ... Everything else is despised and considered useless. In what is deemed useless, however, there is a world of things ... Among these things are the moral judgment, responsibility, and behaviour of the individual. Among these things is the inevitability of death. Everything which makes up the life of an individual.

Natalia Ginzburg consequently turns the tide; she defies public opinion; she deliberately focuses away from what men today consider 'useful' and zeros in on the 'useless,' on the detail in her life and work. In conclusion, it is precisely her compassion for all that is considered 'useless,' her different focus, her modest and understated point of view, that sets her apart and defines Natalia Ginzburg's person and her art.

NOTES

1 Natalia Ginzburg, *Vita immaginaria* (Milano: Mondadori, 1974), 23–4. All further page references will appear in the text. The translation is mine.
2 Natalia Ginzburg won the Tempo Award for *È stato così* in 1947; the Veillon Award for *Tutti i nostri ieri* in 1952; the Viareggio Award for *Valentino* in 1957; the Strega Award for *Lessico famigliare* in 1963; and the Marzotto award for theatre for *L'inserzione*, which appears in *Ti ho sposato per allegria*, in 1969.
3 Natalia Ginzburg, *Le piccole virtù* (*The Little Virtues*). All further page references to *Le piccole virtù* and its translation will appear in the text.
4 See *The Little Virtues*, 69; *Mai devi domandarmi* (Milano: Garzanti, 1970), 91, 96. All further page references to *Mai devi domandarmi* will appear in the text. The translations are mine.
5 Ironically enough, Natalia Ginzburg participated in Italian political life in her later years. See *Mai devi domandarmi*, 151, and *Vita immaginaria*, 140, 144, 168.
6 Italian literary critics assume a tongue-in-cheek attitude toward Natalia Ginzburg's humble-pie stance. See Piero Dallamano, '*Mai devi domandarmi*,' *Paese sera*; M.C. Ottaviani, '*Le piccole virtù*,' *Paragone*; Piero De Tommaso, 'Elegia e ironia in Natalia Ginzburg,' *Belfagor*; Claudio Marabini, 'Riflessioni quotidiane,' *Resto del Carlino*; Pietro Citati, 'Il mondo di Natalia Ginzburg,' *Punto*; and Raffaello Baldini, 'Questo mondo non mi piace,' *Panorama*.
7 Natalia Ginzburg's self-deprecating attitude is typical of female writers. See Chapter VI in Patricia Meyer Spacks, *The Female Imagination*; Clotilde Soave Bowe, 'The Narrative Strategy of Natalia Ginzburg,' *Modern Language Review*; Luigi M. Personé, 'Natalia Ginzburg,' *Nuova antologia*.
8 Sylvia Plath, *The Bell Jar*, 84.
9 Spacks, *The Female Imagination*, 218.
10 Margaret Cavendish, Duchess of Newcastle, *The Life of William Cavendish, Duke of Newcastle, to which is added The True Relation of My Birth, Breeding and Life* (London, 1886), in Spacks, *The Female Imagination*, 193.
11 Spacks, *The Female Imagination*, 218.
12 Soave Bowe, 'The Narrative Strategy of Natalia Ginzburg,' 795.
13 Personé, 'Natalia Ginzburg,' 40.
14 *Vita immaginaria*, 190.
15 Natalia Ginzburg, *Cinque romanzi brevi*.
16 The following critics discuss Ginzburg's plain and simple literary style: Piero De Tommaso in *Altri scrittori e critici contemporanei*, 40; Lilia Crocenzi

in *Narratrici d'oggi*, 93; Antonio Russi in *Gli anni della anti-alienazione*, 135; Giorgio Pullini, '*Valentino*,' *Comunità*, 192; and Renzo Frattarolo, *Ritratti letterari ed altri studi*, 250.

17 Natalia Ginzburg, *Valentino*, 165–6. All further page references will appear in the text.

18 Natalia Ginzburg, *Valentino*, in *Valentino and Sagittarius*, translated by Avril Bardoni, 16–17. All further page references will appear in the text.

19 Natalia Ginzburg, *Lessico famigliare*, 72. All further page references will appear in the text.

20 Natalia Ginzburg, *Family Sayings*, translated by D.M. Low, 60. All further page references will appear in the text.

21 In Italian, the word D.M. Low translates as 'bristling' is *spinosi* or 'prickly,' which leads the reader to think perhaps of the 'spini,' or spines, of a porcupine.

22 See my article 'La simbologia animale nelle opere di Natalia Ginzburg,' *Quaderni d'italianistica*, which discusses the abundant use of animal imagery in our author's works.

23 Giulio Nascimbeni, 'Ginzburg: "Il mio Manzoni giù dal piedistallo?"' *Corriere della sera*. The translation is mine.

24 Natalia Ginzburg, *La famiglia Manzoni*, 10. All further page references will appear in the text.

25 Natalia Ginzburg, *The Manzoni Family*, translated by Marie Evans, 15. All further page references will appear in the text.

26 About the juxtaposition of significant and insignificant facts, see Crocenzi, *Narratrici d'oggi*, 95; Soave Bowe, 'The Narrative Strategy of Natalia Ginzburg,' 793; Luigi Pozzoli, 'Una società senza padre nella recente narrativa italiana,' 39; Pullini, '*Valentino*,' 92; Eurialo De Michelis, '*La strada che va in città*,' *Mercurio*, 134–5.

27 Donald Heiney, 'Natalia Ginzburg: The Fabric of Voices,' *Iowa Review*, 92.

28 Italo Calvino, 'Natalia Ginzburg o le possibilità del romanzo borghese,' *Europa letteraria*. The translation is mine.

REFERENCES

Baldini, Raffaello. 'Questo mondo non mi piace.' *Panorama*, 3 May 1973.

Calvino, Italo. 'Natalia Ginzburg o le possibilità del romanzo borghese.' *Europa letteraria* 2 (1961): 132–8.

Citati, Piero. 'Il mondo di Natalia Ginzburg.' *Punto*, 24 August 1957.

Crocenzi, Lilia. *Narratrici d'oggi*. Cremona: Mangiarotti, 1964.

Dallamano, Piero. '*Mai devi domandarmi*.' *Paese sera* (8 January 1971).

De Michelis, Eurialo, '*La strada che va in città.*' *Mercurio* 2 (1945): 134–5.
De Tommaso, Piero. 'Elegia e ironia in Natalia Ginzburg.' *Belfagor* 17 (1962): 101–4.
– *Altri scrittori e critici contemporanei.* Lanciano: Itinerari, 1970.
Frattarolo, Renzo. *Ritratti letterari ed altri studi.* Pisa: Casa Editrice Giardini, 1966.
Ginzburg, Natalia. *È stato così.* Torino: Einaudi, 1947.
– *Tutti i nostri ieri.* Torino: Einaudi, 1952.
– *Valentino.* Torino: Einaudi, 1957. Translated by Avril Bardoni under the title *Valentino and Sagittarius* (Manchester: Carcanet, 1987).
– *Le piccole virtù.* Torino: Einaudi, 1962. Translated by Dick Davis under the title *The Little Virtues* (New York: Carcanet, 1985).
– *Lessico famigliare.* Torino: Einaudi, 1963. Translated by D.M. Low under the title *Family Sayings* (Manchester: Carcanet, 1984).
– *Cinque romanzi brevi.* Torino: Einaudi, 1964.
– *Ti ho sposato per allegria.* Torino: Einaudi, 1968.
– *Mai devi domandarmi.* Milano: Garzanti, 1970.
– *Vita immaginaria.* Milano: Mondadori, 1974.
– *La famiglia Manzoni.* Torino: Einaudi, 1983. Translated by Marie Evans under the title *The Manzoni Family* (Manchester: Carcanet, 1987).
Heiney, Donald. 'Natalia Ginzburg: The Fabric of Voices.' *Iowa Review* 1 (1970): 92.
Marabini, Claudio. 'Riflessioni quotidiane.' *Resto del carlino*, 22 December 1970.
Meyer Spacks, Patrici. *The Female Imagination.* New York: Knopf, 1975.
Nascimbeni, Giulio. 'Ginzburg: "Il mio Manzoni giù dal piedistallo."' *Corriere della sera*, 5 February 1983.
Ottaviani, M.C. '*Le piccole virtù*' *Paragone* 13 (1965): 106–8.
Personé, Luigi M. 'Natalia Ginzburg.' *Nuova Antologia* 516 (1972): 539–61.
Plath, Sylvia. *The Bell Jar.* New York: Harper & Row, 1971.
Pozzoli, Luigi. 'Una società senza padre nella recente narrativa italiana.' *Famiglia* 9 (1971): 39.
Pullini, Giorgio. '*Valentino.*' *Comunità* 11 (1957): 192.
Russi, Antonio. *Gli anni della antialienazione.* Milano: Mursia, 1967.
Soave Bowe, Clotilde. 'The Narrative Strategy of Natalia Ginzburg.' *Modern Language Review* 68 (1973): 788–95.
Wienstein, Jen. 'La simbologia animale nelle opere di Natalia Ginzburg.' *Quaderni d'italianistica* 8, no. 2 (1987): 263–76.

Feminism and the 'Absurd' in Two Plays by Natalia Ginzburg

SERENA ANDERLINI-D'ONOFRIO

Introduction

Natalia Ginzburg wrote her first eight plays between 1964 and 1971 and published them in 1970 and 1973. These were years of transformation in Italian society, in the areas of education, labour, sexuality, and gender. The writer adopted the well-established convention of the theatre of the absurd and adapted it to her needs. The effort of writing these plays, and the plays themselves, place Ginzburg within the discourse of the Italian women's liberation movement and the two main issues around which it was organized: divorce and abortion (Birnbaum 1986). Ginzburg was too old to be a protagonist in the movement, and too established a literary figure not to take a position on it. In her plays, this position is expressed in the relationships between younger and older women; in her essays, by her responses to questions on women, feminism, and Judaism. The present article consists of three parts. The first is an outline of the Italian women's movement in the 1970s. The second is a textual reading of two plays whose female characters relate as women aware of the social changes brought by feminism: *Ti ho sposato per allegria* (*I Married You for Fun*, 1965) and *Fragola e panna* (1966) (this play is not translated; strawberry [*fragola*] and whipped cream [*panna*] are two favourite Italian ice cream flavours). The third is an account of Ginzburg's distant yet concerned observations of the feminist movement that took place in Italy during her later life. She was ambivalent towards and fascinated by it. Why? My intent is to combine literary, political, social, and psychological criticism to propose possible answers to this question.

Ginzburg Looks at Feminism in Italy

In this section I delineate the sociocultural landscape in which Ginzburg's work developed. She was a part-Jewish Italian woman, born of the kind of bi-racial marriage that was possible in Italy in the liberal climate of the turn of the century. She grew up in the period between World Wars I and II in an anti-Fascist, middle-class family of the left. She was well aware of being a woman writer because there were few of them in Italy at the time. The landscape in which she affirmed herself as a writer gradually transformed into the one in which she came in contact with the new feminism and the global women's movement of the 1970s. My intent is to delineate this transformation from a point of view closer to her own than to mine. This will clarify the reasons for her ambivalence towards, and fascination with, Italian feminism and the women's movement led by Italian women older than myself by about one decade. As a hybrid of two cultures by birth and education, Ginzburg positioned herself in a neutral space with respect to Italian feminism. From there she could support the two major claims that animated the movement – divorce and abortion – while reserving her right to critique feminism when it participated in the creation of cultural camps and contributed to the formation of univocal identities.

The vote of Italian women had its first impact on the national political scene when the Cold War order was already in place.[1] In Italy the Fascist era ended with the fall of Mussolini and the conclusion of World War II. In the West, as defined by the Cold War order, the counter-revolution had already taken back some of the advancements American and British women had obtained in the suffrage era.[2] The Italian Republic replaced the constitutional monarchy that had preceded the Fascist dictatorship. The Socialist and Communist parties, which had been suppressed by Fascism, participated in the writing of the Constitution and in the early governments.[3] This seemed a propitious moment for Italian women to obtain the franchise: ideologic pluralism had just been reinstituted, and the democratic system seemed to freshly grant political citizenship to both genders at the same time. But the women's vote was obtained through political negotiation rather than militancy.[4] It was part of a strategy designed to contain the country's tendency to override the boundaries established at Yalta, a tendency that might make it turn to the Soviet bloc. If it was true, as many Socialist, Communist, and democratic political leaders felt, that women were too afraid of the Catholic church to vote for the left, then their vote would support

Christian Democracy, the party of political Catholicism that was to become the most faithful supporter of the foreign policy of the White House.[5] The suffrage of Italian women can be seen as part of a larger strategy: a Cold War project in which Italy was a pawn positioned at an important junction between what the social order of the Cold War had designated as East and West. For this reason the victory is not one Italian women can simply call their own.

In the 1940s and until the rampant industrial development of the late '50s and '60s, the extended family was a widespread structure of kinship, at least in central Italy (Barbagli 1984, 108–28; Donati 1981, 44–8).[6] Even though women's economic power was increasing owing to industrialization, their juridic power was very limited (Birnbaum 1986, 89–90, 140, 200; Ravera 1978, 243–57).[7] Family and kinship structures were rapidly transforming, but large female homosocial spaces still existed in them, and women had considerable economic control.

The economic expansion of the 1960s, and the attendant urbanization of large rural masses, broke the traditional family clans into smaller nuclear units. The social consciousness that there was a need to control birth rates moved from a privileged middle class to a wider social group which included large sections of the working class as well (Donati 1981, 59–78).[8] Marriages became less stable owing to the deterritorialization of families between rural and urban areas. In the cities, families had starkly reduced female homosocial spaces where adult women could work together because formerly extended families became nuclearized. While this transformation was happening, the media and the new political climate turned the cultural arena constituted by this putatively sovereign country into a market where cultural products from the English-speaking world were voraciously consumed. They were chiefly music, films, and radio and television programs from Britain and the United States.[9] Owing to what was perceived to be, and in a large measure was, a liberalizing influence, the code of morality changed dramatically. Young women claimed their right to experiment with sexuality, explore erotic pleasure before marriage, and satisfy their sexual appetites with men they accepted as sexual partners.[10]

The system was not prepared to manage this transformation. The judiciary legacy of Fascism was a code that designated any action intending to prevent procreation as a crime (Birnbaum 1986, 37; Ravera 1978, 277; Tedesco 1981, 2).[11] Even though the sale of contraceptives was against the law, birth-control pills circulated widely since pro–birth control physicians prescribed them as remedies against migraine (Lantin

1975, 15).[12] Abortion was considered a crime against the race. The only way to untie a bond of marriage was through the Byzantine mechanism of Vatican annulment.[13]

In the Cold War era, Italy was positioned 'at the periphery' of what the Reaganite mythology was to construct as 'the good empire.' It was the cultural landscape at the centre of Ginzburg's thoughts, even though her cultural agency affected a larger, international arena. The women who lived and worked in Italy acquired a sense of their power when the ideology of the counterrevolution was gradually giving way to the impulses of the civil rights era. At this time, and not in the prior era of suffrage, the coordinates of the system that regulated sexual, reproductive, parental, and filial rights were being established. In the 1970s, most progressives and liberals gravitated toward the socialist and communist left. Like Ginzburg, they became advocates of women's rights, helping to pass a timid set of regulations granting limited divorce and reproduction rights (in 1970 and 1978 respectively).

Many male political leaders of the left had been slow in taking up the divorce issue and disagreed with feminist leaders who advocated women's complete control of their reproductive systems. But by and large, the political parties of the left sided with the feminist rank and file to defend the newly acquired rights of divorce and abortion. For two times in a row, the political arena polarized around issues in which the women's movement had invested itself. The results of the referendum on divorce (1974) demonstrated that, as electors and participants in the democratic process, women had a will of their own which could not be manipulated by international or parochial interests. The referendum on abortion (1981) demonstrated that the country was with them. After 1981, the law was no longer threatened by the local 'pro life movement' ('movimento per la vita').[14] In one decade the women who had participated in the Italian feminist movement in one way or another had moved the culture from a preindustrial to a postmodern view of what constitutes family. The first was based on the institution of the extended family in which patriarchal authority was undisputed. The second was a porous structure in which new aggregations formed from what remained of a disintegrating nuclear unit. It was understandable that, for a while, they felt they had the destiny of the country in their hands.

When all these momentous events were happening, Natalia Ginzburg (1916–1992) was in her late fifties and early sixties. Since the end of Fascism, she had exerted a considerable political influence with her writing, even though she was born long before Italian women became political citizens. A widow whose first husband had been killed during the fascist regime, she had been married twice even though divorce was not available.[15] She had neither identified herself as a Jewish writer nor denied her heritage, even though she had used a gentile-sounding pseudonym, Alessandra Tornimparte (rather than her maiden name Levi), to safely publish her first work during the Fascist regime (Marchionne Picchione 1978, 28). Her success had been possible even though her first husband was a Jew like her father, not a 'gentile' like her mother, and even though she had lost him to racial and political persecution (Clementelli 1972, 5–40). Most important, this success happened even though she was a mother of four who had established herself without the help and support of an ongoing women's movement. Some of the female militants and activists of the new women's movement had been born after World War II. They had not been tried by the kind of dictatorship owing to which Leone Ginzburg died (Passerini 1991, 140).[16] Wouldn't it be understandable, even desirable, for a person in her position to feel a certain distance from, perhaps a sense of senior superiority to, the younger women and the enthusiasm with which they approached current issues?

Femminismo was part of a large international movement. But it also had its specific character. A large popular base participated in the mobilizations for the new laws. The momentum produced wide female homosocial spaces in which women who felt part of the movement interacted. Because of its natural and cultural attractiveness, the Italian peninsula was a favourite site of invasions and colonizations from abroad, not least of which is the postmodern tourist industry. In the culture based in this peninsula, the definition of the self was porous and open to the various forms of exogamic hybridization that repeated contacts with outsiders made possible over the centuries (Bono and Kemp 1991, 12–14; Passerini 1991, 161–3).[17] Sexual preference was understood as a personal choice that could be explained by the modern science of psychoanalysis. But the country's history and popular mythology on the subject of erotic expression indicated that love between persons of the same sex, far from having been invented or discovered in the modern era, had been around much longer, and lived through various persecutions in one form or another. It was not easy to persuade a public equipped with this knowledge and sense of the past that psychoanalysis could cure the forms of erotic expression that modernity regarded as perverse. And it was unlikely that this public would be persuaded that desire, in its infinite forms of expression, could be heterosexualized. The sense of national identity was permeable. Fascism had taught the lesson that xenophobia was at best self-destructive. Respect for what was foreign grew to the point of xenophilia. Love for what came from the cultures that were centres of power in the Cold War order compensated for the nationalism that the new democracy had put in the past. The new sense of national identity was based on the concept of resistance, the ability of the self to define itself against external forces by holding a chosen position in self-defence, but without engaging in direct aggression. It was based in the identity constructed by the celebration of the subterranean movements of resistance to Fascism that had been instrumental in helping the Allied forces defeat the regime at the end of World War II (Wilkinson 1981; Ravera 1978). As both a woman and a writer, Ginzburg had found a home and a space in the landscape that put Fascism in the past. When feminism appeared in this landscape she resisted it. One simple reason is that she did not feel part of it. Another less apparent reason is that a women's movement from which she felt excluded threatened her sense of herself as a woman and a writer. What kind of force was this movement going to bring into the cultural landscape? Was it going to remain porous and transformative, or was it going to become stilted and dogmatic? These are questions that a woman like Ginzburg could ask because she was part of Italian feminism despite herself, even though she had no major investments in it.

The Figure of Two-in-One in the Family

For the following textual readings, I use categories I have developed from reading other plays by women, such as the realistic American plays by women of the suffrage era; they also adopted established conventions and adapted them to their needs.[18] These categories are: (1) the dual female protagonist; (2) the figure of two-in-one that this duo constitutes; (3) the labial symbolism of this figure and the structure of labial mimesis; (4) the nuclear, extended, and disintegrating family structures in which the duos live; and (5) the 'straight' and 'queer' codes of reading according to which the plays' meanings can be produced.

The dual protagonist or female duo is a pair of adult female persons usually not related by kinship. In numerous plays by women, it replaces the conventional male hero at the centre of the dramatic structure. The figure of two-in-one is the symbolism that this dual protagonist configures: the dual protagonist is one and two, like the two labia that form the external part of a woman's genitals. The labial mimesis is the new relationship between experience and what is intelligible according to this new mode of ordering experience. The nuclear, extended, and disintegrating families are the transforming structures of kinship in which the relationships of the two characters in the duo take place. The 'straight' and 'queer' code of reading are complementary sets of assumptions that give access to the plays' possible meanings. The first presumes that heterosexuality is natural and therefore things are as they appear to be. The second presumes that a variety of sexual and erotic experiences are natural, while heterosexuality is the only one representable and legitimate. Therefore things are quite different from what they appear to be. Both codes are necessary to understand the plays of Natalia Ginzburg. They construct a virtually bisexual female reader/viewer who is aware of, and attracted to, the variety of possibilities that the queer code opens to view. But she is trapped in a system in which divorce is not possible and abortion is illegal.

In most plays by Natalia Ginzburg, dual female protagonists are situated in social circles that gather around extended families in the process of dissolution. These social formations are realistic of the plays' period in central Italy. A belated industrial revolution has grafted on a prevailing extended-family structure, which was already dysfunctional, obsolete, and drained by emigration. The nuclear model exists but, at least in the internal landscape of its participants, it has never supplanted the extended model. The result is a disjointed extended family with various internal nuclear groups and with related and unrelated single individuals who function as adjunct and produce a certain instability in the couples that form the nuclear units (Donati 1981).[19] The two elements of the labial figure are women with a disparity of either class or generation. In *Ti ho sposato per allegria*, Giuliana is the wife of a young, middle-class professional; Vittoria is her maid and housekeeper. In *Fragola e panna*, Barbara is the teenage mistress and Flaminia the aging wife of an established middle-class businessman, Cesare.

The dramatic structure positions the two female characters at a distance. But the narrative brings them close to each other and makes them emotionally intimate. In the 'straight' and in the 'queer' codes this transgression has different meanings. To a 'straight' viewer, the closeness of the two women appears to be a dramatic device to develop a critique of social manners. It causes the two women to speak to each other about the society in which they live in narrative scenes that construct the events prior to the drama, giving the female characters a diachronic dimension the male characters do not have. Presenting the past from the women's point of view adds to the plays the dimension of social satire in which the women's speech exposes society's hypocrisy and formalism.

This focus on friendship between women reflects the developing sense of equality that can be attributed to the growth of the women's movement. But the social order constructs women as good talkers and bad doers precisely because they are seen as human beings devoid of autonomous eros. The 'queer' code presupposes that they might have a Sapphic or homoerotic secret. If their transgressive closeness is an indication that there is such a secret, the dysfunctional families that host the duos might be the safest closets in which to hide it. The sum of the two codes produces the meaning that the strength of the women's movement is connected in some uncanny way to the possibility of this secret. This hypothesis is reflected in Ginzburg's social commentaries on feminism, women, and Judaism.

Marriage: Who Has 'Fun' with It?

Pietro is at the centre of the kinship structure represented in *Ti ho sposato per allegria.*[20] His mother, his sister Ginestra, his wife Giuliana, and his maid Vittoria are linked to him. The structure does not provide a space for direct communication between women. The culture constructs the mother-in-law, *suocera,* as an enemy of the daughter-in-law, *nuora.* The latter tends to emancipate the son from his dependency on his mother's care, services, and cuisine, enabling him to make independent decisions which might contrast with his parents' views (Barbagli 1984, 506–10). Pietro's mother is a widow. Since the father is absent, she expects special attention from her son, at least until the process of mourning the loss of her husband is complete. But Pietro has married a woman of a class considered significantly inferior. His marriage is exogamic, which is against his parents' views. His mother resents it. She perceives it as a threat to her efforts to keep all the members of the extended family securely in the class that has been conferred to it by her deceased husband.

Ginestra's role in the family is to protect the health of the only parent that Pietro and she have. Their mother claims that her grief over her son's marriage has caused her to fall ill. Pietro's young wife Giuliana is a destitute. She is the reason for the mother's illness. Ginestra implicitly blames her sister-in-law for having to provide extra free-of-charge services to the family. Finally, Giuliana and the housekeeper Vittoria are originally from the same class. They could become friends. But in the social order in which this kinship structure is situated, this would further advance the effect of social degradation that Pietro's exogamous marriage has produced. Therefore, it would also ultimately threaten the livelihood of the housekeeper the family employs.

Pietro and Giuliana's motivations for marrying each other are very different. Pietro is a version of the anti-hero of existentialist and absurdist theatre.[21] He is the scion of an upper-class family whose financial stability is based on both land and money. His mother and sister relate to him as a phallic symbol. Afflicted with existential anxiety, he assuaged it by marrying an adventurous girl of the working class. She was raised by her mother while her father lived with his mistress, with whom he had illegitimate children (19). Giuliana has married Pietro because – or at least from her own admission 'also' because – she was desperate for status. She is quite open about this with him: 'Ero disposta a sposare chiunque, hai capito, quando ti ho incontrato ... così ti ho sposato. Anche per i soldi. Hai capito?' ('When I met you I was ready to marry anybody. Do you understand it? ... So I married you. Also for the money. Did you get it?' [39]).[22] Later she confirms 'è vero che ti ho sposato per i soldi. Anche per i soldi' ('It is true that I married you for the money. Also for the money' [39]). Since their motivations for marrying were unconventional, it makes sense that their wedding was private and nonreligious. Pietro's mother, being a practising Catholic, was not invited (69). She is on the brink of a nervous breakdown over the whole thing when she decides that it is time to meet her daughter-in-law. Her own daughter Ginestra knows that at this time being in charge of her mother's nerves might be particularly difficult. In Pietro and Giuliana's new home, Giuliana and Vittoria have become friends, even though Giuliana is not expected to befriend this 'social inferior' (17–31). This puzzles Pietro, who anticipated that Giuliana would patronize Vittoria, and be somewhat aloof from her as his mother was with her own maids.

In the narrative scenes that tell the past from the point of view of the women, Giuliana steals the centrality of the phallic symbol away from the anti-hero. She replaces him as a central figure. Vittoria comes to clean, and instead spends hours listening to Giuliana's stories about her life before she met Pietro. As she points out, 'Mi tiene qui a discorrere, e io poi mi trovo indietro' ('You keep me here to chatter, and then I fall behind in my work' [18]). But it takes her little pressure to become Giuliana's confidante. Before Pietro, Giuliana had a lover, Manolo. She lived in his apartment. He was married to Topazia, a photographer who visited occasionally. He claimed that Topazia had style and he loved her, but she had left him. He could not divorce her to marry Giuliana because the Italian law on divorce did not yet exist.[23] He kept telling Giuliana that 'non mi amava' ('he did not love me') because 'non avevo nessuno stile' ('I had no style' [23]). With this excuse, he eventually made her pregnant and left. Vittoria is mesmerized by Giuliana's stories about premarital sex, something a married woman is not expected to share with her maid.

Not knowing where to go or what to do, Giuliana remained alone in Manolo's apartment. But her story continues as she tells Vittoria of how she became friends with Manolo's ex-wife. Topazia visited the apartment and found Giuliana instead of him. She did not appear as stylish as Manolo claimed, so Giuliana lost her shyness and opened up to her. She told Topazia of how he used to make her feel ugly and undesirable with his complaints that she 'had no style' and he 'could not love her.' Topazia replied that he used to tell her exactly the same thing! On realizing this, the two women laughed from relief, and immediately became friends. Topazia explained that she no longer blamed Manolo, having come to the conclusion that he was 'un uomo che non gli vanno tanto bene le donne' ('a man who did not really like women' [27]). Then Giuliana proceeded to talk about the baby she was expecting. Topazia said that she would help her raise it, for she could not have children of her own. But, on reflection, Giuliana decided to get rid of it. Topazia took her to a doctor who practised abortion illegally and was successful in helping her. This episode was followed by a period of bittersweet happiness for the two women. They spent a lot of time together, experimenting with a homosocial friendship and freedom that in Italian culture is typical of men's youth and is often denied to women (27–8).

Through this friendship with a woman, Giuliana gathered a lot of self-confidence. She exercised her right not to choose reproduction against a system that denied this choice, and without substantially damaging her health. At this time, happy and looking towards the future, she had met Pietro at a party. The two had married shortly after, the reason simply being that it was 'fun' to do it. Vittoria is proud of her class and of supporting herself with her own salary. Nonetheless, she is drawn to this former social equal, who, by virtue of her friendship with the (ex)-wife of her former lover, seems to have risen to such a secure position, and in such a short time! Giuliana takes the risk of presenting herself to Vittoria as a woman who has married above her class after having aborted a pregnancy from another man. She earns the respect of this social inferior precisely because she is honest with her.

When they find out that Pietro's mother is coming, Vittoria and Giuliana arrange for a *pranzo*, an abundant Italian midday meal. During the meal, the mother reverses her attitude towards Giuliana: when she arrives she calls Giuliana 'signorina,' a title meaning 'miss,' by which the mother denies the fact that Giuliana is married to her son (53). But in the course of the meal, Giuliana becomes 'figlia mia,' a phrase that means 'my (female) child,' by which the mother acknowledges that Giuliana is now part of the family (61). Pietro's mother also offers advice on who might be the best people for Giuliana to have as female friends, and proposes to commission a coat for Giuliana hand-knitted by the mother's best friend, Virginia (61). Despite the continuing disapproval of the mother for the lay wedding and for the informal way in which Giuliana treats Vittoria, this *pranzo* is a success for the alliance of Giuliana and Vittoria. It stabilizes the entrance of Giuliana into the extended family of her husband, the source of economic stability for both Vittoria and Giuliana.

When the mother leaves, Pietro asks for his hat to recapture Giuliana's attention. Vittoria is out. Giuliana cannot find the hat. He is in a hurry and leaves. So the play closes on Giuliana at the centre of the frame of representation, and Pietro rushing out of the picture. In the 'straight' code, the play appears to be primarily a social satire. But the focus on the homosocial interaction of Giuliana and Vittoria is starkly significant. For a phallic symbol, Pietro is a nice fellow. He is also a good provider and does not seem to mind his financial responsibilities. He likes to surround himself with women. But he has a hard time keeping them away from each other. The women's interactions with each other are more interesting than his interactions with them. Consequently, the focus of the narrative shifts towards them.

Pietro is not a hero in the traditional sense. But he takes his centrality for granted since he has the phallus. Ginzburg adapts the convention of the absurd to push him to the margin of the picture. He is primarily concerned with assuaging his existential anxiety and sometimes comes across a bit presumptuous and ridiculous. As the narrative progresses, slowly but surely Giuliana moves from the margin to the central place that Pietro occupied in the beginning. Her 'preference' for women is so interesting that it causes the narrative to focus on her interactions with female allies and peers. He might have married Giuliana because he thinks that lower-class girls are cheerful and it is fun to have them around. But who is having fun in this marriage? The female duo of Giuliana and Vittoria inhabit a disjointed nuclear unit part of an extended family. The 'straight' female viewer sees Giuliana enter the family picture through her solidarity with Vittoria. But the queer female viewer notices that their friendship is a bit 'queer.' She imagines the secret that they might be lovers. If this is possible, Pietro's family is indeed the best closet in which to hide their well-kept secret.

The Mistress, the Wife, and the 'Hero'

The dual female protagonist in *Fragola e panna* is different from the one in *Ti ho sposato per allegria* in composition, presentation, and behaviour. Even though the two women belong to different social classes, emphasis is on their age difference.[24] Giuliana and Vittoria are of the same age, but Flaminia is old enough to be Barbara's mother. This emphasis constructs the 'queer' reading of their emotional intimacy as virtually incestuous and more transgressive than in the former duo. In *Allegria*, Giuliana tells Vittoria of how she became emotionally intimate with Topazia, the (ex)-wife of her former lover. We do not directly meet Topazia. But Barbara and Flaminia are lovers of the same man, Cesare. The interaction which produces their emotional intimacy happens in the drama's present, not in the past that leads to it. Giuliana and Vittoria become best friends and stay together. Flaminia and Barbara learn from each other like a mentor and, to coin a new word, a 'mentee.' Then they part ways like a mother and a daughter who comes to adulthood. Sharing the experience of being in love with Cesare produces their ability to trust women and learn from them.

Cesare is the anti-hero. Like Manolo, he cannot marry Barbara because there is no divorce in Italy. But he presents himself to her as a liberal. Neither does he expect fidelity from his wife, nor she from him. In fact, he claims that she is happy to be his confidante, something that both 'queer' and 'straight' female readers seriously doubt as the play develops. Like Pietro, he is pushed towards the frame of representation by the bond established between two women to whom he is emotionally related. His wife Flaminia is financially secure and in her fifties. His mistress Barbara is poor and eighteen. Unlike Pietro, Cesare is physically absent from the beginning. But until they meet and discuss him, he is all too present in the women's imagination. The play focuses on their first encounter which happens in a female homosocial space at Flaminia's house, in the presence of Flaminia's maid Tosca and her sister Letizia. The two female lovers of the anti-hero become confidantes. Their emotional intimacy is the content that has different meanings in the 'queer' and in the 'straight' codes. Its sexual ambiguity is the measure of the abuse that Barbara has suffered from Cesare. Ginzburg has removed it from the past, and put it in the present. Cesare's irresponsibility is similar to Manolo's, but we can compare it with Flaminia's honesty. She acts as a maternal teacher towards Barbara, and this younger 'social inferior' responds by acting as a filial student.

Barbara gives her own account of how she met Cesare. She was attracted by his affluence and professional success. Raised by her grandmother, Barbara married a man as young and poor as herself, and she has a baby. As she explains to Flaminia, after meeting Cesare, 'mio marito adesso sembrava piccolo, stupido. E la mia casa mi sembrava piccola, brutta, sporca.' ['my husband started to look little, stupid ... my house looked small, ugly, dirty' [137]). Cesare's success and affluence are things that Barbara cannot obtain with her own means on two counts: she is a working-class female with no professional training, and she is a very young mother. When Barbara visits Flaminia and Cesare's house, Cesare is out of town. But Flaminia is afraid to have Barbara near her and in her house (136; 141). Is this a homophobic response to a deep-seated desire to replace Cesare in Barbara's life? Or is it the fear of a woman approaching the end of her fertile age: if she were to express affection for Barbara in a physical manner, would this young woman reject her, as sometimes daughters do to their mothers? Or is it both?

The bond Barbara and Flaminia develop in the course of the play composes the figure of two-in-one in a dialogue between a maternal and a filial voice. It does not produce a stable and physical proximity between the two women. But it enables both mentor and mentee to learn from each other's experience and thereby face their respective situations more realistically. This happens despite the class and age difference between the two. By speaking to each other, these two elements of the labial figure discover they can love each other independently of their relationship with Cesare. Tosca, another ubiquitous housekeeper like Vittoria, and Letizia, Flaminia's sister who is visiting, stand by the formation of this homosocial bond, and almost pander to it with their support. They quietly understand the predicament of the dual protagonist.

Cesare is a successful professional in a midlife crisis. He is seeking to rejuvenate himself with a younger lover. In the 'straight' code, his bravado is his lack of commitment to his lover. In the 'queer' code, it might be his fantasy to share his young lover with Flaminia. When Barbara is out to see Cesare, her mother-in-law babysits. This has put Barbara in an impossible situation with her own family. Her relationship with Cesare has almost succeeded in driving her to suicide, as Oedipus' did with Jocasta, and Hamlet's with Ophelia. But Jocasta did not have another woman in the plot to go see. Ophelia had Hamlet's mother Gertrude, but killed herself before she thought of it. Barbara does not kill herself. The culture that constructs women's monogamy as natural presents Flaminia as her rival. But instructed by Cesare that his wife is his confidante, Barbara visits her. Perhaps Flaminia is a traitor of other women, like Mme De Merteuil, Valmont's lover in *Les liaisons dangereuses,* who uses her bisexual seductiveness to attract women and then turns them over to her husband (Hampton 1988). But Barbara wants to give it a try. As it turns out, Flaminia does not seduce the girl away from her husband. Instead, she takes this younger woman under her wing. 'Ho l'idea che sia stanco di te,' Flaminia cautions Barbara, 'E allora, quando lui è stanco di una donna, taglia la corda, va a Parigi, va a Londra, si tiene lontano più tempo che puó' (I've got the idea that he is tired of you.' 'And then, when he is tired of a woman, he beats it, he goes to Paris, London; he keeps away as long as he can' ([141]).

Barbara explains that since her husband has found out about her lover, he has been crushed. This working man felt 'so little' in the face of her affluent and well-educated lover. He sensed her disaffection from her own family, and started to beat her up out of an impotent rage. She had to leave. Where else could she go, Barbara asks? She declares that given the fact that Flaminia is not taking responsibility for her, 'allora io posso anche buttarmi nel Tevere?' ('I may as well jump in the river Tiber' [142]). Her threat to commit suicide provokes Flaminia. She advises Barbara there are better reasons to live than her own husband Cesare. 'Io non ho avuto bambini, ma se ne avessi avuti, non li avrei lasciati. Piuttosto mi sarei fatta ammazzare' ('I have not had any children, but if I had, I would not have left them. I would rather have been killed' [142]). Flaminia will not allow Barbara to stay for the night, but she gives her some money. Tosca feeds her, and Letizia offers to drive her to a nuns' convent, where she can be safe from both Cesare and her own husband (143–6).

The three older women offer Barbara momentary relief. They cannot change the course of her life, but their interaction ends with a reversal of power between the two generations. The motherly protection that Flaminia and the two other women have bestowed on Barbara helps her to see Cesare in a different light. Now Flaminia begs compassion from a younger person who can still look ahead to a full life. 'Aspetto Cesare, quando viene lo ascolto raccontarmi le sue storie con le ragazze. La chiami una vita allegra? No. È una vita schifosa' ('I wait for Cesare, when he comes I listen to his stories with girls. Do you call this a cheerful life? No. It's a revolting life' [142]). Perhaps the knowledge that there is nothing to envy in Flaminia's life will help Barbara to find the strength to stay alive.

When Cesare returns, the now-absent girl is on the women's minds. A reader who takes divorce for granted expects Flaminia to divorce Cesare. But what is realistic in societies that admit divorce is not yet an option for Flaminia. It is clear that, of the two spouses, she is the one who would have the courage to file for divorce, if there were such a thing. She is empowered by Barbara's trust in her. The manner in which she confronts Cesare is realistic for the social order in which she lives. What makes him think that he has the right to dispose of his wife, look for new flames young enough to be her daughters, and then abandon them with the expectation that she will pick them up? She quits being his confidante because she envies Barbara, not him. 'Io non sono né nobile, né buona. Non ho cuore. Mi sento il cuore secco, piccolo piccolo, una piccola prugna secca ... Sono ferocemente gelosa di lei. Ma non per amor tuo. Sono gelosa nel modo più vile. È una gelosia fatta di invidia, di vergogna, di mortificazione' ('I am neither noble nor good-natured. I have no heart. My heart feels dry, small, a little dry prune ... I am ferociously jealous of her. But not because I love you. I am jealous in the vilest way. My jealousy is made of envy, shame, mortification' [153]).

Flaminia's ability to love has been crushed by a system that uses wives as disposable objects of sexual attention who cannot dispose of their husbands because they cannot divorce them. Barbara has shaken Flaminia out of her inability to feel. Now she is capable of speaking for herself. 'Chissà cosa vede in te, e io invece so quello che sei. Sei niente. Un uomo da niente. E io non ti amo più. Non ti voglio più nemmeno un po' di bene' ('Who knows what she sees in you, but I know what you are. You are nothing. A worthless man. And I don't love you any more. I don't even have the slightest affection for you left' [153]).

A phone call announces that Barbara has escaped from the convent. She is at the hairdresser's where Tosca's daughter works. She is having her hair done with the coupon Tosca gave her. Everyone is relieved at this news, including Cesare. Barbara has not jumped in the river Tiber. She has followed Flaminia's advice to keep going on with her own life. Perhaps Flaminia's frankness instilled a sense of hope in Barbara that helped her get through a difficult moment. Flaminia has succeeded where others failed because she has shared with Barbara the experience of having Cesare in her life. Barbara can trust her because their mutual preference is established.

The meaning of the emotional intimacy of Barbara and Flaminia is both 'straight' and 'queer.' The straight meaning points to the conventional rivalry between wife and mistress, which is shattered by the unusual friendship between the two elements of the dual protagonist. The queer meaning suggests that the desire for a younger lover is a desire to reach back to a lost, imaginary, or inner child men only are allowed to express in Italian society. But the figure of two-in-one formed by a maternal mentor, Flaminia, and a filial mentee, Barbara, is also a figure of one-in-two. Flaminia neither can seduce Barbara nor keep her near herself. Cesare, however, cannot undo the bond the two women have established.

Both women inhabit a system that makes divorce impossible. The play measures its power to keep them tied to their husbands. The phallic symbol is not allowed to separate the two parts of the figure of two-in-one and dominate them by playing both ends against the middle. The married couple Ginzburg presents is one in which the wife is readier than the husband to admit that her marriage has failed and to give it up. In just one day, with words alone, Flaminia has established a bond with another human being stronger than the one Cesare had been able to develop with her in months. But the system that ties her to her husband functions like a nationwide kinship structure that stops this bond from being fully expressed in a love relationship.

Ginzburg Responds to Feminism

On a simple level, one might say that Ginzburg felt ambivalent towards feminism because it threatened the sense of themselves Italian women of her generation had. By the same token, she was fascinated by it because it provided a space in which her desire to write about the younger women who participated in it could be expressed. It was too late for her to personally benefit from either divorce or abortion. But she supported both, even though she probably did not approve of all the divorces and abortions that the new laws allowed. Her reservations were mainly on how feminism constructed identity and on how it denied its erotic subtext. Interpellated, she replied with a certain coldness, but declared an almost unreserved support for the rights women were advocating: 'Non amo il femminismo. Condivido però tutto quello che chiedono i movimenti femminili. Condivido tutte o quasi tutte le loro richieste pratiche' ('I don't love feminism. But I share everything women's movements ask. I share all, or almost all their practical demands' [1974, 182]).

In her view, people who are culturally similar can create forces of social transformation when they unite to achieve certain goals. However, women do not appear to be such a group because what they have in common is natural – their 'gender' is a series of physical characteristics from which no social transformation can be generated. Advocating her position further, Ginzburg compared gender difference with class difference. She explained that while the meaning of the international socialist motto 'proletari di tutto il mondo unitevi' ('proletarians of the entire world unite' [182]) was very clear to her, the parallel international feminist motto 'donne di tutto il mondo unitevi' ('women of the entire world unite' [182]) rang false. As opposed to distinctions of caste, class distinctions are based on axioms that construct individuals as capable of moving from class to class. Class and gender are different types of categories as long as persons cannot change gender in their lifetime. But postmodern surgical technologies allow individuals to move from gender to gender, thus transforming gender into a distinction based on the transformative concept of class, rather than the more conservative concept of caste. Ginzburg could see that what all women have in common is 'natural.' But she was not aware of the possibility that a natural difference can become cultural. By not seeing this possibility, she placed herself inside and outside feminism. She functioned as a mediator between the women who resisted it and those who invested in it.

While she proceeded to suggest the origins of *femminismo* lay in an age-old 'inferiority complex' (183) of Italian women, she also declared 'una cosa sicura è che non esiste fra uomini e donne una differenza qualitativa' ('it is certain that there is no qualitative difference between men and women' [189]). One might assume that in her mind this complex made Italian women emotionally dependent on Italian men. Acculturated in a system that presented male models, these women did not have much to look at to find sources of encouragement and validation, and the sense of inferiority operated in their consciousness. Even though she placed herself above the complex, Ginzburg did not offer much advice on how younger women who did not have her experience of success could acquire the self-confidence she had. In fact, she even seemed to assume that some women should not acquire it, since they did not have 'una vocazione irrevocabile e precisa' ('a precise and irrevocable inner calling' [189]).

In an essay on Jews ('Gli ebrei,' 1974, 174–81), she admitted that when she met another Jewish person she felt a 'secret complicity.' This is an affinity that produces a common effort to survive. It has an erotic subtext inasmuch as it denotes a desire to live through those who are like us. But Ginzburg regarded herself, and was, a hybrid by nature and culture. As both Jewish and gentile, she claimed to resist the secret complicity she felt, as she resisted younger feminists and the attraction they exerted on her. She positioned herself with respect to the people who felt that Holocaust survivors had a right to a promised land, no matter what cost other people would have to pay. In their eyes, a large part of the aggressiveness of Israel against Palestinians was justified. She indirectly attacked them by exposing the feelings she attributed to the Jewish part of herself and then repudiating them as 'un'idea mostruosa' ('a monstrous idea' [180]). As she explained, 'a volte ho pensato che gli ebrei di Israele avevano diritti e superiorità sugli altri essendo sopravvissuti a uno sterminio' ('sometimes I've thought that the Jews of Israel have rights of superiority over others, being survivors of a holocaust' [179–80]). In her mind, this idea initially seemed far less 'monstrous' than the 'final solution' to the deterritorialization of the Jewish people proposed by the Nazis. However, on thinking again, she felt that it was 'un errore' ('an error' [180]). To conclude this excursion in the thought of a constructed univocal Jewish identity, she recuperated her position of neutrality by affirming that 'Il dolore e le stragi di innocenti ... non ci danno ... nessuna specie di superiorità' ('grief and the massacre of innocents ... do not give us ... any kind of superiority' [180]). Thereby, she positioned herself as both insider and outsider of the Jewish community, the referent of that 'us,' and the people for whom she wanted to model a position of fairness and neutrality with respect to the rights of Palestinians.

In her childhood, she had learned to fend off questions about her mixed racial heritage. Being neither completely Jewish nor completely gentile, she said she was 'nothing.' In the new democracy that claimed to valorize pluralism, she claimed 'nothing' as her own space on two counts. She had been reduced to 'nothing' by those who valorized univocal racial identities. Now she claimed that she was neither a feminist nor a nonfeminist. From this position, she stood back and watched the battles younger women were fighting to affirm their rights. She offered support only by calling attention to feminism in her essays published in the periodicals of the day and by examining women's relationships in her plays. Being 'nothing' was a position of neutrality negotiated between competing, warring camps. It was the place where Ginzburg's 'queer' and 'straight' meanings met and were created in the imagination of virtually bisexual female viewers. By assuming again a role of mediator between opposite identities, she replicated her role of child who belongs to two races constructed as enemies.

Conclusion

Ginzburg was and was not part of Italian feminism. As often before, she chose the position of outsider/insider who occupies a neutral space between camps. From this position she advocated that women be granted the rights they claimed. But most importantly, during the growth of Italian feminism she became a playwright. While it is understandable that she was not interested in doing activist street theatre, it is significant that she chose an art form more public than the ones used before. At this time her essays in support of the rights advocated by the women's movement appeared in widely read periodicals and daily papers. Like the American women playwrights of the suffrage era, she was an advocate and an artist as well. Her turn from fiction to plays followed a desire to establish a dialogue with the younger women whose identity formed in the struggles for reproductive and divorce rights. In this dialogue, she wanted to explore the ways in which these women interacted with women like herself. The relatively traditional style she adopted in writing for the stage was an adaptation of the absurdist style established by Ionesco and Beckett. The dual female protagonist adapted this style to her needs. It offered female viewers a mirror of the way in which they interacted with other women like themselves. This figure of two-in-one was a labial symbol, a means to investigate the 'secret complicity' of feminism her essays did not quite explain. Her female characters do not identify as feminists. But the possibility of their friendships makes feminism present in the spaces they inhabit. If the women's movement was a means to compensate for the inferiority complex that came from women's legacy of disenfranchisement, then the secret of the complicity was that feminism enabled women to stop loving men more than themselves and love other women instead. This homoerotic secret inhabited the female homosocial space the movement had created. The figure of labial eros uncannily symbolized it in Ginzburg's ambiguous, compassionate, and ironic absurdist plays.

NOTES

1 Italian women obtained the political franchise on 30 January 1945 (Birnbaum 1986, 48). In 1945 the United States dropped atomic bombs in Japan. This was reasonably constructed as an indication that the 'peace' negotiated at Yalta was the beginning of a 'cold war' between the two superpowers that had emerged from World War II. In 1946 Italian women voted for the first time in municipal elections and in the institutional referendum that abrogated the monarchy (Birnbaum 1986, 53; Ravera 1978, 178–80; Travis 1989, 100; Ravera reports the number of women in office and their deeds). Their vote had a decisive impact in the elections of 1948. By this time, the new Christian Democratic president, Alcide de Gasperi, had negotiated a renewal of the Marshall Plan aid money in exchange for the expulsion of Socialists and Communists from the government (Travis 1989, 103). The united left, including the PCI and PSI, obtained a total of 31 per cent of the vote. The Christian Democrats (DC) obtained 48.5 per cent (Birnbaum 1986, 54; Travis 1989, 106). Based on this victory, the DC had control of the administration until 1963. The PCI and the PSI, who had participated in the government and in the writing of the Constitution, became the opposition. This stabilized the world order of the Cold War since it became clear that Italy, the country where the papacy had its seat, would not turn 'red and atheist.'

2 The term 'counterrevolution' refers to a category defined by Kate Millett in 1970. It indicates the repression of women's sexuality in the three decades between 1930 and 1960. The agents of this repression, Millett claims, were totalitarianism, nationalism, and functionalism (1970, 157 234). The category applies to Italy only transversally: the moment of indecisiveness that, after the franchise, stalled the women's movement in England and the United States did not happen in Italy because the vote had not been obtained. Italian Fascism took power in the early 1920s. By 1930 its totalizing system of subjectification was well in place. Nonetheless, when the issue of reproductive rights came to the attention of the judicial sys-

tem, Italian women had been voters for three decades, even though the legacy of Fascist ideology had not been eliminated from the private sphere.

3 For three years, 1945 to 1948, all the political parties that had been suppressed by Fascism participated in the government (Wilkinson 1981, 218–60; Travis 1989, 86–105; Ravera 1978, 149–224). The year in which the Fascist Party suppressed them was 1926 ('Leggi eccezionali fasciste' ['Exceptional Fascist Laws'], *Nuova Enciclopedia Universale Garzanti*, 1982, 1054.)

4 Birnbaum (1986) indicates that the UDI (Unione Donne Italiane, the women's chapter of the PCI) was instrumental in petitioning for the franchise (54). Even so, the Christian Democrats also supported the franchise (138). This was the party that engineered the political strategy that brought the expulsion of PSI and PCI from the government, with the support of Washington (Travis 1989). Significantly, Ravera, who, even as a feminist, writes as a militant PCI member, explains what the elected women did in the municipal administrations, the constituent assembly, and the governments, but does not explain how women obtained the vote (Ravera 1978; 178).

5 The elections of 1948 were dominated by a Cold War rhetoric in which the communists were accused of being enslaved to Moscow, and the Christian Democrats to Washington (Travis 1989, 104). In this climate, parish priests could exert their influence in their sermons and, less legitimately, through the ritual of confession. Their influence was most effective on female voters. In a testimonial, G.S., a woman who was in preschool in 1948, recalled that when her mother discovered that her father was a member of the Communist Party, she and the other women of the family spent some days reciting rosaries in front of a statuette of the Virgin to 'save' the reprobate. The woman described the episode in tragicomic tones. She also recalled that her female teacher helped her to get over the shock ('Testimonianze,' 1976, 17). This situation is one in which many women of her generation can recognize themselves. Women like G.S.'s mother felt threatened by Communism, for homemaking was their unpaid profession. Bolsheviks were depicted as advocates of free love who would abandon their wives and families if communist ideology prevailed. Furthermore, in the popular imagination and in the local artistic tradition, their symbolic colour, red, was associated with the devil and the flames of hell. On Italian women's suffrage, its motivations and consequences, see also *Essere sfruttate* 1972, 76–7).

6 Modern sociology of the Western family focuses on the distinction between the nuclear and extended, or complex, family. The first model

contains one heterosexual couple and its children only. The second has either unmarried or elderly relatives of the couple, or more than one couple, and children and other relatives. The Industrial Revolution is characterized by the prevalence of the first model. However, in one school of thought, industrial production caused the nuclearization of the family (Le Play 1987); in another, the relation of causality is somewhat reversed (Parsons 1949; Parsons and Bales 1955). Another school challenged the idea that at some point either the extended or the complex family had been prevalent or universal models (Laslett 1970). In modern Italy, Barbagli's data confirm that between 1951 and 1971, in the centre and north, the number of nuclear families increased by 18.1 per cent (53.7 per cent to 61.8 per cent) and the number of extended families decreased by 9 per cent (44.2 per cent to 34.4 per cent). See Barbagli 1984, Table III. 30: 125. These data indicate a dramatic transformation, even though in a longer diachronic perspective the changes might appear transitory rather than permanent.

7 The economic transformation of northern and central Italy in the 1950s and '60s is often called *miracolo economico* (economic miracle). Donati (1981), Seroni (1977), and Ravera (1978) indicate that this miracle profoundly affected power structures within the family (Donati refers to it as 'La 'rivoluzione familiare' ['The Revolution of the Family,' 44]; Seroni, 'La famiglia in una società profondamente trasformata ['The Family in a Profoundly Transformed Society,' 59]). More women found work outside the home and were able to earn salaries. But from a juridic perspective, the inequality of men and women persisted. The father was the sole owner of the family property. He had the *patria potestà* (parental tutelage or power) over the children and the right to decide where the family lived. Adultery was a crime and illegitimate children could not be recognized, even though it was not uncommon for a married man to have an *amante* (mistress) who lived in a separate household and had children of her own. Therefore, unmarried women who had accepted the role of *amante* were unable to obtain legitimacy and child support for their children born out of wedlock. Obviously, the *moglie/amante* (wife/mistress) system condoned and institutionalized male adultery. (See Ravera 1978, 253; Compagno 1974; Figa-Talamanca 1974; Francescato 1983; Ghezzi 1960; and Meloni 1984.)

8 The data Donati presents indicate the following: between 1931 and 1979, the number of births per 1,000 inhabitants decreased from 24.9 to 11.8. Between 1931 and 1941, the decrement was 4.0 points, in spite of the Fascist propaganda to promote procreation. From 1941 to 1971, the decrement

was 4.1 more points (from 20.9 to 16.8), despite the economic miracle and baby boom. Decrements were sharper in the 1970s, with 5.0 points between 1971 and 1979 (from 16.8 to 11.8). (See Donati 1981, Table 2.10: 62.) On the history of birth control in Italy, Birnbaum (1986) reports the following: the first organization to raise the issue was the UDI in 1953 (55). In 1968 the Vatican condemned contraceptives in the Encyclical Humanae Vitae (112). But in 1971, the state repealed the article that forbade the distribution of contraceptives (89).

9 This voracity represented a kind of Fanonian fascination with the colonizer, an anglophilia largely determined by the dominant role of the United States in NATO and during the Cold War. But it can also be interpreted as an antagonism of the baby-boom generation against their parents, who were somewhat anchored to the values of a national culture they had absorbed from Fascist ideology. A major difference between these two generations, at least among the educated classes, was that the parents' second language was mostly French, the children's English.

10 Through the media came models of liberalism in sexual mores; England was known chiefly for its liberal abortion law, the United States for its liberal divorce laws.

11 The Fascist legal code did not make a distinction between abortion and birth control; both were 'crimes against the integrity and health of the race (or lineage)' ('delitti contro l'integrità e la sanità della stirpe') (Tedesco 1981, 5). With respect to abortion, this code survived until 30 March 1976, when the Chamber of Deputies abrogated it (Ravera 1978, 277).

12 The scenario I describe was realistic until article 553 of the Fascist code was repealed in 1971 (Tedesco 1981, 5). As Lantin (1975) explains: 'We looked around. Contraceptives were forbidden. Only a few privileged women were on the pill on false prescriptions. This was 1970' ('Ci guardammo intorno. Gli anticoncezionali erano proibiti. Solo poche privilegiate usavano la pillola con falsa ricetta. Eravamo nel '70') (15). See also Frabotta (1976, 91–7).

13 Juridically, the question of Vatican annulments was related to the question of separation of church and state. Socially, it was related to the question of protecting children and economically 'weak' spouses. If the ecclesiastical tribunal of the Sacra Romana Rota decided that an Italian marriage was null, its civil effects were terminated automatically. But precisely because the former marriage was declared null, no provisions were made for child support, fair division of property, and spousal alimony. A selling point of the Italian divorce bill was that it did protect wives and children from economic abandonment. As *effe* explained in March 1974, 'In fact the Sacra

Rota considers [the annulled marriage] a bond that has never existed, even when one or more children have been born from it. By considering the former marriage nonexistent, it refuses to give it an adequate economic tutelage, unlike divorce' ('La Sacra Rota infatti considera mai esistito un legame neppure se da questo sono nati uno e più figli e considerandolo inesistente rifiuta di dargli una adeguata tutela economica, a differenza del divorzio') ('Note sul divorzio,' 1974, 5; see also Ravera 1978; 254 and 264).

14 The absence of divorce had created a high number of families with illegitimate children. They were born to parents who lived as a married couple (*more uxorio,* as in the Latin phrase the Italian code used) but could not marry because one of them had been married before. Marriages that ended in de facto separations were called *separazioni di fatto*. The 'married' parent could not recognize the children born of the new spousal relationship (Birnbaum 1986, 104; Ravera 1978, 264 and 336–7). Public opinion on reproduction rights depended on information about the illegal abortion system. Obviously, comparisons between births and abortions refer to data collected from legal and criminal (clandestine) procedures. Pro-abortion lobbying groups estimated the number of abortions at two or three million per year and the number of births at about one million (Birnbaum 1986, 87). Donati comments that these figures were 'disproportionate' ('spropositate, 67). Hellman (1987) reports the estimate of the World Health Organization: 800,000 abortions per year. Her comment is that this figure is 'conservative' (42). *effe* reports the number of legal abortions performed in 1979, only one year after the approval of the abortion bill, to be 187,600 ('Una analisi sulla applicazione della legge,' 1980). Since this is probably a small portion of the total of abortions performed that year., the high estimates for the previous period seem reasonable. Hellman reports the number of deaths from abortion at 20,000 women per year (42). The first divorce bill was passed in 1970 (Birnbaum 1986, 83–4); the abortion bill, Law 194, in 1978 (Birnbaum 1986, 90 and 105). Many feminist groups were sceptical about the abortion law. The struggle to obtain it had been waged through the *consultori delle donne* (women's consulting clinics), activist facilities that combined the praxis of giving abortions to women who needed them with the theory of calling attention to the issue. The law transformed these into *consultori della famiglia* (family consulting clinics), institutions where authority was shared with fathers and physicians (Frabotta 1976, 91–7). 'False conscientious objection' was another problem. The law provided health workers with the option of objecting to participating in abortion pocedures based on faith or personal conviction. The medical personnel who had practised abortion illegally had no serious

reasons to declare a conscientious objection, but they often did. This allowed the clandestine industry to continue to prosper, depriving many women of the benefits of the law (for a good case study, see Hellman 1987, 'Abortion in Caserta,' 178–82). The majorities that confirmed the two laws were 60 per cent and 70 per cent respectively (Ravera 1978, 254 and 266–7; Hellman 1987, 1).

15 Leone Ginzburg was an anti-Fascist, a Jew, and an activist. He died in 1945 in a fascist prison cell (Clementelli 1972, 7 and 25–33). Ginzburg's second husband, Gabriele Baldini, was a professor of English. He died in 1969 (Clementelli 1972, 38).

16 As Passerini states: 'The generations that were to bring the Italian women's movement to life were born between the late 1930s and the early 1950s' ('Le generazioni che daranno vita al movimento delle donne in Italia nascono tra la fine degli anni trenta e l'inizio degli anni cinquanta') (Passerini 1991, 140; my translation).

17 This porous self is implied in descriptions like the following: 'To be a subject in the full sense, with respect to oneself and other women, establishes a movement back and forth between the individual and the collective, which occasionally reaches a momentary equilibrium, and sometimes bends towards the collective' ('Essere soggetto in senso pieno, rispetto a se stesse ed altre donne, stabilisce un movimento di andirivieni fra l'individuale ed il collettivo che occasionalmente raggiunge un equilibrio momentaneo, e a volte si piega verso il collettivo') (Passerini 1991, 161; my translation).

18 I refer to the writers discussed in my book *The 'Weak' Subject* (New York: Associated University Presses, 1998).

19 For a typology of Italian families since World War II, see Donati (1981, 7–43); Barbagli (1984); Esposito (1989); Kertzer and Saller (1991); Melograni and Scaloppia (1988); and Prosperi (1980). These male scholars study the family in the context of Italian social institutions. Significantly, female scholars, motivated by the desire to document the need to transform the family in a feminist direction, write about it in the context of the 'feminine question' (*la questione femminile*) and the main points of feminist debate: the Italian divorce bill; the decision process in state-subsidized abortions; women's employment and unpaid housework; and the struggle to obtain equal family rights, maternity leave, and socialized child care. Useful sources are Cutrufelli (1975); Gaiotti de Biase (1979); Pieroni Bortolotti (1974); Saraceno (1977); Seroni (1977); Spano (1972).

20 The play opened on 15 May 1966 at the Teatro Stabile in Turin. The direction was by Luciano Salce, with Adriana Asti as Giuliana, Edda Feronao as

Vittoria, and Renzo Montagnani as Pietro (Vice 1966; Radice 1966, *La Stampa* 1966; Terron 1966). Adriana Asti was the star of the show and also the female actor that inspired Ginzburg (O'Healy 1976, 139–41). Reviewers were perplexed about the 'strange' housekeeper. The most telling remarks are by Vice (1966): 'Edda Feronao is almost a beginner, but she is already overbearingly influential in the aggressive vitality of Vittoria, the housekeeper' ('Edda Feronao, quasi un'esordiente ma già autorevolmente prepotente nella aggressiva vitalità della cameriera Vittoria,' my translation). The play was translated in English and produced in New York in 1972 (Gussow 1972). The established text has appeared in Ginzburg (1970, 11–74; parenthetic page numbers refer to this edition).

21 I refer to the classical examples of this theatre: Camus' *Caligula* and Ionesco's *The Lesson*.

22 Parenthetic translations are mine.

23 The first Italian divorce law was approved in 1970. In 1974 it was confirmed by a popular referendum (Birnbaum 1986, 83, 89, 103–4). In the years before the bill passed, cultural anxiety about divorce was considerable. It is reflected in Giuliana and Pietro's dialogue about getting a divorce abroad (39). In Italy property passes from parents to children, not from spouse to spouse. A widow or a divorced wife can get retirement benefits and child support, but her spouse's property goes to the next of kin. Therefore, even though Giuliana is poorer than Pietro, divorce is not in her best interest.

24 The play was written in October 1966 (O'Healy 1976, 152). The established text was published in Ginzburg (1970, 127–58; parenthetic page numbers refer to this edition). I am not aware of any records that it was translated into English or produced.

REFERENCES

Anderlini-D'Onofrio, Serena. *The 'Weak' Subject: On Modernity, Eros and Women's Playwriting*. New York: Associated University Presses, 1998.

Barbagli, Marzio. *Sotto lo stesso tetto: mutamenti della famiglia in Italia dal XV al XX secolo*. Bologna: Il Mulino, 1984.

Birnbaum, Lucia Chiavola. *Liberazione della donna, Feminism in Italy*. Middletown, CT: Wesleyan University Press, 1986.

Bono, Paola, and Sandra Kemp, eds. *Italian Feminist Thought: A Reader*. Oxford: Blackwell, 1991.

Canetti, Nedo. 'Nota introduttiva.' In 'Perché i comunisti votano e invitano a votare NO ai due referendum sull'aborto,' 3–4. Rome: Ufficio Stampa del Gruppo Comunista del Senato, 1981.

Choderlos De Laclos, Pierre. *Les Liaisons dangereuses*. New York: Knopf, 1992.

Clementelli, Elena. *Invito alla lettura di Natalia Ginzburg*. Milan: Mursia, 1972.

Compagno padrone: Relazioni interpersonali delle famiglie operaie nella sinistra tradizionale e della sinistra extraparlamentare. Florence: Guaraldi, 1974.

Cutrufelli, Maria Rosa. *Des Siciliennes*. Paris: Des Femmes, 1976. First published in Milan: Mazzotta, 1975.

De Lauretis, Teresa. 'The Practice of Sexual Difference and Feminist Thought in Italy.' In *Sexual Difference*. Bloomington: Indiana University Press, 1991.

Donati, Pierpaolo. *Famiglia e politiche sociali: La morfologia famigliare in prospettiva sociologica*. Milan: Angeli, 1981.

Duncan, Greg J., and Saul D. Hoffman. 'Economic Consequences of Marital Instability.' In *Horizontal Equity, Uncertainty and Marital Well Being*. Chicago: University of Chicago Press, 1985.

Esposito, Nicholas. *Italian Family Structure*. New York: P. Lang, 1989.

Essere sfruttate. Collettivo italiano, Elena, Gabriella, Giorgio, Silvia, Luisa. Milan: Mazzotta, 1972. Translated into French as *Être exploitées* (Paris: Des Femmes, 1974).

Figa-Talamanca, Irene. *Induced Abortion in Italy*. Berkeley: University of California Press, 1974.

Frabotta, Biancamaria. *La politica del femminismo in Italia, 1973–1976*. Rome: Savelli, 1976.

Francescato, D., et al. *Personalità e questione femminile: Famiglie tradizionali e la doppia carriera: Contributi di ricerca*. Rome: Bulzoni, 1983.

Gaiotti de Biase, Paola. *Questione femminile nella storia della Repubblica*. Brescia: Morcelliana, 1979.

Ghezzi, Giorgio. *La prestazione di lavoro nella comunità famliare*. Milan: A. Giuffi, 1960.

Ginzburg, Natalia. *Le voci della sera*. Turin: Einaudi, 1961.

– *Le piccole virtù*. Turin: Einaudi, 1962. Translated by Dick Davis under the title *The Little Virtues* (New York: Carcanet, 1985).

– *Mai devi domandarmi*. Milan: Garzanti, 1970. Translated by Isabel Quigly under the title *Never Must You Ask Me* (London: Joseph, 1973).

– *Ti ho sposato per allegria ed altre commedie*. Turin: Einaudi, 1970.

– *Paese di mare ed altre commedie*. Milan: Garzanti, 1973.

– *Vita immaginaria*. Milan: Mondadori, 1974.

Gussow, Mel. 'Theater Reviews.' *New York Times* (23 March 1972) 38: 2.

Hampton, Christopher, dir. *Dangerous Liaisons*. Burbank, CA: Warner Bros., 1988.

Hellman, Judith Adler. *Journeys among Women: Feminism in Five Italian Cities*. Cambridge: Polity, 1987.

Kertzer, David L., and Richard P. Saller, eds. *The Family in Italy from Antiquity*

to the Present. New Haven, CT: Yale University Press, 1991.
Lantin, Danielle Turone. 'Aborto: Solo la donna può decidere.' *effe* (February 1975): 15.
La Palombara, Joseph. *Interest Groups in Italian Politics*. Princeton University Press, 1964.
Laslett, P. 'The Comparative History of the Household and Family.' *Journal of Social History* (1970): 75–87.
Le Play, Frédéric. *La reforme sociale en France*, vols 1 and 2. Paris: E. Dentu, 1987.
Marchionne Picchione, Luciana. *Natalia Ginzburg*. Firenze: La Nuova Italia, 1978.
Melograni, Piero, and Lucetta Scaloppia. *La famiglia italiana dall' Ottocento ad oggi*. Rome: Laterza, 1988.
Meloni, Benedetto. *Famiglie di pastori, 1950–1970*. Turin: Rosenberg & Sellier, 1984.
Millett, Kate, *Sexual Politics*. New York: Doubleday, 1970.
'Norme per la tutela sociale della maternità e sull'interruzione volontaria della gravidanza.' *effe* 6, no. 6 (June 1978): 23–5.
'Note sul divorzio.' D.L.T. *effe* (March 1974): 5.
Nuova Enciclopedia Universale Garzanti. Turin: Garzanti, 1982.
O'Healy, Anne-Marie. 'A Woman Writer in Contemporary Italy: Natalia Ginzburg.' Diss. University of Wisconsin, Madison, 1976.
Parsons, T. 'The Social Structure of the Family.' In R.N. Anshen, ed., *The Family: Its Social Function and Destiny*. New York: Harper, 1949.
Parsons, T., and R.F. Bales. *Family Socialisation and Interaction Process*. Glencoe: Free Press, 1955.
Passerini, Luisa. *Storie di donne e femministe*. Turin: Rosenberg & Sellier, 1991.
Pieroni Bortolotti, Franca. *Socialismo e questione femminile in Italia*. Milan: Mazzotta, 1974.
Prosperi, Francesco. *La famiglia non fondata sul matrimonio*. Naples: Edizioni scientifiche italiane, 1980.
Radice, Raul. 'Allo "Stabile" di Torino *Ti ho sposato per allegria*.' *Corriere della Sera* (15 May 1966).
Ravera, Camilla. *Storia del movimento femminile in Italia*. Rome: Editori Riuniti, 1972.
Saraceno, Chiara. *Dalla parte della donna: La questione femminile nelle società avanzate*. Bari: De Donato, 1977.
Seroni, Adriana. *La questione femminile in Italia*. Milan: Riuniti, 1977.
Spano, Nadia. *La questione femminile nella politica del PCI, 1921–1963*. Rome: Donne e politica, 1972.

La Stampa. 'Il debutto teatrale della Ginzburg nella commedia in scena al Gobetti' (15 May 1966).

Tedesco, Giglia. 'Cosí è nata la legge.' In 'Perché i comunisti votano e invitano a votare NO ai due referendum sull'aborto,' 5–7. Rome: Ufficio Stampa del Gruppo Comunista del Senato, 1981.

Terron, Carlo. 'Novità di Natalia Ginzburg allo Stabile di Torino.' *La Notte* (16 May 1966).

'Testimonianze.' *effe* 4, no. 2 (February 1976): 17.

Travis, David. 'Communism and Resistance in Italy, 1943–48.' In *Resistance and Revolution in Mediterranean Europe, 1939–1948*. London: Routledge, 1989.

'Una analisi sulla applicazione della legge.' *effe* 7 no. 11 (November 1980): 7.

Vice. 'Ritratto di vita famigliare nella "piece" della Ginzburg.' *Il Tempo* (5 December 1966).

Wilkinson, James D. *The Intellectual Resistance in Europe*. Cambridge, MA: Cambridge University Press, 1981.

I nostri figli

di Natalia Ginzburg[1]

Queste mie parole sono rivolte a tutti coloro che come me hanno dei figli: a tutti coloro che sono passati attraverso le mie stesse esperienze e si trovano davanti ai miei stessi problemi.

Fino a quando non abbiamo dei figli, la nostra vita è relativamente facile. Non dico facile in un senso soltanto materiale, ma in un senso più spirituale e profondo. Facile è il coraggio, facile la rinuncia, facile l'entusiasmo e l'impulso finché siamo soli: facile l'amore universale predicato da Cristo, finché la giovinezza è in noi. Ma con la nascita dei nostri figli la giovinezza si spegne. Ci troviamo di colpo sbalzati in una maturità che ci è nuova, ci troviamo diventati adulti ad un tratto, e troviamo sul nostro viso, sulla nostra persona, espressioni ed atteggiamenti che erano soliti ai nostri genitori. Problemi di natura pratica, preoccupazioni giornaliere e minute ci offuscano: molti interessi ed affetti che prima erano acuti in noi muoiono, e pensieri e timori strettamente privati e famigliari ne prendono il posto. Che cosa mangerà il nostro bambino? Con che cosa si balocchérà? Come vestirlo? Come fare perchè sia sempre sano, forte, felice?

Allora si forma in noi una sorte d'egoismo familiare, tenace ed ostinato, quasi un senso di cupa ostilità per ogni cosa del mondo che non sia il nostro bambino. E quelli di noi che più erano liberi da ogni vincolo materiale e terreno, che più erano lontani da tutto ciò che può costituire un interesse chiuso e individuale, vengono ad essere a poco a poco pervasi da questo egoismo. Una esistenza comoda, facile, quieta ci attrae allora irresistibilmente: vi è legato il benessere dei nostri figli, la loro salute, l'appagamento delle loro esigenze più diverse.

È impossibile condannare tali sentimenti, cosí diffusi e comuni, cosí carichi delle più naturali e istintive giustificazioni. Eppure io credo che l'egoismo familiare, se non lo limitiamo e combattiamo in noi stessi con tutte le nostre forze, possa portare le conseguenze più gravi per noi, per i nostri figli, per l'intera società degli uomini. Credo che gli entusiasmi e gli impulsi che hanno acceso la nostra giovinezza dovremmo mantenerli in vita con tutte le nostre forze, attraverso le preoccupazioni più chiuse e meschine. Credo che i figli non debbano costituire un ostacolo, un peso morto, una ragione di viltà, ma uno stimolo e un incitamento: ed è necessario che essi crescano in un clima di animazione e di vastità di pensiero, che trovino in noi che li abbiamo messi al mondo dei compagni giovani e vivi. Se gettiamo uno sguardo sul passato, possiamo facilmente constatare come l'egoismo familiare che ho detto sia stato la caratteristica principale, forse anche la prima sorgente di quegli anni oscuri, privi di ogni interesse politico e d'ogni carità umana, che si chiamarono l'era fascista.

Noi non dobbiamo vivere chiusi nelle nostre case, ma dobbiamo ricordare continuamente che ci sono infinite altre case, infiniti bambini come i nostri che come i nostri hanno bisogno di vestiti caldi, di cibi sostanziosi, di camere soleggiate. E se ci sentiamo impotenti dinanzi alle innumerevoli esigenze che sorgono da ogni dove, dinanzi allo squallore e allo sfacelo che ha portato la guerra, non dobbiamo però chiudere gli occhi e rassegnarci all'inerzia. Che ognuno di noi, nella misura delle sue possibilità, dedichi un poco del suo tempo, un poco del suo denaro, un poco della sua intelligenza alla causa comune: che ognuno di noi si sforzi di imparare a privare di qualcosa non soltanto se stesso ma anche i propri figli: è forse questo il compito più duro e più arduo tra tutti i compiti che ci incombono, ma certo non è il meno essenziale. E che i nostri figli fin da piccoli imparino a dividere i propri beni con gli altri.

Ma si dirà che la beneficenza c'è e c'è stata sempre. Signore oziose che s'interessavano ai poveri ce n'è sempre state: collette ed istituzioni organizzate a scopo benefico ce n'è sempre state. Ma questa amabile e spesso generica attività non mi sembra abbia portato a risultati effettivi. Ciò che manca a noi tutti è il senso sociale, cioè una vera compartecipazione alla vita del prossimo: questo noi dobbiamo raggiungere e questo va insegnato ai nostri figli.

Proviamoci finalmente ad uscire dall'ambito chiuso delle nostre aspirazioni individuali, proviamoci ad amare nei nostri figli non soltanto il loro singolo essere nato da noi, ma l'intera società umana: e non in un modo freddo ed astratto, ma con tutto il nostro umano calore. Che la speranza di un tempo più saggio e felice non vada spenta per sempre.

Our Children

These words of mine are addressed to people who, like me, have children; people who have had the same experience and are facing the same problems as me.

Until we have children our lives are relatively easy. I don't mean easy only in a material sense, but in a deeper, more spiritual sense. Courage comes easy, sacrifice, enthusiasm and energy come easy, when we are alone in the world. Easy comes the universal love preached by Christ, when we are young. But the birth of children extinguishes our youth. We are immediately thrown into a maturity that is completely new to us, we immediately become adults and discover expressions and attitudes on our faces and bodies that were typical of our parents. Problems of a practical nature, minute daily worries cloud us: many interests and cares that we once felt acutely now die in us, and strictly private and family thoughts and fears take their place. What will our child eat? What will he play with? How to dress him? What to do to make sure he's always healthy, strong, happy?

So, a kind of tenacious, stubborn family egoism forms in us and brings with it a sense of dark hostility for everything in the world that is not our child. And even those of us who were most free from all ties to material and worldly things, who were farthest from any trace of private and individualistic interests, find ourselves little by little besotted by this egoism. We are irresistibly attracted by a comfortable, easy, quiet existence that is tied to our children's well-being, their health, the satisfaction of their various needs.

It's impossible to condemn these diffuse and common feelings, charged as they are with the most natural and instinctive of reasons. Yet, I believe that if we do not limit and fight the family egoism within us with all our force it can lead to the most serious consequences for us, for our children, for our entire human society. I believe we ought to keep alive with all our strength, even through the most private and trivial worries, the enthusiasm and energy that lit up our youth. I believe that our children should not be an obstacle, a dead weight, a reason for small mindedness, but a stimulus and an incitement. And it is necessary for them to grow in a lively environment, amid a wide range of thought, and to find in us, their parents who brought them into this world, young and lively companions. If we glance back at the past we can easily see how the family egoism I am speaking about has been the main characteristic, perhaps even the primary source of those dark years, devoid of any political interest and human charity, that were called the Fascist era.

We must not live closed up in our houses. Rather, we must continually remember that there is an infinity of other houses, an infinity of other children who like our own need warm clothes, sustenance, sunny rooms. And if we feel impotent faced with the innumerable needs that come from everywhere, faced with the squalor and disruption that the war has brought, we must not close our eyes and resign ourselves to inertia. Each one of us, to the extent that it is possible, should dedicate a little time, a little money, a little intelligence to the common cause: may each one of us make the effort to learn to deprive not only ourselves of something, but also our children. This, perhaps, is the hardest and most arduous of the tasks we face, but it is far from being the least essential. And may our children, starting from when they are little, learn to share their belongings with others.

But it could be said that charity exists and has always existed. There have always been *Signore* with time on their hands who have concerned themselves with the poor; collections and organized charitable institutions have always existed. But it does not seem to me that this pleasant and often generic activity has led to great results. What we all lack is social sense. In other words, genuine sharing in the life of our neighbours. We must reach this and must teach it to our children.

Let's try finally to leave behind the closed environment of our individual aspirations, let us try to love in our children not only the single being born of us, but human society in its entirety. And not in a cold or abstract manner, but with all our human warmth. May the hope for a wiser and happier time not be extinguished forever.

NOTES

1 'I nostri figli' first appeared in *L'Italia libera* 2, no. 198 (31 December 1944).

2 This translation and the two that follow first appeared in David Ward, *Antifascisms: Cultural Politics in Italy, 1943–1946. Benedetto Croce and the Liberals, Carlo Levi and the 'Actionists'* (Madison, NJ, and London: Fairleigh Dickinson University Press, 1996). They are reprinted here with kind permission.

Chiarezza

di Natalia Ginzburg

Il fascismo prescriveva al popolo una soddisfazione perenne. Nel fascismo non c'erano suicidi, ma gli uomini 'cadevano inciampando fatalmente nelle propria rivoltella carica'; non c'erano poveri, perchè tutti erano assistiti e soccorsi dalla Befana fascista, dalla Giornata della Madre e del Fanciullo, da altre istituzioni benefiche, e i volti delle madri prolifiche e delle vecchie centenni sorridevano dai giornali. La radio decantava senza tregua le vittoriose campagne di guerra, le industriose operazioni di pace, i brillanti successi diplomatici, le imponenti manifestazioni sportive; la voce stessa di chi parlava allora per radio esprimeva una costante e compiaciuta soddisfazione, un perenne ottimismo; in un mondo di treni popolari, di balli del Dopolavoro, di piacevoli escursioni sciistiche organizzate dalla Gil trascorreva la sana e laboriosa vita del popolo, e non c'era posto per i malcontenti, per i dubbiosi, per i tormentati. È inutile dire come a questo ottimismo nazionale ostentato e artificioso si contrapponesse nella realtà il tedio e lo squallore. Fu quella banale semplificazione della vita a fare in noi più violento il bisogno di una esistenza intima e tormentata; fu appunto quella semplificazione a renderci tutti più complessi e difficili, più involuti in ogni nostra espressione ed azione, a negarci ogni possibilità di una vera chiarezza.

Se volgiamo un rapido sguardo sugli anni trascorsi, noi, accanto al linguaggio vuoto e sontuoso dei giornali di allora, troviamo una letteratura di varia forma, che però tutta portava come segno contraddistintivo un'assoluta impotenza ad esprimersi in maniera intelligibile e schietta, un'assoluta incapacità di chiarezza. Gli scrittori non riuscivano a raccontare fatti e sentimenti che avessero un contenuto vitale, un contenuto elementare e semplice, accessibile a ognuno, ma si perdevano invece in una oscura e nebulosa ricerca di avventure irreali, di sensazioni ultraterrene e magiche. Questa ricerca dell'irreale da parte della letteratura d'allora non era soltanto il tentativo di sfuggire una realtà troppo tediosa e tetra, ma era anche un tentativo di difesa e di salvaguardia della propria personalità contro le insidie che la circondavano, per conservare una certa purezza.

La tortuosità del linguaggio, l'oscurità e le complessità dei sentimenti germogliati nel silenzio del nostro animo, di continuo soffocati e repressi, non era che la naturale reazione a una forma di vita nazionale pietosamente sciatta e mediocre, spoglia d'ogni poesia. Ma tale reazione non poteva portare a risultati felici e poetici, perché in un governo artificioso ed errato nei primi principi non vi possono essere, o assai raramente, risultati poetici e felici. Quando quello stato di perpetuo ottimismo e di compiaciuta soddisfazione nei quali il fascismo soleva cullarsi non fu più possibile davanti all'evidenza dello sfacelo, davanti 'alle province invase e città distrutte,' esso dovette fatalmente perire, precipitando nella fossa che s'era scavata con le sue proprie mani, 'inciampando nella sua rivoltella carica.'

E a me sembra che fra tutti i beni che con la morte del fascismo ci sono stati restituiti, il maggiore e più prezioso sia forse la possibilità di un ritorno alla chiarezza nei suoi aspetti più molteplici e vari. Allora il nostro linguaggio non poteva essere limpido e chiaro, perché la nitidezza e la chiarezza sono attributi della verità, e la verità ci era proibita. Allora eravamo tutti quanti sovraccarichi di parole, perché le parole erano la sola cosa che ci restasse in un tempo dove ogni possibilità di benessere intimo e pubblico ci era negato. Ma come liberarci di tutte le tenebre e i veli dietro i quali ci siamo nascosti per tanti anni? Come ritrovare noi stessi? A chi per molto tempo fu negato il pane, riesce difficile ogni nutrimento; a chi per molto tempo visse al buio, è penosa in un primo momento la luce del sole. Il fascismo ha oppresso i giorni migliori della nostra giovinezza, è penetrato nella nostra anima e l'ha avvelenata. È arduo liberarsene a ognuno di noi, anche a coloro che l'hanno respinto fin dal suo primo apparire. Ma io credo che il primo atto da compiere sia questo, ritrovare noi stessi: ricondurci alle forme più elementari e spontanee nella parola, nei rapporti umani, nei pensieri e nei sentimenti.

Clarity

Fascism ordered people to be permanently satisfied. There was no place for suicides under Fascism. Rather, men 'fatally tripped over their loaded guns'; nor were there poor people, everyone being helped and tended to by the Fascist Befana, by Mothers' and Children's Day, by other charitable institutions. And the smiling faces of fertile mothers and hundred-year-old women beamed down from newspapers. The radio continuously sang the praises of the victorious war campaigns, the industrious peace operations, the brilliant diplomatic successes, the grandiose sporting events. The radio announcer's voice expressed a continuous and complacent satisfaction, a permanent optimism. The healthy and hard-working life of the people was spent in a world of popular trains, of dances organized by the After Work Associations, of pleasant skiing trips organized by the Fascist Party youth groups. There was no place for the unhappy, the doubters, the tormented. It is unnecessary to say that this parade of artificial national optimism was in contrast to the tedium and squalor of reality. It was this banal simplification of life that created in some of us the violent need for a more intimate and tormented existence; it was that simplification that made us more complex and difficult, more introspective in our every expression and act, and denied us the possibility of true clarity.

If we glance back at recent years we find, alongside the empty, sumptuous language of the newspapers, a literature of various forms. The distinguishing mark of all of it, however, was an absolute impotency to express itself in a limpid and intelligible way, an absolute inability to be clear. Writers were unable to narrate lively or elementary or simple facts and feelings that were accessible to all. They got lost in a dark and obscure search for unreal adventures, magic otherworldly sensations. The literature of this period's search for the unreal was not only an attempt to escape an overly tedious and gloomy reality, but also an attempt to defend and safeguard its own personality and conserve a certain purity against the threats that surrounded it.

The tortuous nature of the language, the obscurity and complexity of continually suffocated and repressed feelings that had sprouted in the silence of our souls was nothing other than a natural reaction to a pitifully shabby and mediocre form of national life stripped of all poetry. But such a reaction could not lead to felicitous poetic results because in a government that was artificial and wrong in its first principles there cannot be, or only rarely, felicitous poetic results. When the state of permanent optimism and complacent satisfaction in which it used to delude itself was no longer possible, in the face of the evidence of disruption, and the 'invaded provinces and destroyed cities,' inevitably Fascism had to perish, falling into the ditch it had dug with its own hands, 'tripping over its loaded gun.'

And it seems to me that among all the good that has been given back to us with the death of Fascism, the greatest and most precious good is perhaps the possibility of a return to clarity in its most varied and complex aspects. Back then our language could not be clear and limpid because sharpness and clarity are attributes of truth, and truth was not allowed. Back then we were all overloaded with words because words were the only thing we had at a time when all possibility of intimate and public well-being was denied us. But how to free ourselves of all the darkness and the veils behind which we have hidden for so many years? How to find ourselves again? For whoever has been long refused bread all nutrition becomes difficult; for whoever has lived long in the dark the first moment in the sunlight is painful. Fascism oppressed the best days of our youth; it penetrated our soul and poisoned it. It's difficult for each one of us to free ourselves of it, even for those who opposed it when it first appeared. But I believe that the first thing to do is this, find ourselves again: go back to the most elementary and spontaneous forms in words, in human relationships, in thought and in feelings.

NOTE

1 'Chiarezza' first appeared in *L'Italia libera* 2, no. 198 (11 December 1944).

Cronaca di un paese

di Natalia Ginzburg

Ho vissuto per tre anni in un paese dell'Italia del Sud. Per tre anni ho veduto tramontare il sole sulle colline tondeggianti e spoglie, per tre anni ho veduto mietere il grano, per tre anni ho mangiato il pane bianco e insapore, impastato con le patate, che fanno laggiù.

Il paese era diviso in due dalla strada. Da un lato c'era la pineta e il castello, vigneti e campi, e più in alto la linea sinuosa delle brulle colline. Dall'altro lato c'erano gli orti, i larghi pascoli e il fiume. Il fiume era povero d'acqua, ma un uomo una volta riuscí ad affogarci. Non so come abbia fatto.

Il castello apparteneva a un marchese che era andato in America. Si diceva che avesse una ventina di stanze, quattro bagni e delle seggiole d'oro. Tutti si ricordavano il marchese con i suoi capelli neri dalla ciocca bianca, tutti ricordavano il tempo che andava a caccia con i cani. C'era un uomo in paese che gli aveva fatto da ruffiano. Adesso i cani li teneva lui. I cavalli del marchese invece li teneva il fornaio, e li portava a bere alla fontana due volte nella giornata. Erano bei cavalli muscolosi, di un color biondo, con la coda bianca.

Il paese era formato da due specie di persone: i borghesi e i contadini. Borghesi erano il brigadiere, il segretario comunale, il dottore e il veterinario. È difficile descrivere il tenore di vita, la forma mentale e morale d'una borghesia in un paese di tremila abitanti. E tuttavia mi sembra che la cosa meriterebbe studio e interesse. Questa gente aveva poco da fare e passava la maggior parte del tempo a scrivere lettere anonime alla Questura del Capoluogo, denunciandosi scambievolmente. Ho dimenticato di dire che della borghesia faceva parte anche il ruffiano del marchese, un uomo rosso in faccia, col ciuffo sulla fronte. Era il padrone di una autopubblica ed era l'autore più attivo di lettere anonime.

Il dottore era un vecchio zoppo che puzzava di sigaro. D'inverno portava un pastrano bordato di castorino; d'estate una leggera giacchetta di cascame di seta e un cappello di paglia. I suoi occhi neri e pungenti parevano capocchie di spillo. Da giovane era stato una persona raffinata e colta: gli piacevano i libri e la musica e aveva scritto e pubblicato dei versi. 'Ma a vivere in mezzo ai cafoni mi son perso di coraggio – diceva – mi son perso di coraggio.' Qualcuno diceva che da giovane era stato anche un medico bravo. Ma il fatto era questo, che i cafoni lui li detestava e non desiderava che guarissero quando erano malati. Se una donna gli portava a vedere un bambino malato, diceva: 'Saranno i vermi, come dite voi,' e spingeva in fretta la donna alla porta intascando dieci lire e tre uova. Quando andava in cucina la moglie gli chiedeva: 'Hai fetato?' Lui metteva le uova sulla tavola e sedeva a pranzo in silenzio. La moglie lui la detestava e non le rivolgeva mai la parola. Era una donna che aveva ormai sessant'anni, ma pareva molto più giovane, e ogni mattina si radeva la barba che le cresceva sulle guance piene e bianche, e quando se ne andava ancheggiando per le vie del paese, col soprabito di seta nera, col viso incipriato e gli occhi verdi e splendenti, ognuno ricordava il tempo che era stata l'amante del marchese e si mangiava le tordi e le pernici che lui prendeva a caccia. Il dottore lo chiamavano **becco cornuto**, anche adesso, dopo tanti anni.

Il dottore, quando venivano a chiamarlo di notte, s'arrabbiava e rifiutava d'alzarsi, ma se uno andava a lamentarsi del dottore in giro, la moglie subito lo denunciava per sentimenti antifascisti con una lettera anonima. Ma la sola passione del dottore erano i parti, quando venivano a chiamarlo per un parto difficile era tutto contento, e si alzava magari anche di notte. Cosí se invece di chiamar lui chiamavano l'ostetrico della città, gli facevano un'offesa atroce, e la moglie scriveva subito una lettera anonima. Di donne che morivano di parto ce n'erano tante, ma il dottore diceva che era colpa loro per il gran sudiciume che avevano, che non volevano sentir ragione, e al dottore non gli davano retta.

Nelle belle sere d'estate, mentre il sole tramontava sulle colline e le pecore tornavano dal pascolo sollevando una nuvola di polvere, mentre il barbiere suonava la chitarra sulla porta della sua bottega con una frotta di ragazzi scalzi intorno, il dottore, il veterinario e il brigadiere passeggiavano lentamente lungo la strada. A vederli cosí parevano buoni amici, e nessuno avrebbe pensato che passavano il tempo ad accusarsi l'uno con l'altro in Questura di sentimenti antifascisti, di truffe annonarie, di sevizie, di ogni sorta di cose. Camminavano lentamente, parlando: parlavano del tempo che abitavano altrove in città, parlavano della gioia di abitare in città e del disgusto che provavano a vivere in mezzo ai cafoni. Ma in realtà essi non avrebbero più potuto avvezzarsi a vivere altrove, non avrebbero più potuto rinunciare ai cafoni e all'ebbrezza del potere. Il brigadiere, alto, pallido, col suo grande mantello svolazzante, il veterinario con i calzoni a sbuffo e i denti guasti, e il dottore appoggiato al suo bastone avevano nelle loro mani le sorti del paese e lo sapevano bene. Camminavano interminabilmente fino a buio lungo tutto il paese, assaporando la propria grande potenza e il timore che li circondava. Il brigadiere aiutava i contadini ricchi a imboscarsi e riceveva in dono prosciutti e farina. Quintali di farina venivano scaricati di notte sulla porta della caserma, e il ruffiano del marchese stava affacciato alla sua finestra a guardare e scrivere lettere anonime.

Queste lettere anonime non avevano alcun risultato, probabilmente venivano cestinate, senza essere lette, ma ognuno ne aveva un sacro terrore e l'incubo oscuro ne pesava su tutto il paese. Soltanto i poveri non avevano paura delle lettere anonime, e vivevano una vita loro, fuori d'ogni intrigo, badando ai quattro cavoli piantati a casa e badando a rubare legna nella pineta senza farsi cogliere dal milite forestale. Il giorno che li chiamavano in guerra, ci andavano e crepavano lontano, e quelli che restavano a casa, il dottore non veniva a vederli quando erano malati, dato che non avevano galline. D'estate la dissenteria si portava via sempre sei o sette bambini, e un anno che al dottore gli portarono un bambino con la tosse convulsa, lui disse che non era tosse convulsa e lo mandassero pure a scuola, e tutti i bambini in paese si pigliarono la tosse convulsa.

Un tempo, molti anni prima, i poveri avevano un sussidio dal Comune, ma adesso questo sussidio nessuno lo vedeva più da un bel pezzo, e in realtà se lo mettevano in tasca il segretario comunale e il podestà. Il podestà non era un borghese, era soltanto un contadino ricco con vacche e maiali, ed era anche una persona per bene, prima che lo facessero podestà. Il brigadiere e il veterinario l'avevano voluto apposta un podestà che poco sapeva scrivere e non dava disturbo, e in Comune ci andava di rado e badava a zapparsi le patate.

Ma poi a fare il podestà ci aveva preso gusto e anche lui aveva messo un po' d'importanza, e anche lui aveva imparato a truffare con la farina, a vedere come rubavano gli altri, che era una smania che prendeva ciascuno. Cosí s'era arricchito ancora peggio e i suoi maiali facevano invidia, e a vederli c'era chi diceva: 'Tutta la crusca dell'assegnazione se la mangiano i porci del podestà.'

Ma la moglie del veterinario una sera mandò la serva a rubare l'insalata nell'orto del podestà, e la moglie del podestà se ne accorse e si fecero una chiassata, e allora il veterinario andò di persona alla Questura a dire che il podestà sapeva appena scrivere, e passava i suoi giorni a pascolar le vacche, che non era nemmeno dignitoso per chi lo vedeva; e il nuovo podestà fu allora il ruffiano del marchese, che almeno aveva un'autopubblica e si vestiva come un signore.

Ma i veri abitanti del paese erano i contadini, i **cafoni**, come li chiamava il dottore, e a loro non importava davvero chi fosse il podestà, perché tanto tutti rubavano, e i podestà sono fatti per questo. A loro importava soltanto dei pochi stracci che avevano addosso, e di quei quattro cavoli nell'orto, e della pioggia e del sole: il dottore diceva sempre loro che erano ignoranti e sporchi, e che per questo morivano tanti bambini, ma loro invece pensavano che non era vero, e che i bambini morivano perché non c'era un dottore bravo. Ogni volta che si trovavano col dottore o col brigadiere, si mettevano subito a parlare della miseria che avevano a casa, ma era solo una vecchia abitudine e in verità non erano scontenti, perché non sospettavano neppure che si potesse vivere in un altro modo, e al freddo ci s'erano avvezzati, alla fame ci s'erano avvezzati, e amavano le loro case con le pareti annerite dal fumo e la padella involta in un giornale ingiallito, i loro quattro cavoli fuori nell'orto, i pochi soldi nascosti nel paglione del letto, la conca di rame, e anche loro sarebbero stati incapaci di vivere altrove, come il brigadiere e il segretario: senza rubare, senza leticare, senza lamentarsi.

Chronicle of a Village

I lived for three years in a Southern Italian village. For three years I saw the sun set on the round and bare hills, for three years I saw the grain harvested, for three years I ate the tasteless white bread, kneaded with potatoes, they make down there.

The village was split into two by the road. On one side there was the pine wood and the castle, vineyards and fields, and higher up the sinuous line of the bare hills. On the other there were the plots of land, pasture, and the river. The river had very little water, but once a man managed to drown in it. I have no idea how he did it.

The castle belonged to a Marquis who had gone to America. It was said the castle had twenty or so rooms, four bathrooms, and some golden chairs. Everyone remembered the Marquis with his black hair and white tuft, everyone remembered when he went hunting with his dogs. There was a man in the village who used to be his *ruffiano* [procurer]. He now looked after the dogs. As to the Marquis' horses, the baker had them, and took them to the fountain twice a day to drink – fine, muscular horses, blond in colour, with white tails.

The village was made up of two kinds of person: bourgeoisie and peasants. The sergeant, the town clerk, the doctor, and the veterinarian were all bourgeois. It is difficult to describe the tenor of life, the mentality and morality of the bourgeoisie in a village of three thousand inhabitants. And yet it seems to me that this is of interest and deserves study. These people had very little to do and spent most of their time informing on one another by writing anonymous letters to the police station in the regional capital. I forgot to say that the Marquis' *ruffiano* was also one of the bourgeoisie. He was a red-faced man, with a fringe on his forehead. He was the owner of a car and was the most active author of the anonymous letters.

The doctor was an old lame man who stank of cigars. In the winter he wore an overcoat with a beaver trim; in the summer a light jacket made of scraps of silk and a straw hat. His black, piercing eyes looked like the heads of a hair pin. In his youth he had been refined and learned: he liked books and music and had written and published some verses. 'But living in the midst of peasants I lost my courage,' he would say, 'I lost my courage.' It was said that he had been a good doctor in his youth. But the fact was, he detested the peasants and didn't want them to get better when they were sick. If a woman brought him a sick child to examine he'd say, 'It must be worms, as you lot say,' and then quickly push the woman to the door pocketing ten lire and three eggs. When he went in the kitchen his wife asked him in dialect, 'Lay any eggs today?' he would put the eggs on the table and sit through lunch in silence. He detested his wife and never spoke a word to her. She was at least sixty years old, but looked much younger, and every morning she shaved the beard that grew on her full white cheeks. And when she would roll her hips down the village streets dressed in her black silk overcoat, her face powdered and her green eyes flashing, everyone remembered the time she had been the Marquis' lover and she used to eat the thrushes and partridges that he used to hunt. Even today, many years later, they still call the doctor *becco cornuto* [cuckold].

When they used to call the doctor out at night he would get angry and refuse to get up. But if someone in the village complained about the doctor his wife would immediately write an anonymous letter and denounce him for anti-Fascist sentiments. The doctor's only passion was births. When they called him out for a difficult birth he was all happy and even got up during the night. If instead of calling him they called the obstetrician from the city, they offended him deeply, and his wife immediately wrote an anonymous letter. There were many women who died during childbirth, but the doctor said it was their fault on account of their filthiness, and that they didn't want to listen either to reason or to him.

On beautiful summer evenings, while the sun was setting on the hills and the sheep raised clouds of dust as they came back from pasture, while the barber played his guitar outside the door of his shop surrounded by a gang of bare-footed kids, the doctor, the veterinarian, and the sergeant promenaded slowly up and down the street. Seeing them like that they looked like good friends, and no one would have thought that they spent their time in the police station informing on one another about their anti-Fascist sentiments, ration swindling, cruelty, and every sort of thing. They would promenade slowly, talking: they would talk of when they used to live elsewhere in the city, of the joy of living in a city and of the disgust they felt at living in the midst of the peasants. But in truth they could never have got used to living anywhere else, they could never have given up the peasants and the drunkenness of power. The sergeant, tall, pale, his large fluttering cloak, the veterinarian with his baggy trousers and rotten teeth, and the doctor leaning on his stick had the future of the village in their hands, and well they knew it. They would walk interminably up and down the entire village until darkness fell, relishing their great power and the fear that lay all around them. The sergeant helped the rich peasants when they needed to evade conscription in return for *prosciutto* ham and flour. At night tons of flour would be unloaded outside the barracks door, and the Marquis' *ruffiano* would stand at his window watching and write anonymous letters.

These anonymous letters had no effect. They were probably thrown into a basket without being read. Nevertheless, everyone held them in holy fear and their dark nightmare hung over the entire village. The only people not afraid of the anonymous letters were the poor. They lived a life of their own beyond all intrigue looking after the few cabbages they had planted at home and looking to steal wood from the pine forest without getting arrested by the guards. The doctor, the day the peasants were called up to fight in the war, where they went and died in a distant land, no longer examined those who stayed behind when they were sick because they didn't have any eggs. In summer six or seven children died of dysentery. One year when they brought him a child with convulsive coughing the doctor said it wasn't a convulsive cough and that it was alright to send him to school, and so all the kids in the village got the convulsive cough.

Once, many years ago, the poor received some financial help from the town hall, but now they hadn't seen any for a long time. In truth, the town clerk and the mayor were pocketing it themselves. The mayor was not one of the bourgeoisie; he was only a rich peasant who owned cows and pigs. And before he became mayor he was a decent person. The sergeant and the veterinarian had wanted as mayor someone who hardly knew how to write, wouldn't disturb them, go only rarely to the town hall, and concern himself with tending his potatoes.

But he took to being mayor, began feeling self-important and learned how to swindle flour, saw how the others stole, which was a craze that affected everyone. So he got richer still and his pigs were the envy of all, so much so that whoever saw them would say: 'All the bran that's meant for us gets eaten by the mayor's pigs.'

But one evening the veterinarian's wife sent her maid to steal some lettuce from the mayor's plot, and the mayor's wife saw her and caused a huge scene, and so the veterinarian went in person to the police station and said that the mayor barely knew how to write, and spent his days grazing his sheep, which was not dignified for those who saw him. And the new mayor was the Marquis' *ruffiano*, who at least had a car and dressed like a gentleman.

But the real inhabitants of the village were the peasants, or the *cafoni* as the doctor disrespectfully called them. They cared little who was mayor because they knew that everyone stole, and that mayors are made to do this. They cared only for the few rags they wore, the few cabbages in their plots, the rain, and the sun. The doctor always used to tell them they were stupid and dirty, and that was the reason so many babies died. But they didn't think this was true and that the babies died because they didn't have a good doctor. Whenever they were in the company of the doctor or the sergeant they immediately began talking about the misery in their homes, but it was only an old habit and they were not really unhappy because they had no inkling that they could live in any other way. They were used to the cold, they were used to being hungry, and they loved their homes and their smoke-blackened walls and the frying pan wrapped in a yellowed newspaper, their few cabbages outside in their plots, their savings hidden in the straw mattress, or in the copper pot. Like the sergeant and the town clerk, they too could never live anywhere else: without stealing, without being happy, without complaining.

NOTE

1 'Cronaca di un paese' first appeared in *L'Italia libera* 3, no. 7 (2 January 1945).

The Wig

A Play by Natalia Ginzburg

Translated by Jen Wienstein

(*A woman is sitting on the bed. She picks up the receiver.*)

Hello? Operator? I'd like to make a long distance call to Milan. 80–18–96. And I ordered a raw egg. They brought me my tea but no egg. The tea was like water. Yes, operator. No, forget it. No, my husband's not having tea. He'll have a café au lait later. So can you get me Milan? Yes, the same number. Oh God, now I can't find it. 80–18–96. No, not direct. No, I already told you. I don't want to dial direct.

(*She goes to the mirror and starts to put on make-up. In the next room someone is whistling softly.*)

Massimo? I'm calling Milan. Cut out the whistling! My skin is so dry and yellow – sickening. It's no wonder. What a night! The mattress was full of lumps. And I was cold. The covers in this hotel are like cobwebs. And I want you to know that my nose hurts. It's swollen and it won't stop bleeding. Massimo, this cotton is still full of blood. It makes me sick to see my own blood. Other people's blood doesn't bother me. But my own ... If you dare slap me again, I'll leave and you'll never see me again. My jaw is killing me and my nose. God, get out of that lousy bathroom. What's the point anyway? When you get out of the bath, you look dirtier than when you got in. Funny. I look clean even if I don't wash. This poor wig is finished. It looks like a rag since you tossed it. There's still mud on it. What a shame. It was a gift from you. The only thing you ever gave me in six years of marriage. Because you're cheap. You're cheap with me. With yourself you're very generous. You bought yourself that jacket. Now – when we're broke. And it doesn't even look good on you. You're too short to wear raspberry velvet. This lousy hotel! I ordered a raw egg. Where is it?

(*The phone rings.*)

Finally. It must be my mother.

Hello, Mom? Hi, Mom. I've been trying to get through for an hour. No, I don't dial direct because Massimo doesn't want me to. He's cheap. Not when it comes to his wardrobe. He just bought himself a raspberry velvet jacket – an awful thing. He's so short – you should see what he looks like in it. You haven't seen him in a long time. He let his hair grow. You haven't seen him with his hair long. He has a long golden mustache and hair down to his shoulders. Yes, that's true. Maybe I haven't spoken to you in a while but I've written to you. I didn't write that he let his hair grow? Funny.

Guess where I'm phoning from? Montesauro. A small town on the top of a hill. It's snowing. We're in the Collodoro Hotel. No, it's not a good hotel. Hardly. I ordered an egg. I never got it. I had to put a sweater on top of my nightgown it's so cold in here. What are we doing here? Good question. I don't know what we're doing here. The kids, no. The kids are in Rome with the cleaning lady. No, they have such a good time with her. She's cheerful. Always singing. Trustworthy. She's great. She doesn't do anything but she's great. Lucky – me? Lucky in what? The cleaning lady? Yeah. Maybe I'm lucky with the cleaning lady but with everything else I'm pathetic.

Yes. Right. Thank goodness we didn't drag the children along. Yes, because it's snowing. There we were on our way to Todi and the Dauphine breaks down on the autoroute. It made an awful noise and just stopped. It was snowing. We didn't know what to do. So we took our two valises and the paintings out of the car and started to walk. We must have walked for a half-hour. And finally we reached an emergency phone. My feet were soaking wet. No, I didn't have boots. Why not? Because I didn't bring boots because when we left Rome the weather was beautiful. I was wearing my deerskin jacket and my black maxi-skirt. No, no tights. From there we called a mechanic and he came to tow away the car. He thinks the battery has to be changed. He suggested this hotel. When we got here we had some old meatballs for supper and then we threw ourselves into bed. My feet were like ice. Massimo was furious. He was pulling out his hair. He carried his bed into the bathroom. He says he sleeps better when he's alone.

Mom. I phoned you for a reason. We need money. We left Rome with very little money. How could we know that the battery would conk out? So send me a money order for 200,000 lire. Yeah, I'm sorry. I hope to give it back one day. Eighty thousand for the battery and the rest – well, we need it. We left Rome on a Saturday so we couldn't go to the bank. Anyway, what do we have in the bank? Nothing. Close to nothing. We thought we'd get to Todi the same night and we would have managed somehow. We have friends in Todi. Make sure you wire me the money. Don't send it by mail. We're here in this hotel and Massimo is nervous. He's pulling out his hair and he's got a lot of hair. Lots of long hair. He just smacked me and made my nose bleed. My nose is still plugged up with cotton. My nightgown is bloody. No, Mom, it's true. I'm not making up anything. Me? What did I do? Nothing. I just told him that I don't find his paintings so beautiful. They're all the same. He's always making those flowery little meadows with a huge eye stuck on top. I'll tell you the truth. I'm sick of that eye. I dream about it at night. It's wide open with long turned-up eyelashes. It's huge. It's yellow. It looks like a fried egg.

Mom. Listen. Write it down. Put on your glasses because if you don't, your handwriting will be sloppy and then you won't be able to understand what you wrote. Hotel Collodoro. Not Pollodoro. Collodoro. Montesauro. Province of Todi. What do you mean, it's not a province? Sure it's a province. Don't forget that it's snowing here. Yes, I know I already told you. But until we get that money we can't leave this place. Not much. We don't have much. What we have isn't even enough to pay the hotel room. Where is our common sense? Well, when we get to Todi, we are going to stay with our friend Rosaria. She's a social worker. Rosaria is supposed to introduce us to an elderly gentleman – a lawyer who buys paintings. We're bringing him six paintings. The same old eye. No, we can't call Rosaria from here and ask her for a loan. Massimo says it's not right. Anyway, Rosaria is broke. Massimo brought along a book but I don't have anything to read. Just an old issue of *Annabella* that I found in the room. No radio. I didn't bring one. He's soaking in the bathtub with his book. It's called *The Psychology of the Unconscious.* Freud, I think. He has a habit of reading in the bathtub. He stays hours and hours in the water and he gets out looking dirtier and scruffier than when he got in. Oh, here's my egg! No, don't hang up. Wait. I'll eat while I'm talking. I asked for breadsticks. They brought me a roll that's hard as a rock. What? Is the egg fresh? It seems fresh. Ma, my life is falling apart and you're worried about whether or not the egg is fresh?

Ma, I don't think that Massimo and I can live together anymore. I don't know. I can't stand him. And he can't stand me either. We're constantly fighting. No, Ma. We're not just going through a difficult period. It's worse than that. We even had a huge fight before leaving Rome. We were at the kitchen table. I told him that I really didn't feel like going to Todi with him. He answered me in English that if I didn't go with him he would throw me out of the house. He was speaking English because of the kids. So I told him – in English – that he couldn't throw me out of the house because the house is mine. We bought it with the money Daddy left me. It's in the children's names but I have the use of the house. He was eating a persimmon. He took the persimmon and smashed it on the floor. And so I took a spoon and started cleaning up the mess. The girls? They weren't scared. They were enjoying the whole thing. While I was on my knees cleaning up, he ripped the wig off my head and whipped it out the window. It flew through the air and landed in a puddle of water on the downstairs neighbor's roof. And so I had to send the cleaning lady downstairs where the pharmacist lives and she and the pharmacist (with a mop) managed to fish my wig out of the puddle – all wet and muddy. Then I told the cleaning lady to dress the girls and take them to Villa Borghese. When I was alone with Massimo all of a sudden I got very angry and I started kicking his paintings that were on the floor in the entrance. He started screaming like a madman so I locked myself in my room and I started brushing my wig. After a while he begged me to open the door. He was almost crying. He said he was very sorry and begged me to go to Todi with him because he says I give him confidence. I don't know how he can say that I give him confidence when I'm always telling him over and over again that I don't really like his work and that that eye is a joke. Anyway, I said I would go but I should have stayed home because as soon as we got into the car we started to fight again.

Ma. Yes. I know. He's not a bad guy. He's good – good as gold. He's a bit of a ruffian but good – good as gold. I know. But I can't stand him anymore. Yes, he's successful. Quite. Yes, he's respected. Sure. He's healthy. I'm also healthy. And the children are healthy. But Ma, what's health got to do with this? Yes, I know. We have two adorable daughters. Sure we'd do anything for our children. But I can't stand him anymore. Yes. I know I had two children with him but now I can't stand him anymore.

Ma, I have to tell you the truth. I have someone. What? Yes, Massimo knows. I've told him over and over again. No, no. Don't start getting neurotic or I won't tell you anything else. I have someone. His name is Francesco. What lover! Lover is not exactly the right word. He never touched me. Well – hardly ever. He's always very very busy. He's the publisher of a weekly magazine. He's a politician. Yes, famous. Rich? What rich? He's completely broke. He has to support all those children. No, he's not a good-looking young man. He's not so good-looking and he's certainly not young. He's 49 years old. Yes, Ma. He's not so good-looking because he's balding slightly and he also has an enormous nose. Yes. Enormous. What do I see in him? You want to know what I see in him? I don't know.

No, I'm not a home-wrecker. His wife doesn't give a hoot. They're more or less separated. He lives upstairs. He has an enormous apartment. On Gesù Street. His wife and kids live downstairs. But the kids are always coming up. There's a hullaballoo in that apartment. Incredible. Doorbells, typewriters, telephones, kids. Kids everywhere! I'm always tripping over some kid. And the wife is always coming up with his groceries because they have separate kitchens. His wife? Yeah, she's nice to me. She's a good-looking woman, slightly chubby. They're obsessed with cooking, the two of them. He's always so busy but never too busy to check the spaghetti sauce simmering on the stove. They're very Catholic. Left-wingers, but Catholic. I had to end up with these two Catholics.

The trouble is that I'm afraid I'm pregnant. No, not Massimo. Francesco. No, he hardly ever touched me but the one time he touched me I became pregnant. It was a Sunday. We put the chain on the door. No, not in our house, in his house. On Gesù Street. The kids were ringing the doorbell and ringing the doorbell, and we didn't answer. It was too much. I'm whispering because Massimo doesn't know about this. No, he doesn't know that I'm pregnant. No, I didn't tell him. I didn't even tell Francesco. When I get back to Rome, I'll tell him. I don't want an abortion. I wouldn't think of it. I want this child. Yes, Ma, it'll have an enormous nose. I don't give a damn what kind of a nose it'll have. I want to live with Francesco. No, I'm not out of my mind. I'm in love. The problem is – he doesn't want to. He has no time. He has no room for me. No, the apartment is enormous. If I live with him, there's room for me and the kids. There are loads of rooms. He has no room for me in his life. His life is too crowded, too full. So I don't know what to do. I'm desperate.

It'll pass. You're telling me it'll pass. But I want to live with him no matter what. My mind is made up. Unfortunately he doesn't agree. But

I'll convince him. Yes. He's also very much in love, but he's confused. He's not sure this is the real thing. And then he says that between my kids and his kids, we can set up a nursery school. So, you see? What do you want to do? Come down and speak with whom? With Massimo? You won't resolve anything by speaking with Massimo. No. No, don't move. Stay where you are. Stay where you are and send me that money order. By wire. Bye, Ma. I'm going to hang up now. You're upset? No. Don't be upset. You'll see, everything will work out. How? I don't know. No, I'm not crazy. I'd better hang up now because we've already spent a pile of money on this call. Don't forget the money order. Hotel Collodoro. Collodoro. Yes, thanks Ma.

(*She hangs up the receiver, goes back to the mirror, and continues putting on make-up.*)

Massimo! I want you to know that my mother is sending the money tomorrow. Poor Ma. She was a little upset. Shocked. Shocked and upset. I told her everything. I even told her something you don't know about. That I'm pregnant. We only made love a couple of times but I'm pregnant. Do you hear me? You must hear me because you've stopped whistling. It's still snowing. What will we do today? God knows. Cooped up in this room. If I only had the crossword puzzle. Massimo! There's a pool of water on the floor. What's happening? Your paintings are getting all wet. I'll dry them carefully with some cotton. You see I take care of your paintings even if I don't like them. But you – you mistreat my things. You destroy them. My poor wig! You ruined it. It's pitiful. You bought it for me. Do you remember? With the money from one of your paintings. It was one of the first ones you sold. It was a simple meadow. But the 'eye' was already there – perched on a flower like a little bug. It was four years ago. We were happy then. Sometimes I miss those days so much. I loved you then. You didn't have that long moustache yet. And all that long messy hair. You had a brush cut. Your head looked like a toothbrush. You know, I don't think that guy is going to buy any of your work. Rosaria's dreaming. It was a complete waste of time to come here. I'm so cold. Get out of that bath or I'll shoot you. I'm pregnant. Do you understand? With Francesco's child. And I don't want an abortion. I'm going to live with Francesco and I'm going to take the girls with me. Anyway, you don't care too much about the kids. You can stay there on Cerchi Street. I'll leave you the house. I can't give it to you because it belongs to the kids. You'll pay me rent. Seventy thousand lire a month. No, eighty. I'll stay on Gesù Street. God, my nose is bleeding again. Get out of that bath! Help me! Bring me a towel! My sweater is all stained. I don't have another sweater. I have only this one.

(*She knocks loudly at the bathroom door. She pushes the door and it opens.*)

He's not here. God, he's not here. Where did he go? His clothes are gone. He must have gone out by the terrace door. He couldn't have just left. He wouldn't just dump me in this idiotic town.

(*She picks up the receiver.*)

Hello, operator? Have you seen my husband by any chance? Oh, really. He's in the dining room? Doing what? Having a café au lait? Tell him to come right back upstairs. Tell him I don't feel well. Tell him to stop eating right this minute and come upstairs because I'm going crazy here. I'm sick. I'm cold. I'm fed up and I don't know what to do and if he doesn't come right up, I'm taking a pair of scissors and I'm going to cut his stupid paintings to pieces!

Bibiliography

Note: Only the first editions are mentioned, unless there are revised versions of them.

Fiction

La strada che va in città e altri racconti. Turin: Einaudi, 1942. Reprinted in *Cinque romanzi brevi.* Translated by Frances Fresnaye under the title *The Road to the City: Two Novelettes* (London: Hogarth Press, 1952).

È stato così. Turin: Einaudi, 1947. Reprinted in *Cinque romanzi brevi.* Translated by Frances Fresnaye under the title *The Dry Heart*, in *The Road to the City: Two Novelettes*

Tutti i nostri ieri. Turin: Einaudi, 1952. Translated by Angus Davidson under the title *All Our Yesterdays* (Manchester: Carcanet, 1985).

Valentino (includes *Valentino* and *Sagittario*). Turin: Einaudi, 1957. Reprinted in *Cinque romanzi brevi.* Translated by Avril Bardoni under the title *Valentino and Sagittarius: Two Novellas* (New York: Seaver, 1988).

Le voci della sera. Turin: Einaudi, 1961. Translated by D.M. Low under the title *Voices in the Evening* (London: Hogarth Press, 1963).

Lessico famigliare. Turin: Einaudi, 1963. Translated by D.M. Low under the title *Family Sayings.* (New York: Dutton, 1967; rev. ed., Manchester: Carcanet, 1984). Also translated by Judith Woolf under the title *The Things We Used to Say* (Manchester: Carcanet, 1997).

Cinque romanzi brevi. Turin: Einaudi, 1964.

Caro Michele. Turin: Einaudi, 1973. Translated by Sheila Cudahy under the title *No Way* (New York: Harcourt Brace Jovanovich, 1974).

Famiglia (includes *Famiglia* and *Borghesia*). Turin: Einaudi, 1983. Translated by

Beryl Stockman under the title *Family: Two Novellas* (New York: Seaver Books, 1988).

La famiglia Manzoni. Turin: Einaudi, 1983. Translated by Marie Evans under the title *The Manzoni Family* (New York: Seaver, 1987).

La città e la casa. Turin: Einaudi, 1984. Translated by Dick Davis under the title *The City and the House* (Manchester: Carcanet, 1986).

Essays

Le piccole virtù. Turin: Einaudi, 1962. Translated by Dick Davis under the title *The Little Virtues* (Manchester: Carcanet, 1985).

Mai devi domandarmi. Turin: Einaudi, 1970. Translated by Isabel Quigly under the title *Never Must You Ask Me* (London: Joseph, 1973).

Vita immaginaria. Turin: Einaudi, 1974.

Serena Cruz, o la vera giustizia. Turin: Einaudi, 1990.

Theatre

Ti ho sposato per allegria e altre commedie. Turin: Einaudi, 1966. Only one play has been translated, *L'inserzione/The Advertisement*, by Henry Reed, in *The New Theatre of Europe* (London: Faber, 1969).

Paese di mare. Turin: Einaudi, 1973.

Opere. 2 vols. Milan: Mondadori, 1986–7.

www.ingramcontent.com/pod-product-compliance
Lightning Source LLC
LaVergne TN
LVHW040758070826
844660LV00025B/1184

* 9 7 8 1 4 8 7 5 8 7 2 7 7 *